Learn Salesforce Lightning

The Visual Guide to the Lightning UI

Felicia Duarte
Rachelle Hoffman

Apress®

Learn Salesforce Lightning: The Visual Guide to the Lightning UI

Felicia Duarte
La Puente, California, USA

Rachelle Hoffman
Sunland, California, USA

ISBN-13 (pbk): 978-1-4842-2993-4
https://doi.org/10.1007/978-1-4842-2994-1

ISBN-13 (electronic): 978-1-4842-2994-1

Library of Congress Control Number: 2017962634

Cover image by Freepik (www.freepik.com)

Managing Director: Welmoed Spahr
Editorial Director: Todd Green
Acquisitions Editor: Susan McDermott
Development Editor: Laura Berendson
Technical Reviewer: Phil Weinmeister
Coordinating Editor: Rita Fernando
Copy Editor: Kim Wimpsett

Distributed to the book trade worldwide by Springer Science+Business Media New York, 233 Spring Street, 6th Floor, New York, NY 10013. Phone 1-800-SPRINGER, fax (201) 348-4505, email orders-ny@springer-sbm.com, or visit www.springeronline.com. Apress Media, LLC is a California LLC and the sole member (owner) is Springer Science + Business Media Finance Inc (SSBM Finance Inc). SSBM Finance Inc is a **Delaware** corporation.

For information on translations, please email rights@apress.com, or visit www.apress.com/rights-permissions.

Apress titles may be purchased in bulk for academic, corporate, or promotional use. eBook versions and licenses are also available for most titles. For more information, reference our Print and eBook Bulk Sales web page at www.apress.com/bulk-sales.

Any source code or other supplementary material referenced by the author in this book is available to readers on GitHub via the book's product page, located at www.apress.com/9781484229934. For more detailed information, please visit www.apress.com/source-code.

Printed on acid-free paper

Table of Contents

About the Authors

Felicia Duarte is the chief operating officer of Cloud Creations, Inc., a full-service Salesforce consulting and implementation firm in Los Angeles. She oversees the daily operations of the company, including 70+ active implementations at any given time. Her technical expertise on the Salesforce platform is contrasted by her retail management experience, including SEO, web analytics, and social media marketing. In 2017, she filmed Salesforce Admin Certification training courses for ITPRO.TV. In her time off, she enjoys quality time with her two young boys, Michael and Ayden.

Rachelle Hoffman is the chief technology officer of Cloud Creations, Inc., a full-service Salesforce consulting and implementation firm in Los Angeles. Her years of experience on the Salesforce platform include the retail and business services industries. Her marquee clients include Southern California Edison, Smart & Final, Paramount Pictures, and other Fortune 500 Cloud Creations clients. You can reach the firm at `www.cloudcreations.com`. In her spare time, she enjoys spending time with her husband Tyson, being outdoors, playing with her dogs and relaxing with family and friends. She continues to further her education every chance she gets and loves being part of the Salesforce community.

About the Technical Reviewer

Phil Weinmeister, Salesforce MVP, is the senior director of product management at 7Summits, where he is focused on delivering impactful, transformative communities on the Salesforce platform and building innovative components, apps, and bolts that drive those communities. Phil is 18x Salesforce certified and has delivered numerous solutions to a variety of organizations on the Force.com platform since 2010. A graduate of Carnegie Mellon University with a double major in business administration/IT and Spanish, Phil now resides in Powder Springs, Georgia. He spends most of his "free" time with his gorgeous, sweet wife, Amy, and his children, Tariku, Sophie, Max, and Lyla. When he's not trying to make his kids laugh, cheering on the Arizona Cardinals, or rap battling his wife, Phil involves himself in various church-related activities with friends and family in the Cobb County area.

Phil authored *Practical Salesforce.com Development Without Code*, released in 2015, and will release another book through Apress in 2018. His second Salesforce book will serve as a guide for building and managing communities on the Salesforce platform.

Stay updated on Phil's most recent insights and blog posts by following him on Twitter (@PhilWeinmeister).

Foreword

Two years ago, we launched Salesforce Lightning. It was (and if I'm being honest, still is) an audacious undertaking.

Our mission with Lightning was to completely reinvent Salesforce to provide a new modern user experience that set a new standard for customer relationship management (CRM) and build it all on a new, robust, and scalable enterprise application framework. We wanted to make Salesforce easier, more intuitive, and virtually limitless in its potential. And we wanted it to empower everyone in our community to be their best, including trailblazers, admins, customers, partners, and our employees.

Since launching Lightning, we've seen an outpouring of enthusiasm from our community, unlike anything I've ever seen in enterprise software. It's been awe-inspiring.

One of the best things about Lightning is that it helps us innovate faster. With each release, we're expanding the scale and scope of Lightning and doing more than I ever thought possible.

Since launching it just two years ago, we've done the following:

- Redefined the modern selling cycle with Sales Cloud Lightning

- Reimagined the modern contact center with Service Cloud Lightning

- Streamlined navigation to make it easier to move between Salesforce apps

- Empowered admins and trailblazers with a no-code framework so they can easily customize the Salesforce user interface (UI) for their organizations

- Helped more than 100,000 customers deploy Lightning

- Sparked a new level of creativity and momentum in our ecosystem with more than 1,000 new Lightning-ready apps from partners such as DocuSign, Evernote, and FinancialForce that can be simply dragged and dropped into Salesforce

- Created entirely new products that previously weren't possible, such as Salesforce Einstein, an artificial intelligence (AI) offering for CRM, and Lightning Bolt, which offers industry-specific portals for our Community Cloud

- Empowered countless salespeople, service agents, and marketing pros to sell, service, and market faster, smarter, and the way they want

Every day our community gives us feedback—sometimes positive, sometimes critical, but always constructive. And every day, our entire product team (me included) pores over that feedback, and it helps us get better and better. Lightning is what it is today because of you. So, thank you for all you do to help us make Salesforce and Lightning better and better with each release.

Lightning is the future of Salesforce. So, buckle up because we're just getting started.

Mike Rosenbaum
EVP of CRM apps, Salesforce

Acknowledgments

I wish to thank everyone who helped us complete this book. Without their effort and support, we would not have been able to bring this to a successful completion.

Thanks to our editors, Susan and Rita, for their effort, time, and patience. Thank you for this opportunity and all your help.

Thanks to Phil Weinmeister, for his knowledge and expertise as our technical reviewer.

Thanks to Justin Davis, for his support and guidance throughout this process.

Most important, I'd like to dedicate this book to my children, Michael Frank and Ayden James. Don't give up. There is always something to learn.

—Felicia Duarte

Introduction

"Do business faster."

—Cloud Creations

Just like our company tagline, we believe you can "do business faster" with Salesforce Lightning. We wrote this book to provide training on the innovative Lightning Experience in a clear and visual way. As executives in a Salesforce consulting company, we understood the challenges that other organizations faced when it came to user acceptance of a new experience. We wanted to provide material that was easy to follow, with real-life examples, so administrators and users are set up for success.

Learn Salesforce Lightning is a step-by-step visual guide that offers immediate and valuable solutions to the new set of UI tools included in Lightning.

You'll learn to do the following:

- Navigate the Salesforce Lightning Experience
- Migrate from Salesforce Classic to Lightning
- Make customizations
- Configure dynamic reports and dashboards
- Build logic to automate the system with Process Builder
- Manage your data and security
- And much more

This book is for Salesforce administrators, business users, developers, and IT members. Our goal is to prepare you to onboard one of the most innovative and fastest customer relationship management (CRMs) solutions on the market: Salesforce Lightning.

CHAPTER 1

Introducing Salesforce Lightning

Salesforce is currently the number-one customer relationship management (CRM) solution for business management. Delivering a robust platform and groundbreaking technology, Salesforce provides solutions for sales, service, and marketing departments. The Lightning Experience provides a new user interface that delivers a faster platform, dynamic capabilities, and enhanced aesthetics. Businesses have reported an increase in win rates, more collaboration, improved productivity, and faster reporting following the switch to Lightning (see Figure 1-1).

Learn About Lightning Experience

Introducing Lightning Experience See how Lightning Experience can revolutionize the way your team gets work done.	Watch Video
Compare Lightning Experience and Salesforce Classic Verify that the features and customizations your users need are available in the new interface.	Compare
Get Ready to Migrate to Lightning Experience Learn more about Lightning Experience and the best practices for rolling out the new interface to your users. And get a badge while you're at it!	Start Trail

Figure 1-1. *Salesforce Lightning Experience*

© Felicia Duarte, Rachelle Hoffman 2018
F. Duarte, R. Hoffman, *Learn Salesforce Lightning*, https://doi.org/10.1007/978-1-4842-2994-1_1

Lightning Pages

The Lightning pages focus attention on what matters most. Important information is displayed "above the fold," or positioned at the top half of the screen, so users can view key points quicker.

Additionally, layouts are consistent and easy to navigate. See the comparison of an account record in Classic (see Figure 1-2) versus the same record in Lightning (Figure 1-3).

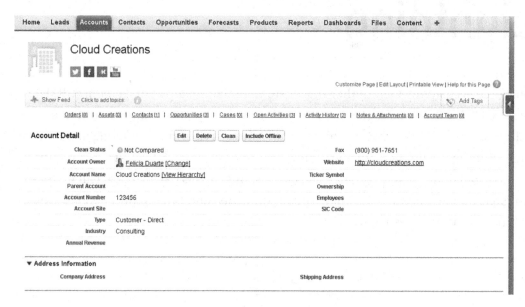

Figure 1-2. *Salesforce account record in Salesforce Classic*

Figure 1-3. *Salesforce account record in the Lightning Experience*

Migrate to Lightning Experience

Migrating to the Salesforce Lightning Experience is straightforward. The following steps describe how to access the Migration Assistant. The Migration Assistant will check your organization's readiness for Lightning and walk you through a series of steps to enable Lightning for your organization. This is a great first step on your Lightning journey.

Note   These steps are not required but highly encouraged. Salesforce has spent considerable time thinking through potential migration pitfalls and has tried to address them within the Migration Assistant.

Migration Assistant

Follow these steps:

1.   In Classic, select Setup (see Figure 1-4).

Figure 1-4. *Setup area in Salesforce Classic*

2. From the Setup menu, click the Get Started button (see Figure 1-5).

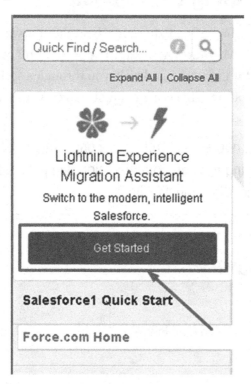

Figure 1-5. *Get Started button in Setup*

3. From here, you have three available resources to learn more about the Lightning Experience. You can select from the options in Figure 1-6.

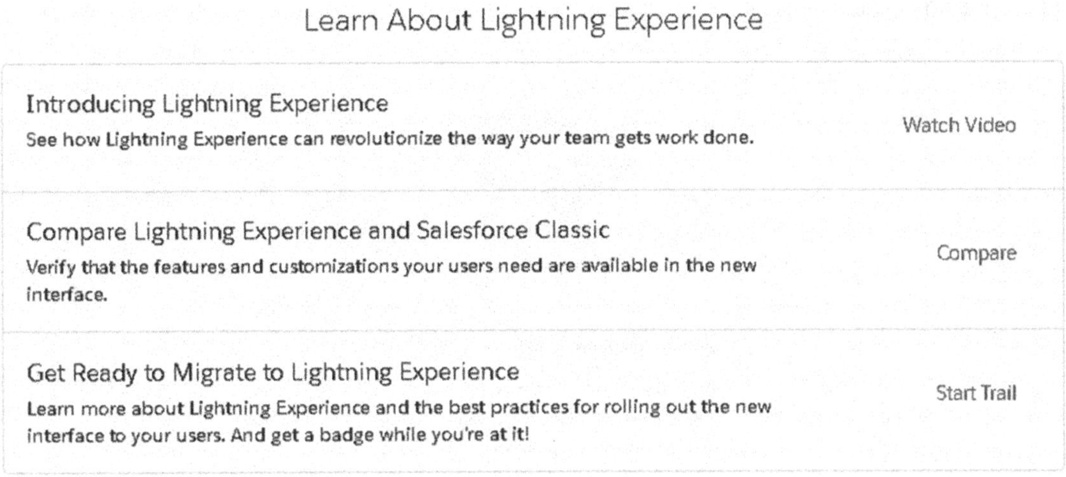

Learn About Lightning Experience

Introducing Lightning Experience	Watch Video
See how Lightning Experience can revolutionize the way your team gets work done.	
Compare Lightning Experience and Salesforce Classic	Compare
Verify that the features and customizations your users need are available in the new interface.	
Get Ready to Migrate to Lightning Experience	Start Trail
Learn more about Lightning Experience and the best practices for rolling out the new interface to your users. And get a badge while you're at it!	

Figure 1-6. *Learning resources for Salesforce Lightning*

4. Click Next Step to get started.

Check Readiness

To get started, Salesforce will request access to your organization to analyze your current setup (Figure 1-7).

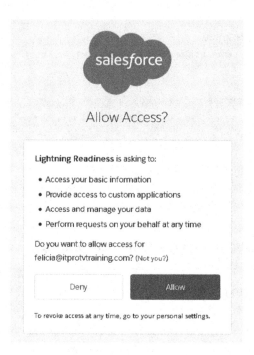

Figure 1-7. *Allowing access to Lightning Readiness*

Once you click Allow, shown in Figure 1-7, you must select which Salesforce product you want to access (see Figure 1-8).

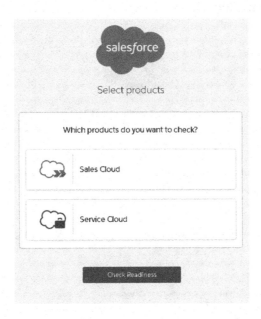

Figure 1-8. *Product selection to check for Lightning Readiness*

Select the appropriate Salesforce product and click Check Readiness. Salesforce will analyze your current setup and email a readiness report (see Figure 1-9). New organizations can skip this step.

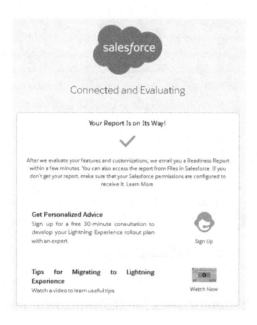

Figure 1-9. *Lightning migration options*

Preview

You can preview how your organization works in the Lightning environment. This is a great feature to test any issues that may have been brought up in your readiness report. If you encounter any issues in this switch, you can make changes on the spot. To test this, navigate to the Preview tab and click Preview, as shown in Figure 1-10.

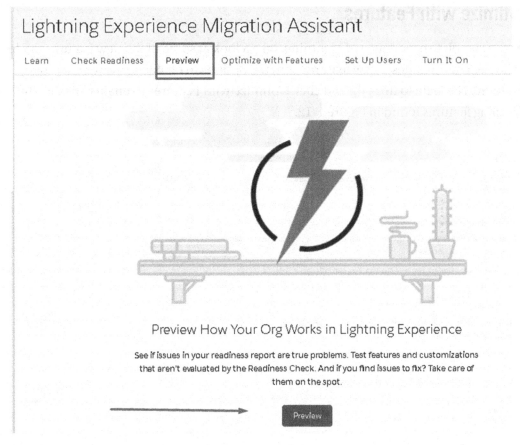

Figure 1-10. *Preview tab in the Migration Assistant*

As you can see in Figure 1-11, you are instantly switched to Lightning in Preview mode.

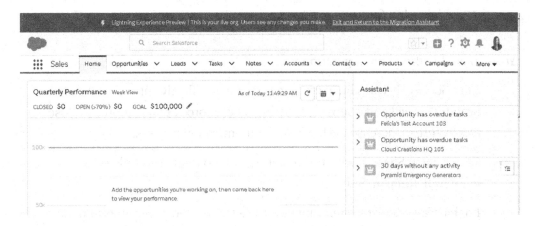

Figure 1-11. *Lightning Experience in Preview mode*

Optimize with Features

For the complete experience of Lightning, take a look at some of the new features made available. This includes a new feature for news, options to enable activities and notes, and more. Navigate to this tab, and click Optimize with Features to enable/disable the Lightning features found in Figure 1-12.

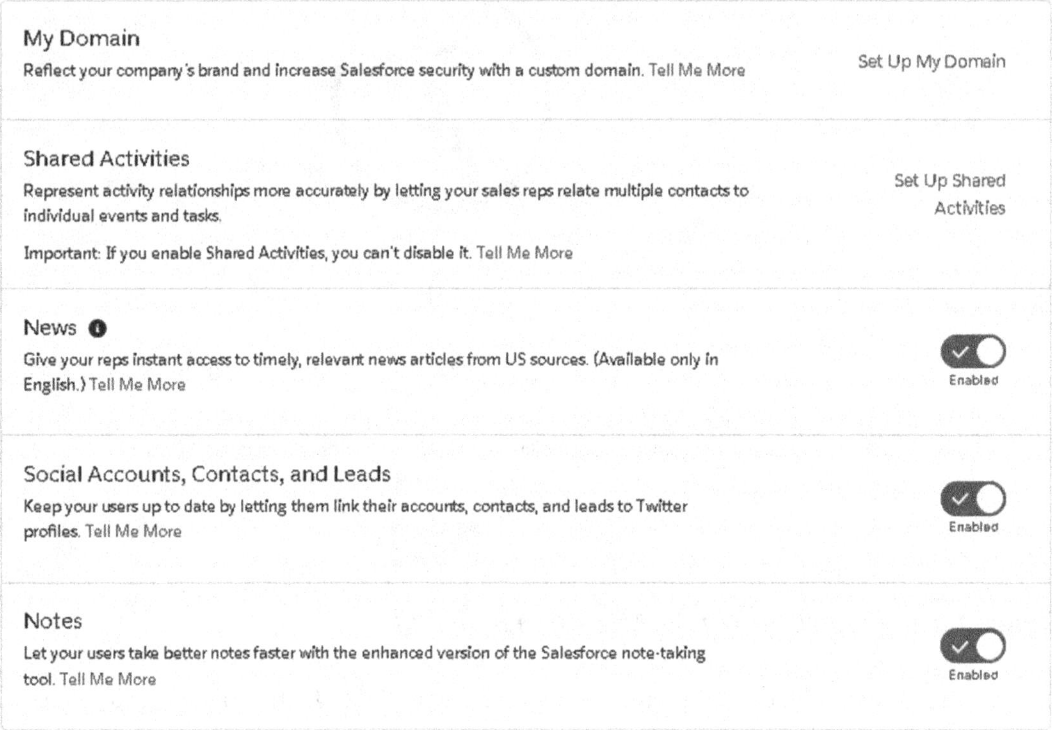

Figure 1-12. *Lightning features to enable*

You can enable the following options:

- Click Set Up My Domain to create a URL that is reflective of your company's brand. This will add a subdomain to your Salesforce organization URL. Use this feature to increase the login and authentication process.

- Click Set Up Shared Activities to allow users to relate multiple contacts to an individual activity.

- Enable News to display relevant news article about your accounts and their industries. This information is pulled by accounts listed in your organization.

- Enable Social Accounts, Contacts, and Leads to allow users to connect better with your accounts by syncing social media accounts.

- Enable Notes to utilize the enhanced version of notes that includes automatic saving in edit mode, an option to add images, and share features.

Set Up Users

You can control who has access to the Lightning Experience. You can choose to roll this out to groups of users, individual users, or all users.

Note   Standard profile users have access to Lightning by default, while custom profile users do not. Click Learn How to change these settings.

Navigate to the Set up Users tab shown in Figure 1-13 to fine-tune this experience and select which users make the switch.

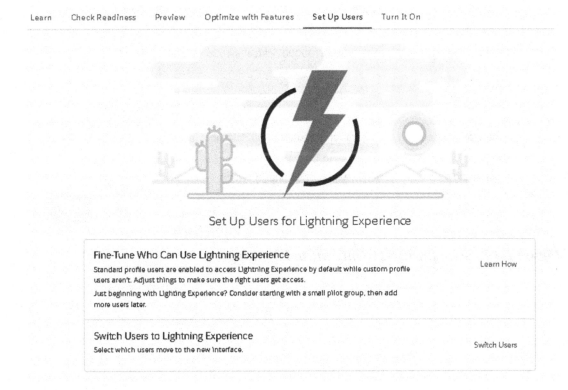

Figure 1-13. *User setup*

Follow these steps to switch users:

1. Click Switch Users.

2. Select appropriate users by clicking the + next to their name (Figure 1-14).

3. Click Save.

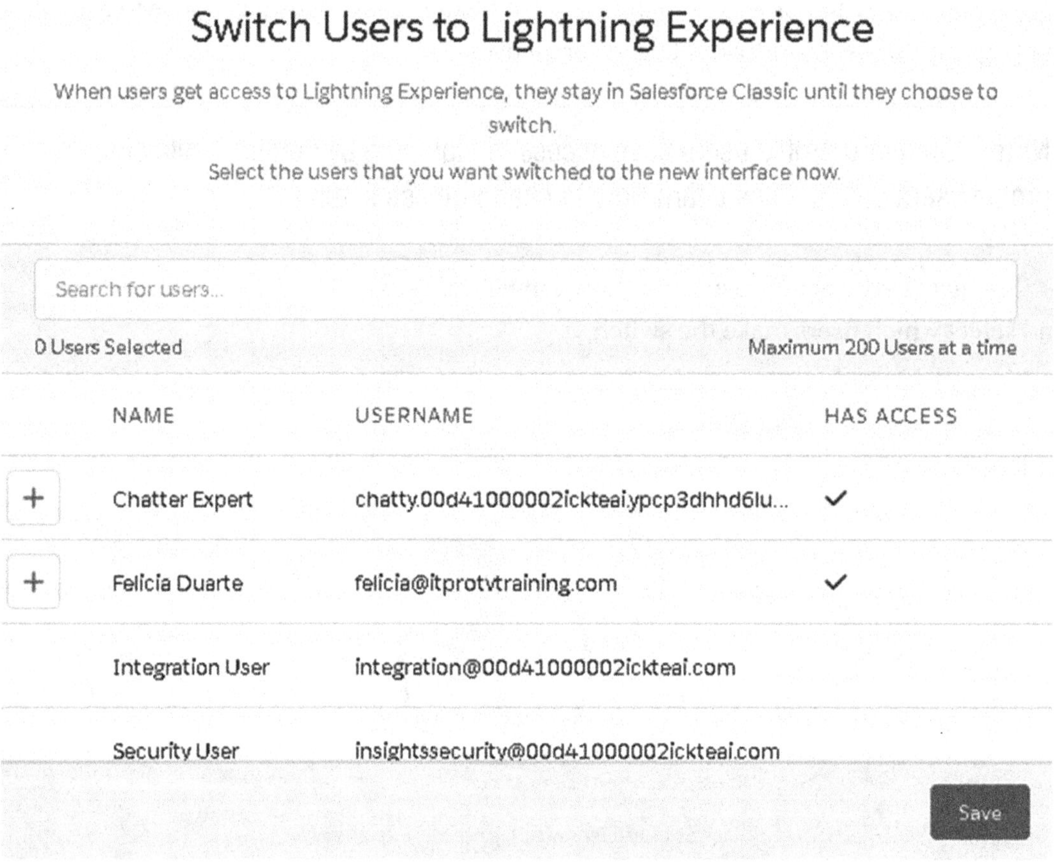

Switch Users to Lightning Experience

When users get access to Lightning Experience, they stay in Salesforce Classic until they choose to switch.

Select the users that you want switched to the new interface now.

	NAME	USERNAME	HAS ACCESS
	Search for users...		
	0 Users Selected		Maximum 200 Users at a time
+	Chatter Expert	chatty.00d41000002ickteai.ypcp3dhhd6lu...	✓
+	Felicia Duarte	felicia@itprotvtraining.com	✓
	Integration User	integration@00d41000002ickteai.com	
	Security User	insightssecurity@00d41000002ickteai.com	

Save

Figure 1-14. *Selecting users to migrate to Lightning*

Rollout Approach

Execute a rollout strategy that works best for your company. For larger organizations, it is recommended that you have a phased rollout approach. This approach is advantageous when migrating large organizations and complex setups. There are a few benefits to this approach, including the following:

- This approach allows you to conduct user acceptance testing. Use this to identify any challenges or issues with the new experience. You can collect feedback from your users and fine-tune changes before executing to the entire organization.

- Make progress on your implementation by breaking this up into pieces. This ensures that progress is being made while staying on top of new features and changes.

The suggested rollout approach starts with new users, a pilot group of users, and lastly all users.

Turn It On

Hurray! The final step! Once your organization is ready to make the move to Lightning, select the Turn It On tab shown in Figure 1-15. Switch the tab to Enabled to finish.

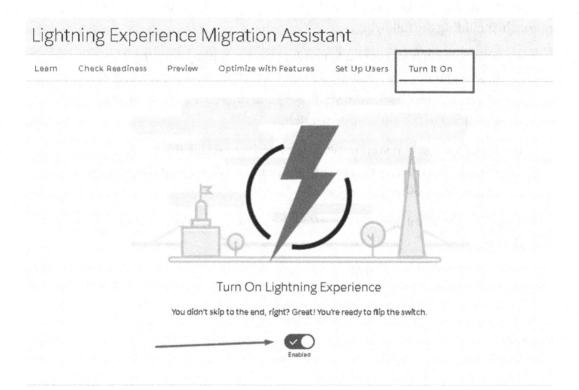

Figure 1-15. Turning on Lightning to finish

> **Note**   With the right permissions, users have the option to toggle between Classic and the Lightning Experience. From the Classic interface, select your username and click Switch to Lightning Experience, as shown in Figure 1-16. From the Lightning Experience, click Switch to Classic, as shown in Figure 1-17.

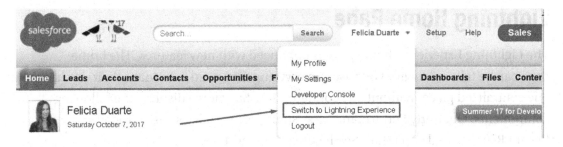

Figure 1-16. *Switching from Classic to Lightning*

Figure 1-17. *Switching from Lightning Experience to Salesforce Classic*

Lightning Home Page

The Lightning Experience home page is enhanced with new features. The home page can be tailored to give your users everything they need to manage their day in one centralized place. Without any configuration, Salesforce displays the following components: Quarterly Performance, Assistant, News, Today's Tasks, Today's Events, Recent Records, and Top Deals. See Figures 1-18 and 1-19.

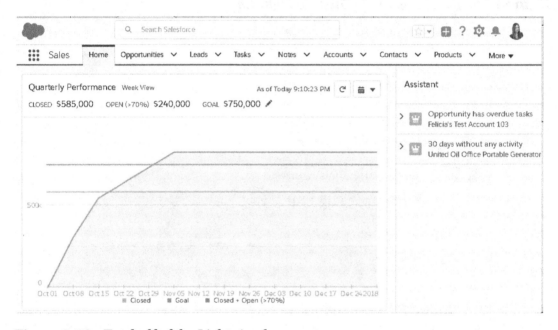

Figure 1-18. *Top half of the Lightning home page*

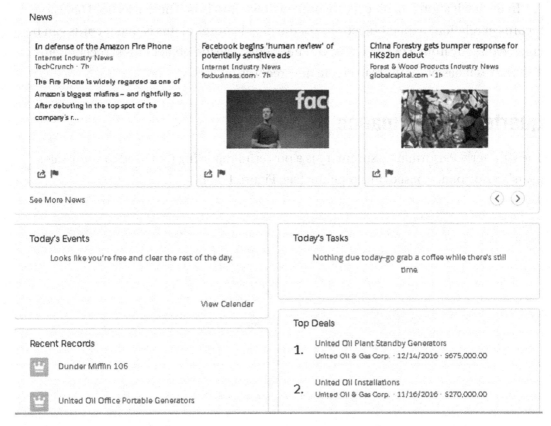

Figure 1-19. *Bottom half of the Lightning home page*

Navigation Bar

The navigation bar uses tabs to hold objects, as shown in Figure 1-20. In database terms, an *object* is a table. Objects hold groupings of information that may be related. This includes the records that live in them. Records are considered the rows that you find within a table. You will hear this terminology referenced throughout this book. For more information on objects, records, and fields, navigate to Chapter X.

In Lightning, each tab is actionable.

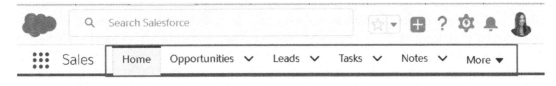

Figure 1-20. *Navigation bar*

In the navigation bar, objects are broken down into lists. These lists hold Salesforce records in relation to their object. One of the neat features of this is that records can be created directly from a tab. Each list can be used to see the object's most recent items. This makes it easier for users to create new records on the fly.

Quarterly Performance

The Quarterly Performance summary is a powerful reporting tool used to show sales users' performance based on a pipeline (see Figure 1-21).

Figure 1-21. *Quarterly Performance component located on the home page*

Closed records display the user's closed opportunities.

Open (>70%) displays the sum of all records with a probability greater than 70 percent.

If the user is part of a team, the team's opportunity sums will be showcased on this report. Otherwise, the data represented will be the user's owned opportunities.

Setting a Goal

To set a goal, follow these steps:

1. Click the pencil icon and enter an amount, as shown in Figure 1-22.

Figure 1-22. *Select the pencil icon to edit your quarterly goal*

2. Click Save.

The chart automatically calculates and updates the chart. Click C to refresh the data. Click 📅 ▾ to filter the data by week or day (Figure 1-23).

Now your sales users can start their day with a data visualization of their sales progress.

News

This new feature is a great way to display news articles related to your accounts and their industries. Once enabled, as discussed in the "Enhanced Features" section, news information can be displayed on your home page. When news is accessed from the home page, information is displayed based on recently viewed records and tasks and events for those records. See Figure 1-23.

Figure 1-23. *News component found on the home page*

Click See More News to navigate to the News tab, as shown in Figure 1-24.

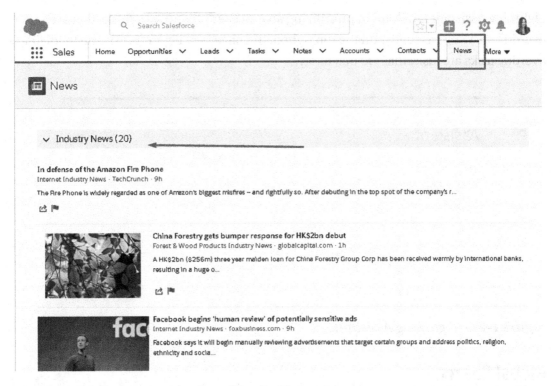

Figure 1-24. *Industry news found in the News object*

This tab displays a list of news articles titled Industry News. Information populated here is related to your accounts and their industry.

Assistant

Lightning Assistant is helpful in prioritizing an end user's daily tasks. Tasks that are overdue are showcased first on the top right of the page (see Figure 1-25). The following overdue tasks are tasks that are due today.

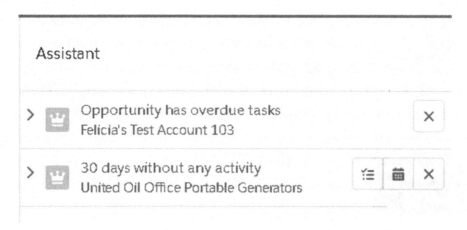

Figure 1-25. *Lightning Assistant*

Global Search

The Salesforce global search bar appears at the top of every page. Use this area to search across any object in Salesforce. It's best practice to search for a record before creating a new one to avoid duplicate data. Use wildcards and operators for greater search results.

Use an asterisk (*) to find records that match at the middle or end of your search, and use a question mark (?) to find records that match only one character at the middle or end of your search.

For example, a search for *Ay** at the end will find and display results for a contact named Ayden. It will also find and display results for Andy Young (Figure 1-26).

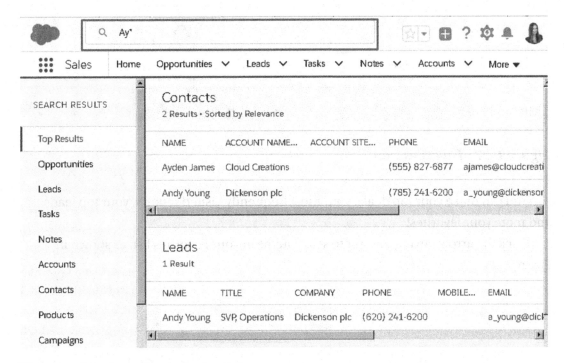

Figure 1-26. *Search results for Ay**

Favorites List

The Favorites icon is a new tool in the Lightning platform. Favorites are customized shortcuts to records and items most frequently visited, such as favorite individual records, list views, dashboards, and more.

To make an item a favorite, click the star button in Figure 1-27. This powerful tool makes it easy to find your favorite records from different object locations, all in one place.

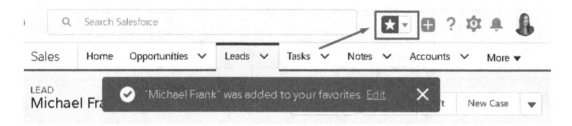

Figure 1-27. *Favorites icon*

You can make your top deals, your most frequently visited reports, your top leads, and more your favorites!

Click the arrow next to the star to select items in your Favorites list, as shown in Figure 1-28.

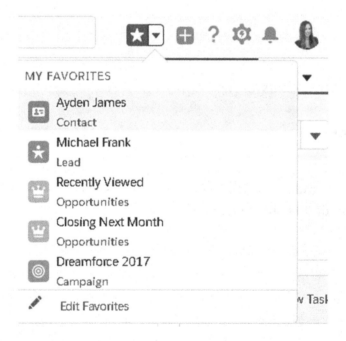

Figure 1-28. *List of favorites*

Lightning Actions

The + button shown in Figure 1-29 can be used to quickly create records in Salesforce. Use this quick-create feature to create a new activity, lead, contact, opportunity, case, or call directly from the home page.

Figure 1-29. *Lightning actions*

Click any of the available options to instantly display a quick-create window at the bottom right of the screen.

In the Lightning Experience, multiple windows can be opened from the home page to enhance user productivity and speed. Up to three windows can be displayed at once (see Figure 1-30).

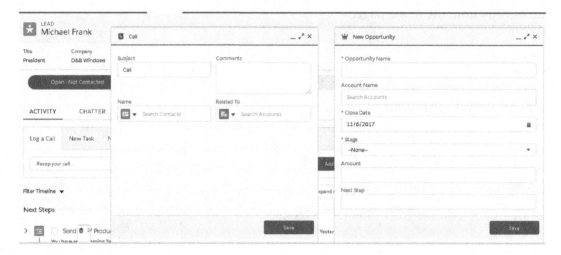

Figure 1-30.   *Utility bar*

Help and Training

Salesforce has many great support resources including videos, walk-throughs, and an interactive learning tool called Trailhead. From the home page, click the question mark (shown in Figure 1-30) to access these resources. Each page has a help menu with links to helpful resources. Use this area to log a case and get support, give feedback, and view release notes.

Salesforce provides three seasonal releases a year: spring, summer, and winter. Each release offers more than 150 new features. The image displayed at the bottom right of this menu (shown in Figure 1-31) tells which release your organization is currently in.

Figure 1-31. *Help and training*

Setup

Setup is an area used most frequently by Salesforce administrators. In Lightning, the Setup page has improved! The setup area has a more logical and easier-to-navigate layout. System administrators and users with the appropriate permission settings can access this area. Select Setup from the toolbar to navigate here (see Figure 1-32).

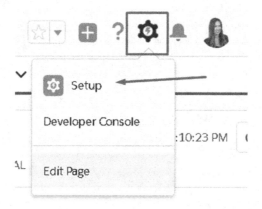

Figure 1-32. *Lightning Setup home page*

Setup has these categories: Administration, Platform Tools, and Settings. View the Most Recently Used Places in Setup to seamlessly continue any admin work. Use the Quick Find to easily find the admin tools necessary for custom work.

Click the Create button to quickly access the most common tools, including creating new objects, workflows, tabs, templates, and users (see Figure 1-33.)

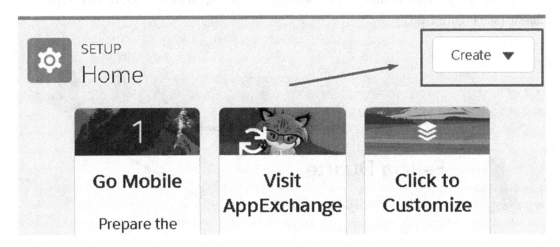

Figure 1-33. *Create button*

Notifications

View all notifications in one place, including approval requests and chatter mentions. Click the bell icon to see a list of notifications (see Figure 1-34).

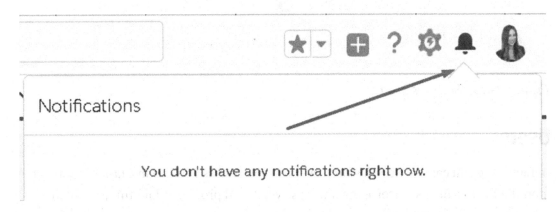

Figure 1-34. *Notifications area*

View Profile

Use this section to make changes to personal settings, log out, or switch to Salesforce Classic (see Figure 1-35).

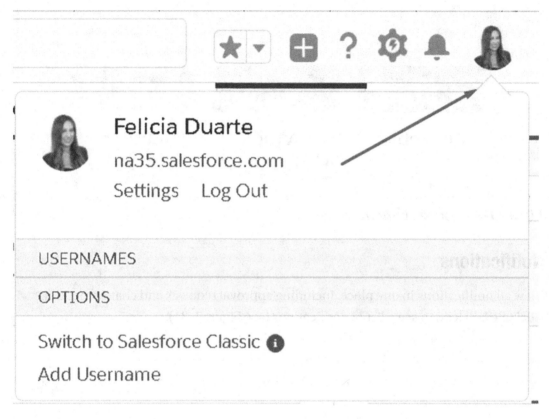

Figure 1-35. Settings area

Users

In Lightning you can create Salesforce users just as easy as you can in Classic. Users are identified with a license, username and password, and profile. In Lightning you can create new users, deactivate users, edit user settings, and more.

Create a New User

To assign licenses and record ownership, you must first create a user. Each user must be assigned a license. To free up a license, you can deactivate a user and assign accordingly. In Quick Find, search for and select Users, which is located in the Administration section.

Navigate to the User home page (see Figure 1-36) to create an individual user, edit information about an existing user, add multiple users, and reset passwords.

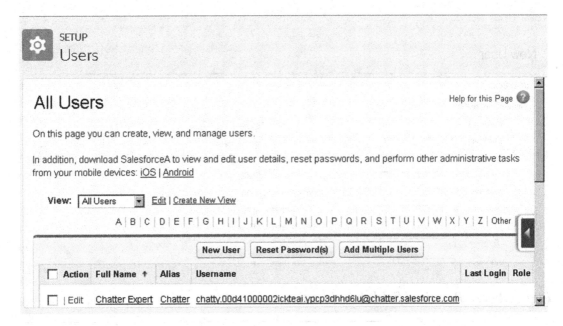

Figure 1-36. *User setup home page*

Create and Edit User Information

Follow these steps to create a new user:

1. Click New User.

2. Fill in all the required fields marked in red. This includes Last
    Name, Alias, Email, Username, and Nickname (see Figure 1-37).

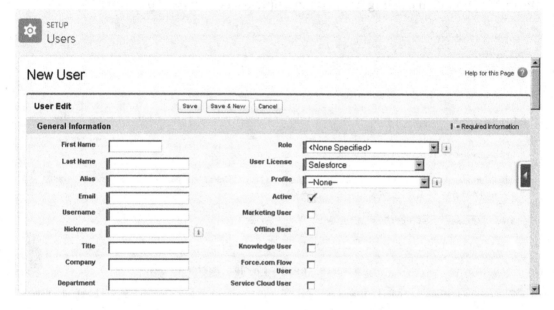

Figure 1-37. *Required fields to add a new user*

Note The email address must be in the form of a valid email address but can
be used for multiple organizations. However, the username must be a unique
username and in a correct email format.

For example, `felicia@cloudcreations.com` is a proper email format.

---

3. Assign the appropriate license in the User License field.

4. Assign a profile using the Profile field.

5. Select Marketing User to give the assigned user access to your
    organization's marketing tools.

6. Select Offline User to give the assigned user offline access.

7. Select Knowledge User to give permission to make changes to Knowledge Base articles.

8. Select Force.com Flow User to grant the ability for a Force.com licensed user to run flows.

9. Select Service Cloud User to grant access to Service Cloud.

10. Select Site.com Contributor User to allow access to Site.com.

11. Select Work.com user to assign a work.com user feature license.

12. Select Salesforce Classic User to enable access to Salesforce Mobile Classic.

13. Apply the appropriate locale settings such as time zone, locale, and language (Figure 1-30).

14. Click Save.

Salesforce sends a notification email to the user immediately to generate a new password. To stop this, deselect "Generate new password" at the bottom of the screen.

Add Multiple Users

You can save time by adding multiple users at once. To add multiple users on the User home page, click Add Multiple Users, as shown in Figure 1-38.

Figure 1-38. Add Multiple Users button

The next page will break down the number of licenses available for each license type, as shown in Figure 1-39.

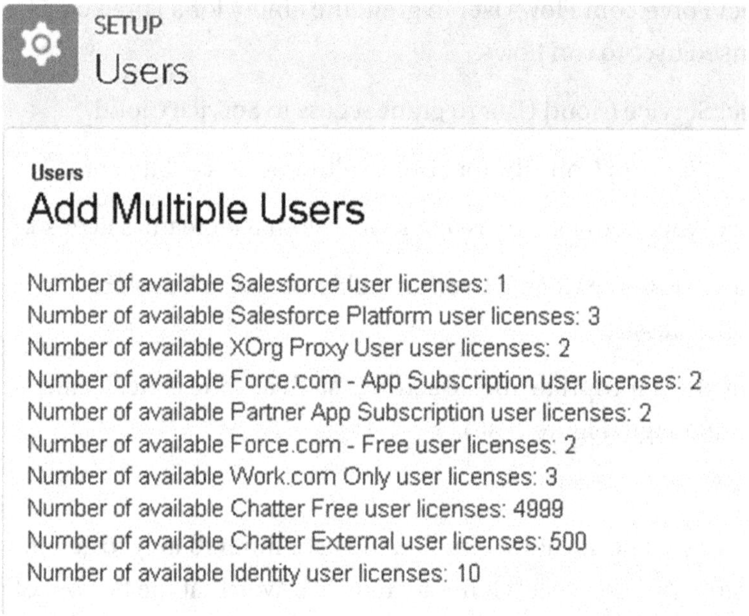

Users
Add Multiple Users

Number of available Salesforce user licenses: 1
Number of available Salesforce Platform user licenses: 3
Number of available XOrg Proxy User user licenses: 2
Number of available Force.com - App Subscription user licenses: 2
Number of available Partner App Subscription user licenses: 2
Number of available Force.com - Free user licenses: 2
Number of available Work.com Only user licenses: 3
Number of available Chatter Free user licenses: 4999
Number of available Chatter External user licenses: 500
Number of available Identity user licenses: 10

Figure 1-39. *Breakdown of available licenses*

Scroll to the bottom of the page and select the user license that you want to add for all users, as shown in Figure 1-40.

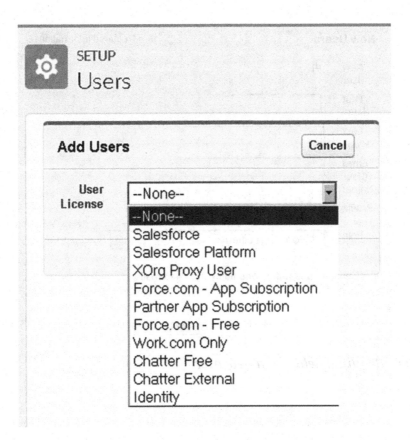

Figure 1-40. *Selecting the user license for a mass group of users*

Note   When adding multiple users, they must be users with the same license type.

Once you select the appropriate license type, fill in the details for the user and click Save, as shown in Figure 1-41. Not all user fields are available in this process.

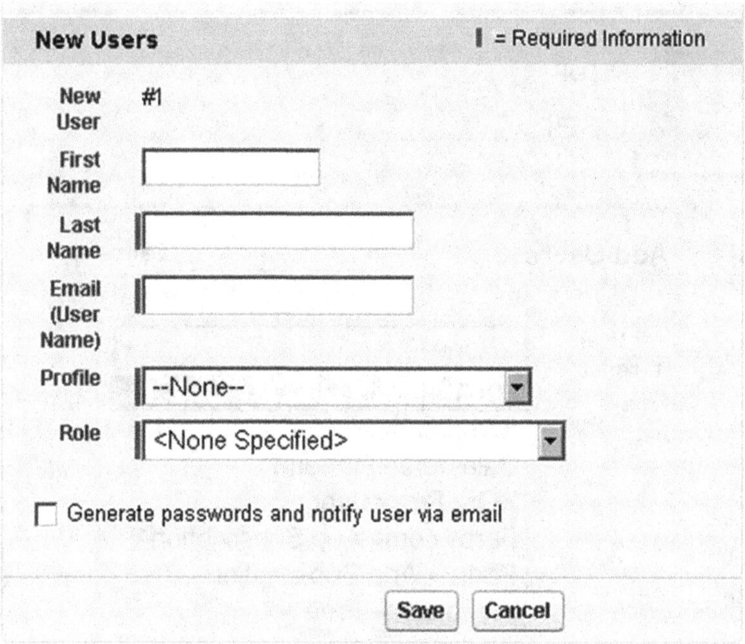

Figure 1-41. *Required fields for a new user*

Deactivate a User

In Salesforce, you can't delete a user, but you can deactivate a user to prevent them from logging in. Deactivating a user frees up a license that can be assigned to another user (see Figure 1-42). When you deactivate a user, the user is removed from all sharing privileges and groups.

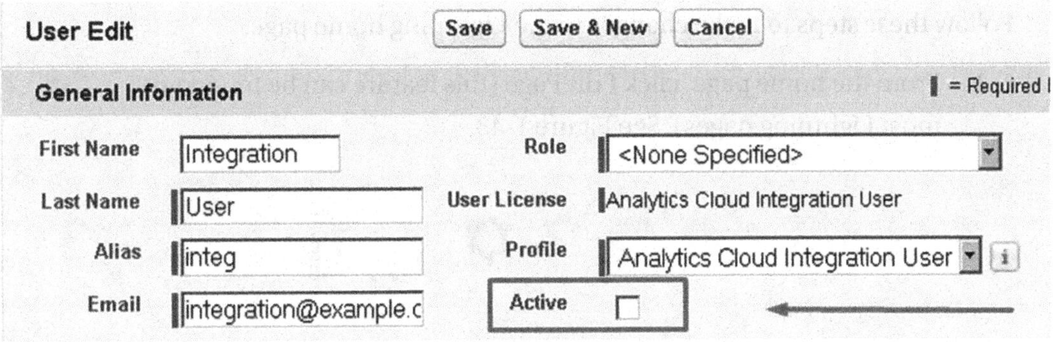

Figure 1-42. Active check box on a user's page

Records owned by this user can still be transferred to an active account. These are the deactivation steps:

1. Navigate to the User section in Setup.

2. Select the name of the user that should be deactivated.

3. Click Edit from the user record page.

4. Deselect Active from the user profile.

5. Click Save.

Lightning Pages

Lightning allows you to create custom pages to display and arrange key information for specific groups of users. You can increase adoption and user acceptance by building out clear and easy-to-use pages. By creating apps, you can minimize the type of information that is exposed to make the Salesforce organization easier to adopt. The App Builder is a new drag-and-drop tool to customize the interface without code (see Figure 1-43).

Follow these steps to make changes to the Lightning home page:

1. From the home page, click Edit Page (this feature can be found on most Lightning pages). See Figure 1-43.

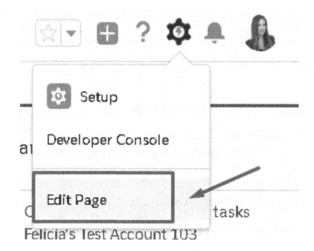

Figure 1-43. *Edit Page in the Setup drop-down*

2. Arrange which components you want accessible for your users to see. See Figure 1-44.

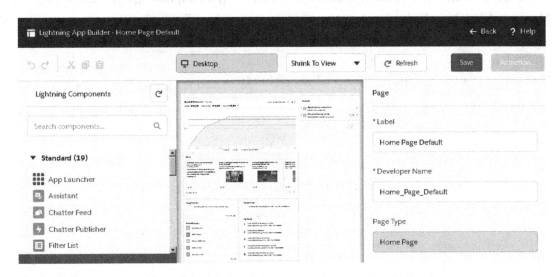

Figure 1-44. *Lightning App Builder*

3. In the left panel, choose from the available Lightning components and drag and drop to the desired section on the home page. The right panel will request details specific to the component chosen.

Create a New Lightning App

From Setup, search and select App Manager to open up the Lightning Experience App Manager. Click New Lightning App to create a new app (see Figure 1-45).

Figure 1-45. Creating a new Lightning app

To create a new app, follow these steps:

1. Fill in the required fields (those marked with an asterisk).

   The app name is what will appear in the navigation bar.

   The developer name is the API name and must be unique across other apps in your organization.

2. For App Branding, upload an image such as a company logo to customize the page (see Figure 1-46).

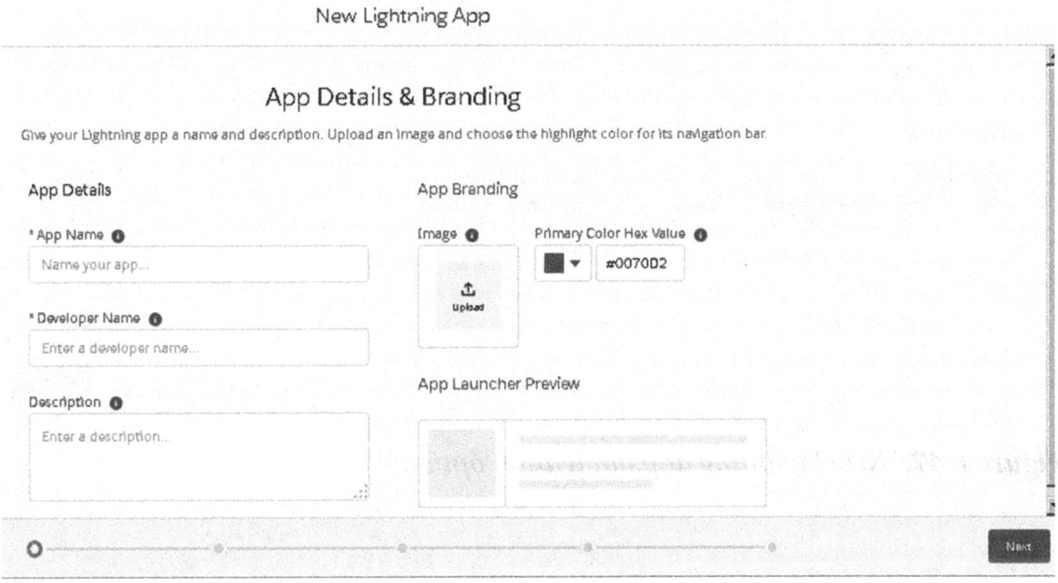

Figure 1-46. *App details*

3. Once you fill out the appropriate fields, click Next.

4. Select the navigation style. Choose Standard to display the
   navigation bar at the top or Console to open records in a new
   workspace tab (see Figure 1-47).

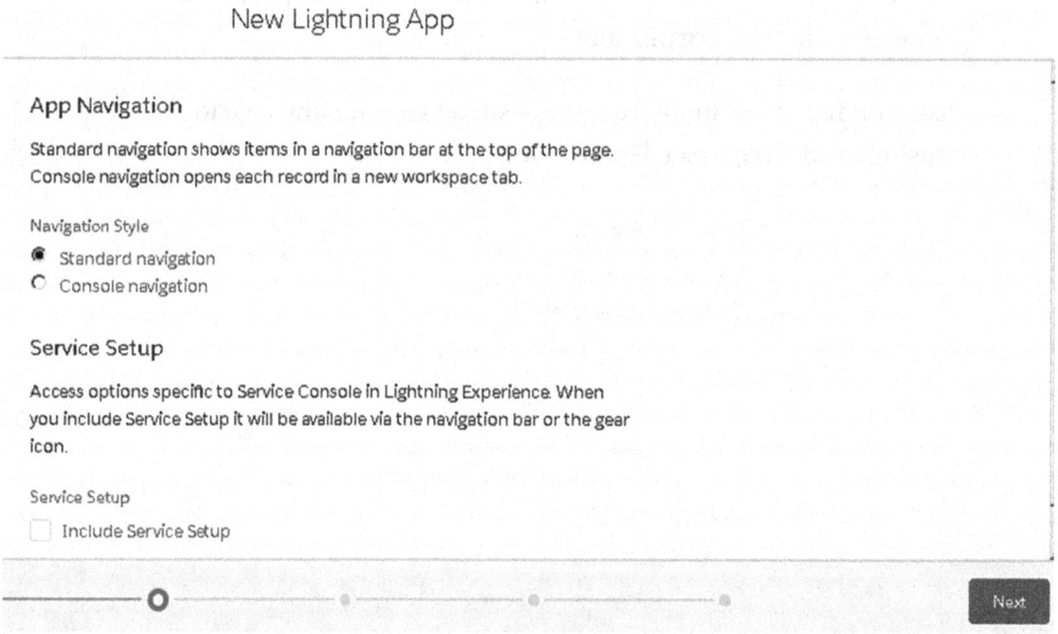

New Lightning App

App Navigation

Standard navigation shows items in a navigation bar at the top of the page.
Console navigation opens each record in a new workspace tab.

Navigation Style

◉ Standard navigation
○ Console navigation

Service Setup

Access options specific to Service Console in Lightning Experience. When
you include Service Setup it will be available via the navigation bar or the gear
icon.

Service Setup

☐ Include Service Setup

Next

Figure 1-47. *New Lightning app navigation options*

5. Click Next.

6. Click Add to add the utility bar (see Figure 1-48).

Figure 1-48. *Steps to enable utility bar for an app*

7. Select the items that should be displayed in the new app. The order of your selected items will display at the top of the page from left to right (see Figure 1-49).

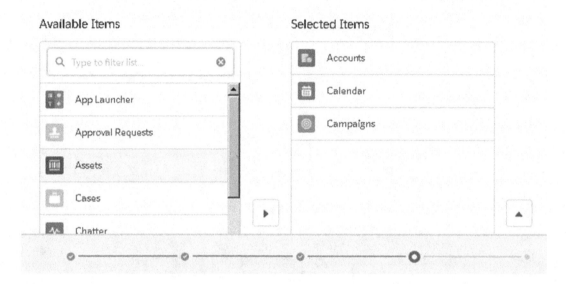

Figure 1-49. *Adding tabs to new app*

Note   It is best practice to create different apps for different groups of users. When creating these apps, it's recommended that you display only the items that are relevant to those groups of users. It can be overwhelming and frustrating when there is too much unnecessary information for your users.

For example, a sales app should show only sales-related items. Leads, accounts, contacts, and opportunities are examples. For your service agents, they most likely do not need to see opportunities. Create an app for your service agents to see only service-related items such as contacts and cases.

8. Click Next.

9. Select the profiles that should have access to this app (see Figure 1-50).

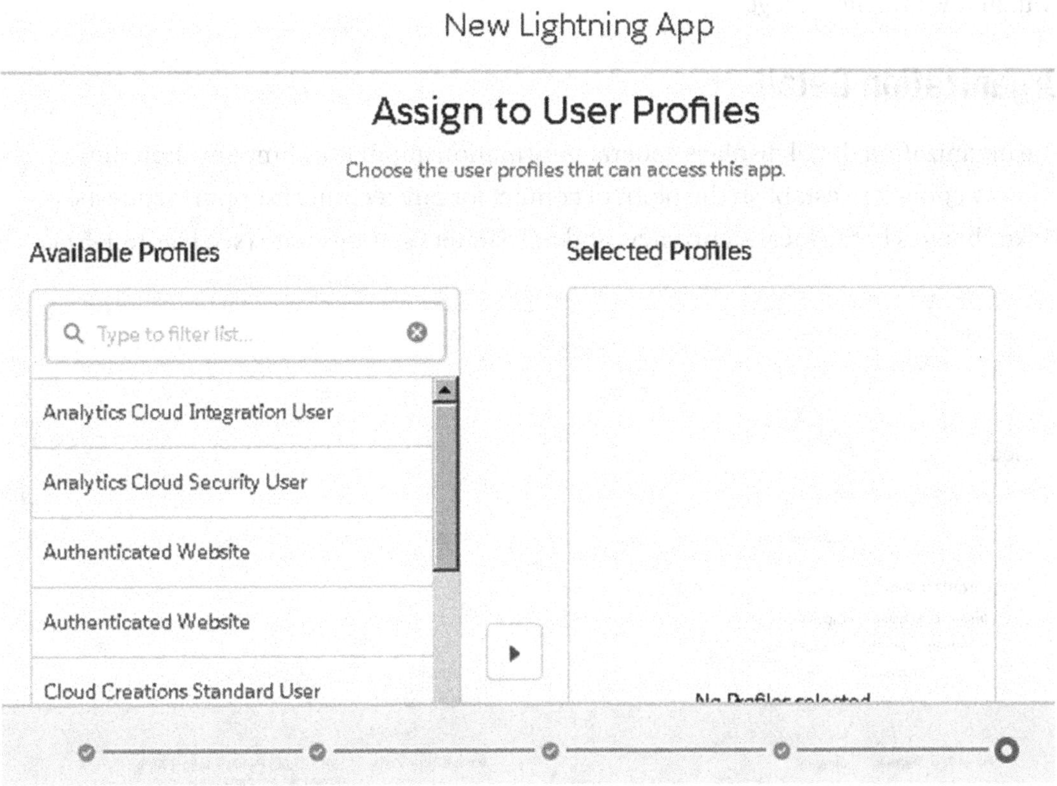

New Lightning App

Assign to User Profiles

Choose the user profiles that can access this app.

Available Profiles   Selected Profiles

Q Type to filter list...

Analytics Cloud Integration User

Analytics Cloud Security User

Authenticated Website

Authenticated Website

Cloud Creations Standard User   No Profiles selected

Figure 1-50. Assigning users to an app

10. Click Save and Finish Now. You can find the newly created app in the App Launcher.

Company Settings

Company settings are comprised of the settings that can be customized, such as fiscal year, business and holiday hours, language settings, and other important information.

Company Information

Search for and select Company Information in the Quick Find area. The Company Information section holds important information about the organization, license availability, and data usage.

Organization Detail

The organization detail displays general information about the company. Edit the primary contact to establish the point of contact for any technical support requests. Make changes to the locale, currency, and newsletters settings here (see Figure 1-51).

Figure 1-51. *Organization detail*

Storage Usage

Each organization has storage limits. Storage is divided into two categories: data and file storage. To view your storage limits, storage usage, and percentage utilized, navigate to your company settings.

Click View next to Used Data Space or Used File Space to view your organization's current storage use.

The storage usage is broken down and shows the percentage of utilization across the two. Information is also broken down by object, as shown in Figure 1-52. Use this breakdown to identify which records occupy the most space.

Storage Usage

Help for this Page (?)

Your organization's storage usage is listed below.

Storage Type	Limit	Used	Percent Used
Data Storage	5.0 MB	396 KB	8%
File Storage	20.0 MB	2.2 MB	11%

Current Data Storage Usage

Record Type	Record Count	Storage	Percent
Opportunities	40	80 KB	20%
Contacts	27	54 KB	14%
Cases	26	52 KB	13%
Leads	24	48 KB	12%
Accounts	21	42 KB	11%
Campaigns	5	40 KB	10%
Solutions	10	20 KB	5%

Figure 1-52. *Storage Usage breakdown*

User Licenses

This section displays the total number of licenses available, the total used, and the remaining number of licenses available for each license type. This includes the standard Salesforce license, which is the most commonly purchased and assigned (see Figure 1-53).

User Licenses

User Licenses Help (?)

Name	Status	Total Licenses	Used Licenses	Remaining Licenses	Expiration Date
Salesforce	Active	2	1	1	
Salesforce Platform	Active	3	0	3	
Customer Community Login	Active	5	0	5	
XOrg Proxy User	Active	2	0	2	
Work.com Only	Active	3	0	3	
Customer Portal Manager Custom	Active	5	0	5	
Identity	Active	10	0	10	
Customer Community Plus	Active	5	0	5	
Silver Partner	Active	2	0	2	
Gold Partner	Active	3	0	3	

Show 10 more » | Go to list (23) »

Figure 1-53. *User licenses*

Permission Set Licenses

Permission set licenses entitle users to access features and various tools that are not included in their user license. This can include a Service Cloud console user, a CRM user, Analytics Cloud accessibility, and more.

Feature Set Licenses

Feature set licenses include additional features on top of the standard user license. These can include Data.com, knowledge users, marketing users, and more.

Usage-Based Entitlements (BETA) Licenses

This feature is available for a limited amount of time for an organization. These tools can vary but are typically made available temporarily.

Fiscal Year

Set the fiscal year in Salesforce with your existing quarterly and annual account periods in Salesforce. This information is important to have for reporting and forecasting purposes.

Modify Fiscal Year: Standard

To modify the standard fiscal year, navigate to the Fiscal Year section in Setup and follow these steps (see Figure 1-54):

1. If the Gregorian calendar year is followed by your company, choose Standard Custom Year. (Select Custom if the standard fiscal year is not followed.)

2. Select Fiscal Year Start Month.

3. Set whether the entered month is based on the ending or start of the month.

4. Click Save.

5. Choose Standard or Custom Fiscal Year.

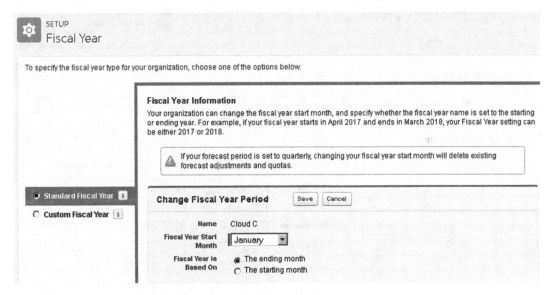

Figure 1-54. *Making changes to your organization's fiscal year*

Business Hours

Business hours define how the customer support team interacts with Salesforce. Specify the hours the support team is available to resolve cases. Salesforce will adjust the hours to sync with escalation rules, milestones, cases, and entitlement processes. Use the following steps to get started:

1. Select Business Hours in the Quick Find area.

2. Click New Business Hours to navigate to the edit page (see Figure 1-55).

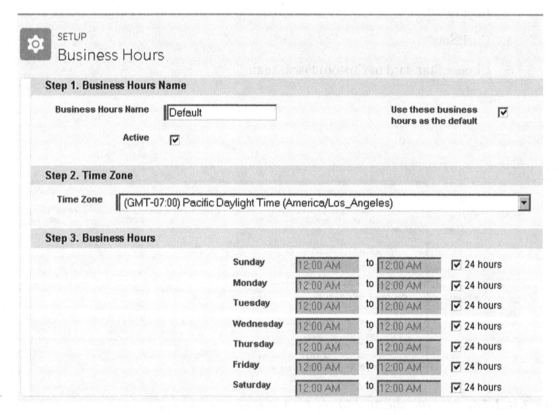

Figure 1-55. *Making changes to your organization's business hours*

3. Give it a specific name.

4. Select the time zone.

5. Specify the business hours.

6. Click Active to activate these hours.

7. Click Save to use these business hours as the default.

Summary

This chapter served as an introduction to the new intelligence and sophistication of Salesforce Lightning. In this chapter, we covered how to migrate from Classic to Lightning and prepared your organization for success with getting set up. The next chapter will discuss how to get the most out of Sales Cloud in Lightning.

CHAPTER 2

Sales Cloud Lightning

The Sales Cloud gives sales and marketing professionals the ability to increase sales productivity and revenue at lightning speeds. You can see the complete customer journey from a prospective lead to an active customer by recording leads, accounts, contacts, opportunities, and campaigns. In Sales Cloud Lightning, leads are captured, nurtured, and seamlessly converted into active accounts or prospects. Sales leaders can then manage their sales pipeline with opportunity tracking to effectively close more deals (Figure 2-1).

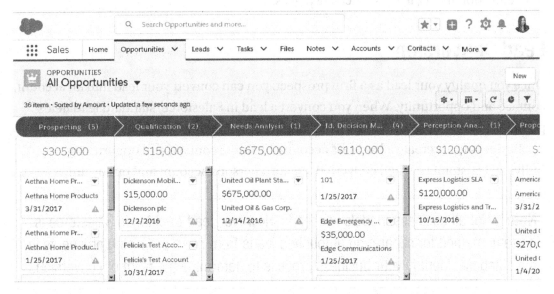

Figure 2-1. *New kanban feature on the Opportunities object in Sales Cloud*

© Felicia Duarte, Rachelle Hoffman 2018
F. Duarte, R. Hoffman, *Learn Salesforce Lightning*, https://doi.org/10.1007/978-1-4842-2994-1_2

Lead Management

Across different business models, a lead in Salesforce can be an individual, organization, or entity. The Lead object can act as a holding bucket of all prospects stored in Salesforce. Leads come from a variety of sources. So, it's a good idea to use the lead area to track important information about your leads, including contact information and notes.

Your leads may come from various entry points and may be a result of your marketing efforts. Use the Lead object to manage and nurture your leads as they are being worked through the qualification process. This can include leads that come from your web site via a Web to Lead, purchased lists, referrals, networking events, and others. Use this information to tell which channels your best leads come from.

For example, create a lead record for the prospect you met at your latest marketing event. Include important contact information about your lead, add notes, and create follow-up tasks to prevent leads from slipping through the cracks. Generate a report to see where most of your qualified leads come from. Use this information to put your marketing dollars in the most effective places.

Lead Conversion

Once you qualify your lead as a firm prospect, you can convert your lead into an account, contact, and opportunity. When you convert a lead in Salesforce, standard lead fields populate the new account, contact, and opportunity records.

Business leads create a business account, business contact, and opportunity. Individual customers, when converted, create a persons account and opportunity.

Note   Not all business models use leads. However, lead tracking in Salesforce is a useful method for separating untouched leads from more promising prospects in the database. Identify your business process to determine the point of conversion.

Understand the Lead Page

In the Lightning Experience, the lead record contains important information about the lead including contact details, activity tracking, campaign history, chatter, and news.

Sales leaders can work through their most qualified leads faster with the help of Lead Workspace toolbar. This toolbar makes it easy for reps to take their leads through the lead conversion process.

Figure 2-2 shows a lead record in the Lightning Experience. This page layout consolidates key information with a highlights panel, an activity section, and the Lead Workspace toolbar.

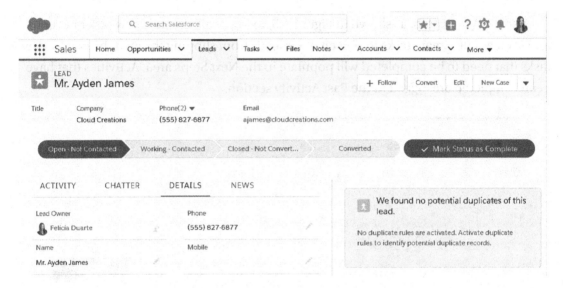

Figure 2-2. *A lead record page in the Lightning Experience*

The highlights panel, shown in Figure 2-3, displays key information at the top of the page. By default, this includes lead salutation, first name, last name, title, company, all phone fields, and email. This feature makes it easier for your users to work through leads quickly.

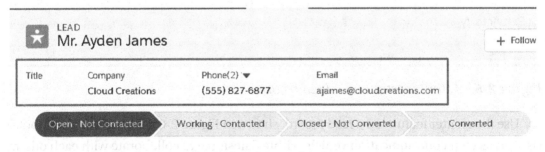

Figure 2-3. *Highlights panel on a lead record*

The interactive toolbar shown in Figure 2-4 is called the Lead Workspace. This area helps users follow a series of configurable steps in the conversion process, referred to as *sales path*. Encourage users to update the lead status as they work to qualify leads.

Figure 2-4. *Lead Workspace toolbar*

Use the Activity tab, as shown in Figure 2-5, to log a call, create a new task or event, and send email. Create tasks to prevent your leads from slipping through the cracks. Any tasks that need to be completed will populate in the Next Steps area. Activities that have been completed are logged in the Past Activity section.

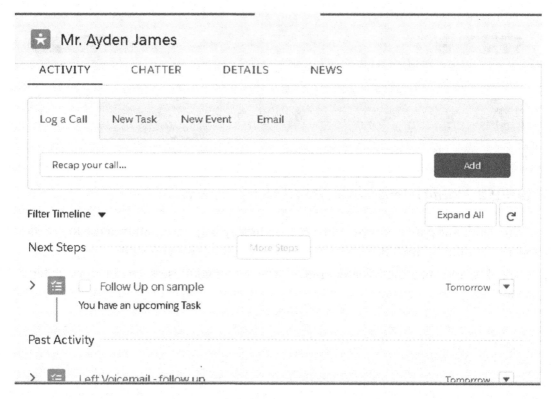

Figure 2-5. *Activity section on a lead record*

Use the chatter feature on a lead record, shown in Figure 2-6, as a collaboration tool. Use this as your communication vehicle within Salesforce to collaborate with each other. Post updates, ask questions, and create polls.

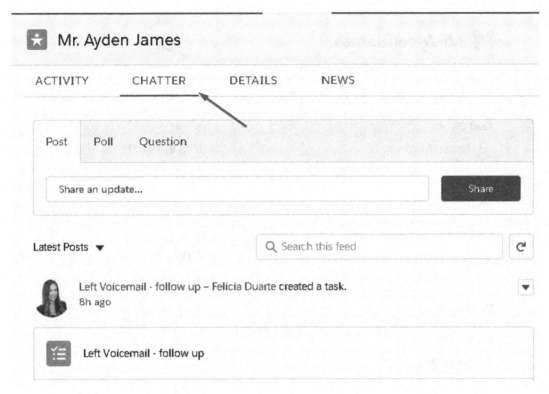

Figure 2-6. *Chatter tab on a lead record*

The Details tab shown in Figure 2-7 displays information related to the lead. This includes any standard and custom fields made visible to the user.

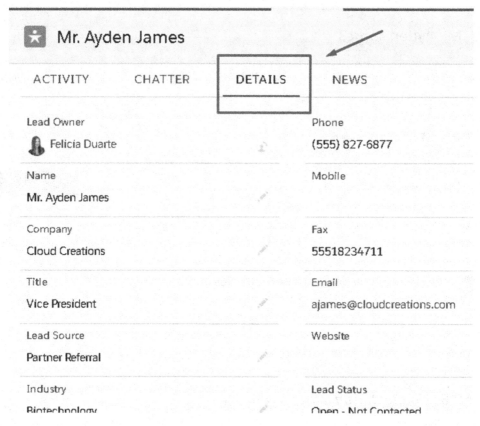

Figure 2-7. *Details tab on a lead record*

Use the News tab shown in Figure 2-8 to find news articles related to your lead. You can also sync your organization with Twitter to see up-to-date Twitter feeds and related connections.

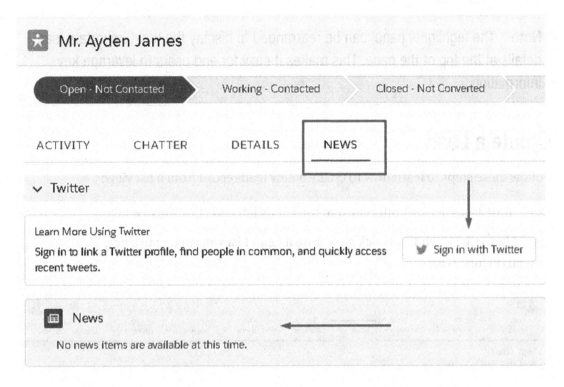

Figure 2-8. *News section on a lead record*

To the far right of the page on a default lead layout, shown in Figure 2-9, you can identify potential duplicate records. If there are any duplicates found, that information will populate this section.

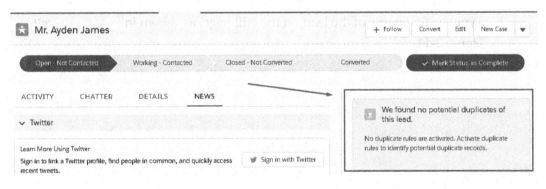

Figure 2-9. *Duplicates area on a lead record*

Note   The highlights panel can be rearranged to display the most important lead details at the top of the page. This makes it easy for end users to leverage key information.

Create a Lead

Follow these steps to learn how to create a new lead record from a list view:

1. Click the ⌄ button next to the Leads tab and click New Lead.

   Alternatively, you can click New from a Lead List view to create a new lead (Figure 2-10).

Figure 2-10. *New button on a lead from a Lead list view*

2. Type the first name of the lead on the edit page, as shown in Figure 2-11.

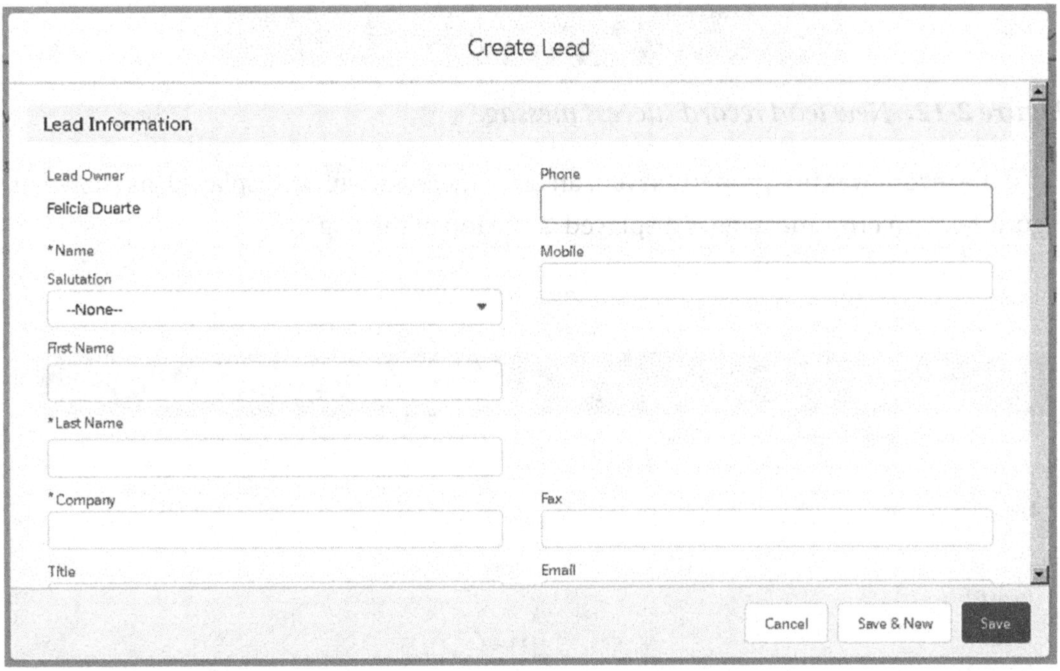

Figure 2-11. Edit page of a lead record. Fill in the appropriate lead details here.

3. Type the last name of the lead, which is required to save any lead record. Type the company name; this is the name of the business the lead is associated with.

Note   When converted, the first and last names will generate the contact's first and last names. The company name is used to create an account record and maps to the Account Name field.

Last Name and Company Name are required lead fields. If data is not filled in these fields, the record will not be saved. It's ideal to fill out more data on a lead record. You should consider adding any additional important information about your lead.

---

4. Click Save to save the record. Click Save and New to save the current record and be directed to create a new lead.

5. When a lead is created successfully, a success message will display at the top of the page, as shown in Figure 2-12.

Figure 2-12. *New lead record success message*

If the record was not properly saved, an error message will be displayed, as shown in Figure 2-13. An error message is displayed at the top of the page.

Create Lead

Review the errors on this page.

These required fields must be completed: Last Name

Lead Information

Lead Owner

Felicia Duarte

* Name

Salutation

--None--

First Name

Michael

* Last Name

Complete this field

Phone

Mobile

Figure 2-13. *Error message received after trying to save a record without filling in all required fields marked in red*

Note   Required fields are marked with a red asterisk, as shown in Figure 2-11. These fields must be populated with information in order for the record to be saved. If the field does not have an asterisk, it is not required and can be left blank, assuming there are no other validation rules in place.

How to Convert a Lead

Follow these steps to learn how to convert a lead in Salesforce:

1. Open an existing lead record.

2. From the lead record page, click the Convert button shown in Figure 2-14.

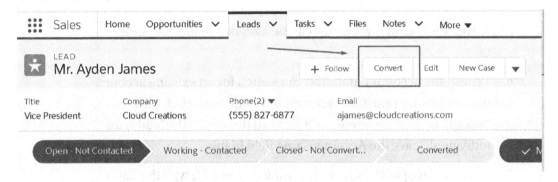

Figure 2-14. *The Convert button on a lead record*

3. Fill in the appropriate details located on the Convert Lead edit page, as shown in Figure 2-15.

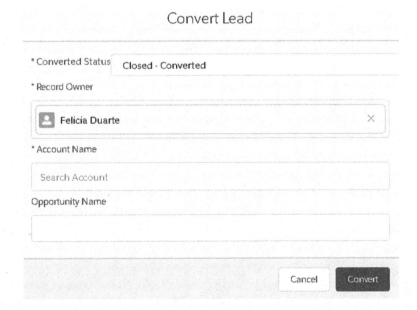

Figure 2-15. *Convert page includes converted status, record owner, account name, and opportunity name*

4.   Enter the converted status. Closed - Converted is the default
     conversion status.

Note   The lead status field captures a value that corresponds to a converted or
unconverted status. Select the appropriate lead status. By default, Converted is the
default status.

---

5.   Assign the record owner. This can be assigned to any Salesforce
     user.

6.   Type in the account name. You can search for an existing account
     or create a new one. If the account does not exist, click New
     Account to create a new account record directly. If the lead is an
     individual, leave the Account Name field blank.

7.   To create an opportunity record while converting, type the name
     of the opportunity. Leave this field blank if an opportunity does
     not exist.

8.   Click Convert and view the conversion confirmation page, as
     shown in Figure 2-16.

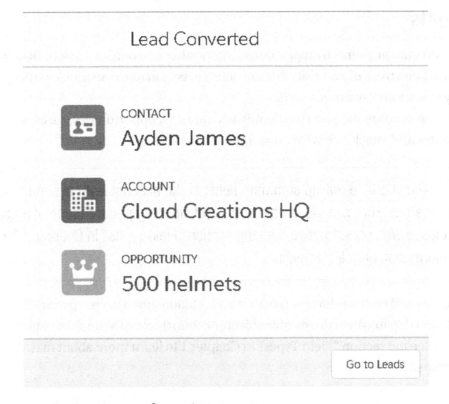

Figure 2-16. *Conversion confirmation page*

Accounts and Contacts

An account in Salesforce can be an organization, company, or institution, while a contact can be an individual associated with a business.

For example, you may have an upcoming meeting with Michael Scott at Dunder Mifflin Paper Co. in regard to a potential opportunity about your product or services. Track information about Michael Scott and Dunder Mifflin Paper Co. in Salesforce. Create a new account and call it Dunder Mifflin Paper Co. Next, create a contact record for Michael Scott to relate the two.

Tip   It's best practice to search for something before creating a new record to avoid duplication.

Accounts

You can sort your accounts by type, status, or any other standard or custom field in Salesforce. Keep track of accounts that are active versus inactive, within a particular industry or territory, and much more.

From the Account list, you can identify key contacts, opportunities, cases, and related notes and attachments for an at-a-glance view.

Note   You can create roll-up summary fields at the account level to summarize specific metrics. For example, create a roll-up field to aggregate the total amount for all Closed Won opportunities. See the section "Field Types" in Chapter 1 for more information on roll-up fields.

Accounts and contacts have a master-detail relationship. This is a parent-child relationship in which the master object (Account) controls the detail object (Contact). See the section "Field Types" in Chapter 1 to learn more about master-detail relationships.

Create a New Account

Accounts can be created or imported directly into Salesforce, without having to be converted. Create an account record to track information at the account level, such as employee count, account number, web site, etc.

1. From the toolbar, click ⌄ next to the Account tab.

2. Click New Account.

3. Fill in all required fields marked with an asterisk, including the account name (Figure 2-17).

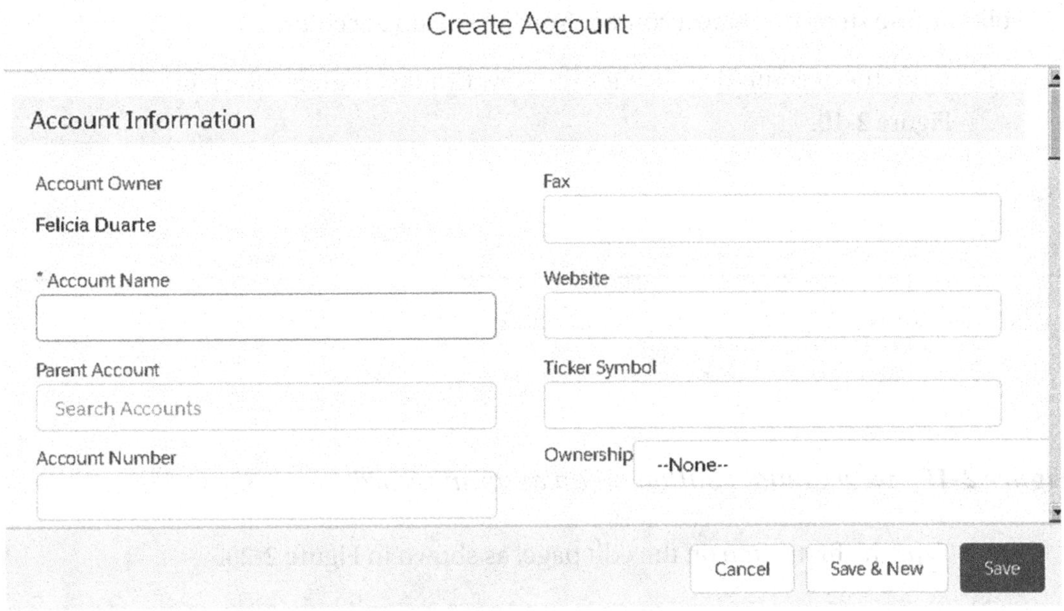

Create Account

Account Information

Account Owner

Felicia Duarte

Fax

* Account Name

Website

Parent Account

Search Accounts

Ticker Symbol

Account Number

Ownership   --None--

Cancel   Save & New   Save

Figure 2-17. *Account record in edit mode*

4. Click Save to save an account record. A success message will
    appear when properly saved, shown in Figure 2-18.

ACCOUNT
Dunder Mifflin

✓ Account "Dunder Mifflin" was created.   ✕

Figure 2-18. *Account success message*

Contacts

Use the contact record to capture individual information, including email addresses,
phone numbers, birth dates, and more. Use this information to boost client
relationships. Create encrypted fields to store secure information at the contact level, for
example, Social Security numbers and credit card information.

As mentioned earlier, accounts and contacts have a master-detail relationship.
To create a relationship between the two, make sure to enter the account name when
creating a contact.

Tip   Create the contact from the account record to quickly relate the two.

Follow these steps to create a contact from an existing account:

1. From the account record, click the New Contact button shown in Figure 2-19.

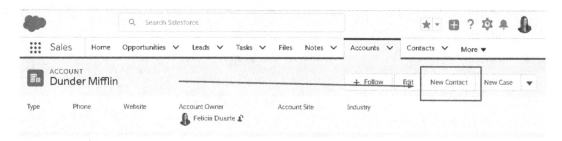

Figure 2-19. *New Contact button on an account record*

2. Type the first name on the edit page, as shown in Figure 2-20.

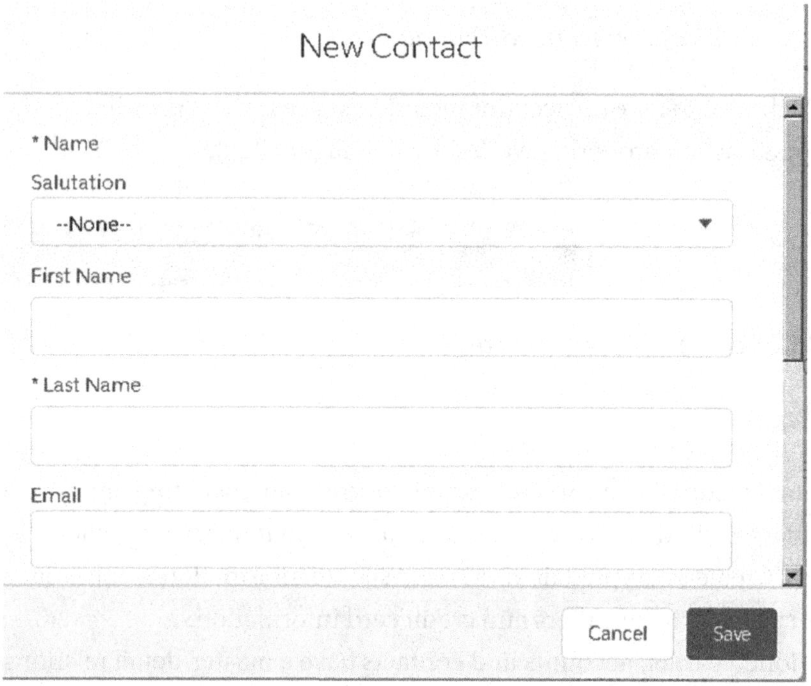

New Contact

* Name
Salutation

--None--

First Name

* Last Name

Email

Cancel   Save

Figure 2-20. *Edit page for a new contact*

3. Type the last name (this is required to save any contact record).

4. The account name is prefilled with the name of the account record you started in. Fill in any additional information about the contact.

5. Click Save to save the record and relate Michael Scott with Dunder Mifflin. Once properly saved, a success message will appear, as shown in Figure 2-21.

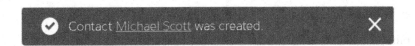

Figure 2-21. New contact success message

Now, in the account record you can see the new contact record, as shown in Figure 2-22.

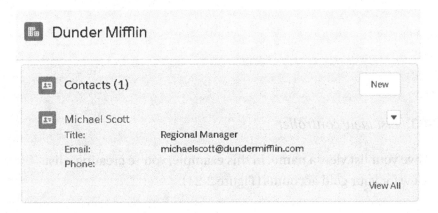

Figure 2-22. An account with its related contacts. Click New to relate more contacts.

List Views

List views make it easier to sort Salesforce data within each object. Leverage list views to call on specific groupings of records. For example, create a list view to only see active accounts, hot leads, and opportunities in the negotiation stage, and so on. Records are automatically displayed in any list view when the criteria are met. Take action on these lists with Salesforce's importing and mass updating capabilities.

The new user interface (UI(in Lightning makes it easier to visualize data. Add charts to your views and use the new drag-and-drop feature to move records across different stages.

Create a List View

Follow these steps to create a new list view:

1. To create a list view, select the tab of the object desired. For example, select the Accounts tab to create an Account List view.

2. Select the list view controller boxed in red, shown in Figure 2-23, and click New.

Figure 2-23. *List view controller*

3. Give your list view a name. In this example, you're creating a list view for your gold accounts (Figure 2-24).

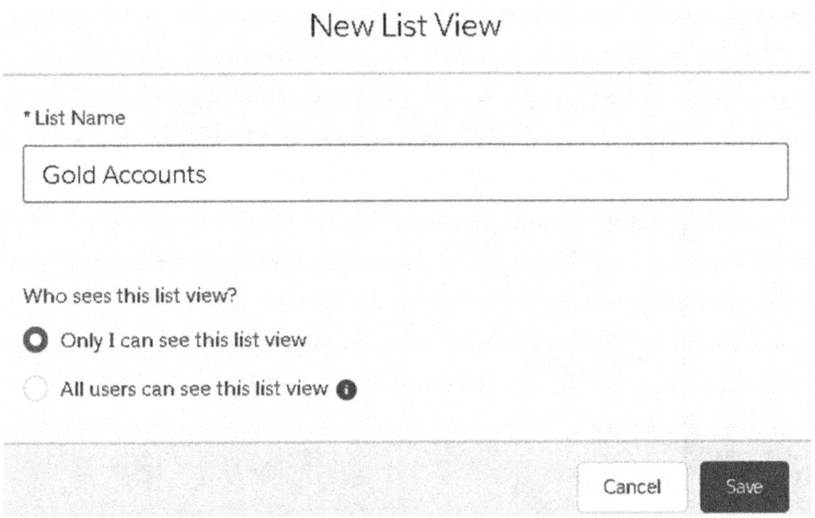

New List View

* List Name

Gold Accounts

Who sees this list view?

○ Only I can see this list view

○ All users can see this list view ●

Cancel   Save

Figure 2-24. *New list view edit page*

4. Select the appropriate level of access. If this is a list view that should be visible only to you, select "Only I can see this list view."

5. Click Save and view the new list in Figure 2-25.

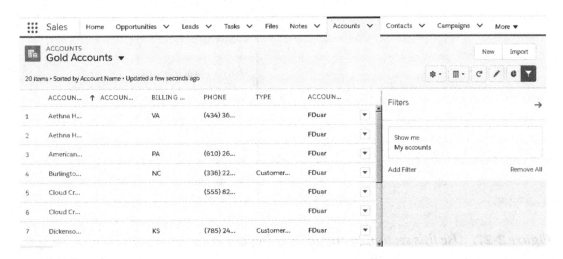

Figure 2-25. *List view after selecting Save*

6. Apply filters to your list views to segment Salesforce data, as shown in Figure 2-26.

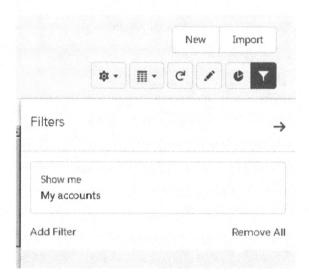

Figure 2-26. *The filter area in a list view*

7. Apply a filter to your Salesforce data using the filter section in Figure 2-27. Click Add Filter.

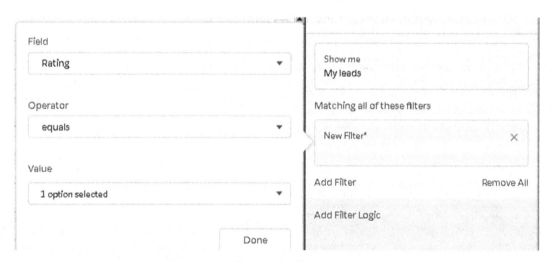

Figure 2-27. *Use this section to create filter logic*

8. Set the Field, Operator, and Value options of the filter, as shown in Figure 2-14. (See the Reports area for more information on operators.)

Example   To create a list of only hot leads that I own, I created a filter. The values to this filter include "show only lead records where I am the owner" and Equal to Hot for the Rating field.

9.   Click Done and Save.

Take Action on List Views

Records can be edited inline in a list view by clicking the pencil icon or double-clicking in the field. To save records that have been modified in a list view, click Save at the bottom of the page (Figure 2-28).

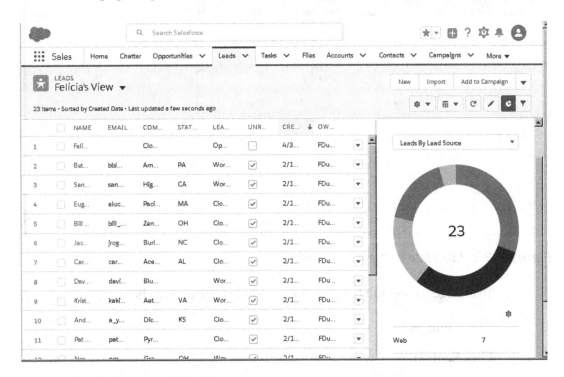

Figure 2-28. *Charts within lists*

Experience the enhanced update to list views in the Lightning Experience. Salesforce introduces a new UI to list views with its report charts and kanban functionality. Report charts can be displayed as bar graphs and donut charts.

Kanban Feature

Make lightning-fast changes in Salesforce with the new kanban feature. Instantly update the status of multiple records within a list view by utilizing the new drag-and-drop feature shown in Figure 2-29. In the kanban view, each record is displayed as a widget that can be dragged and dropped across the lead status pipeline. This enhanced feature makes it easier to visualize and organize your data.

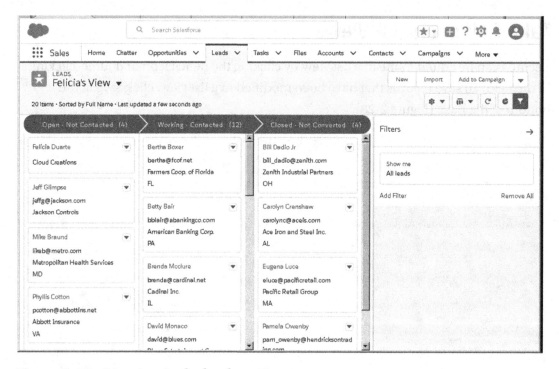

Figure 2-29. *List view in the kanban view*

1. To change the default list view from a grid list to kanban, click the
   button.

2. Click Kanban.

3. Drag and drop records to the appropriate column to instantly update the status.

Mass Change Status

To change the status for a group of records at once, create a list view for that set of data.

1. Select the records that should be updated either individually or for all, as shown in Figure 2-18.

2. From the list view, click 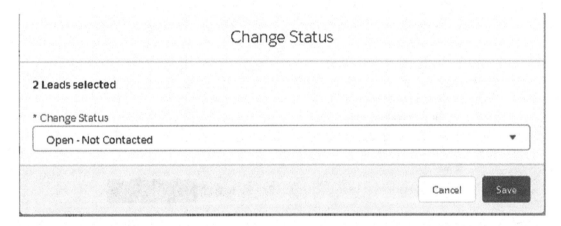 .

3. Next, click Change Status. It's important to know that only the first three actions are displayed. Any additional status values are grouped under the arrow.

4. From the Change Status pop-up, select the updated status shown in Figure 2-30. From here, you can change the status for a group of records with one click.

Change Status

2 Leads selected

* Change Status

| Open - Not Contacted | ▼ |

Cancel   Save

Figure 2-30. *Steps to change the status for a mass group of records*

5. Click Save and view updated changes to selected records.

Create an Email Template

Standardize company emails in one central place with ease. Use merge fields to populate templates with custom values from a given record. Simply create and store on-the-spot email templates directly from an account, contact, or opportunity.

1. From a contact record, select Email, as shown in Figure 2-31.

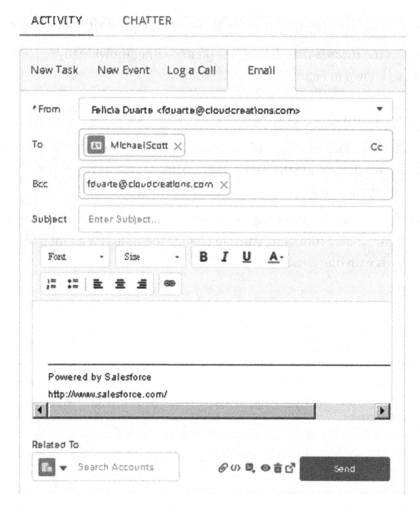

Figure 2-31. *How to create and save an email template*

2. Type the email of the recipient(s).

3. Type the subject of the email.

4. Compose the email in the body of the text.

5. Select ⟨/⟩ to include merge fields.

6. Click 📋 to save it as a new template.

Send an Email

From the Activity section in Salesforce, you select the Email tab to send an email. Enter the email of the recipient and subject, as shown in Figure 2-31.

1. Click the Activity tab from any record.

2. Type the subject for the email.

3. Type the body text for the email.

4. To relate the email to another record in Salesforce, search and enter the record in the Related To section.

5. Click Send.

Note   To access stored templates, click 🖃 and select Insert Template. Choose from the list of available templates.

Opportunities

Opportunities allow you to hold key information about any potential deal, order, or anything that may generate revenue (Figure 2-32). Deal tracking is an integral part to any business. Maximize and accelerate sales efforts effectively by keeping track of all open deals.

Use this powerful tool to prevent deals from slipping through the cracks.

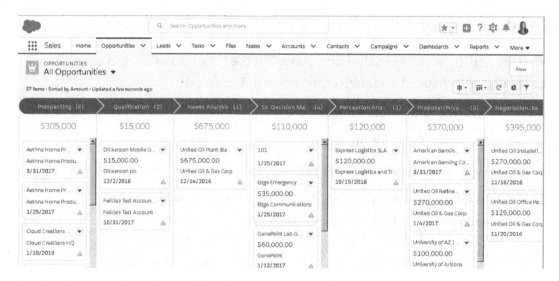

Figure 2-32. *Opportunity list view*

Create a New Opportunity

Track key information to help close open deals. Track samples that were sent, latest touch points, and next steps. Utilize or customize the Stage field to track where the deal is in the sales pipeline. Use the close date to forecast the expected close date of this deal.

1. Click the Opportunities menu.

2. Click New Opportunity and fill in the required fields found in Figure 2-33.

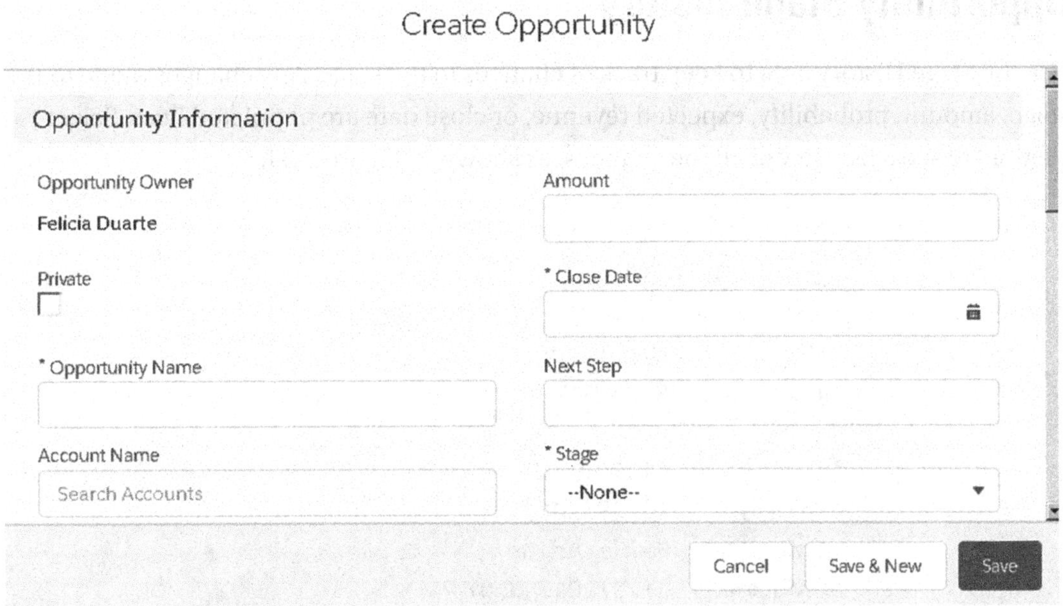

Create Opportunity

Opportunity Information

Opportunity Owner   Amount
Felicia Duarte

Private   * Close Date
☐

* Opportunity Name   Next Step

Account Name   * Stage
Search Accounts   --None--   ▼

Cancel   Save & New   Save

Figure 2-33. *Edit page on an opportunity*

3. Type the opportunity name.

4. Type the expected close date and fill in any additional details
   about the opportunity. It's recommended to fill in more details
   about the opportunity.

5. Select the stage of the opportunity record.

6. Click Save to save an opportunity record.

7. Salesforce relates the account and opportunity records once
   saved.

Tip Not sure what to name the opportunity? Try to keep uniformity in your
opportunity nomenclature and be specific. For example, Quantity + Product or
Service of Interest.

Opportunity Stage History

Use the Stage History area to keep track of changes to the stage. Any changes made to the stage, amount, probability, expected revenue, or close date are populated here. Select View all to see a list view of all the changes, as shown in Figure 2-34.

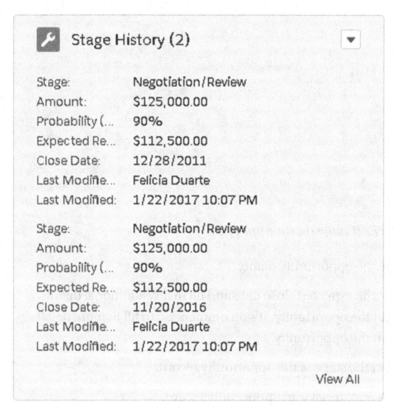

Figure 2-34. Stage History list on an opportunity record

Products

Products represent the product or service offered by your company. Store important product information in this object for sales reps to leverage during the sales process. The product description and pricing are powerful information for sales reps to leverage when out on the field or on a call.

Use products to associate with opportunities or quotes. Seamlessly update the opportunity amount to forecast potential incoming revenue. Use this information to report on best sellers, and so on.

Create a Product

Follow these steps to create products in Salesforce:

1. Click the Products tab (shown in Figure 2-35).

Figure 2-35. *Products tab*

2. Click New (Figure 2-36).

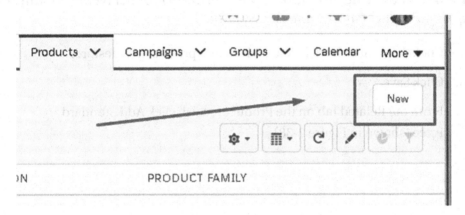

Figure 2-36. *New button on the products list view*

3. Enter the product details. Type a descriptive name for the product and provide a description (Figure 2-37).

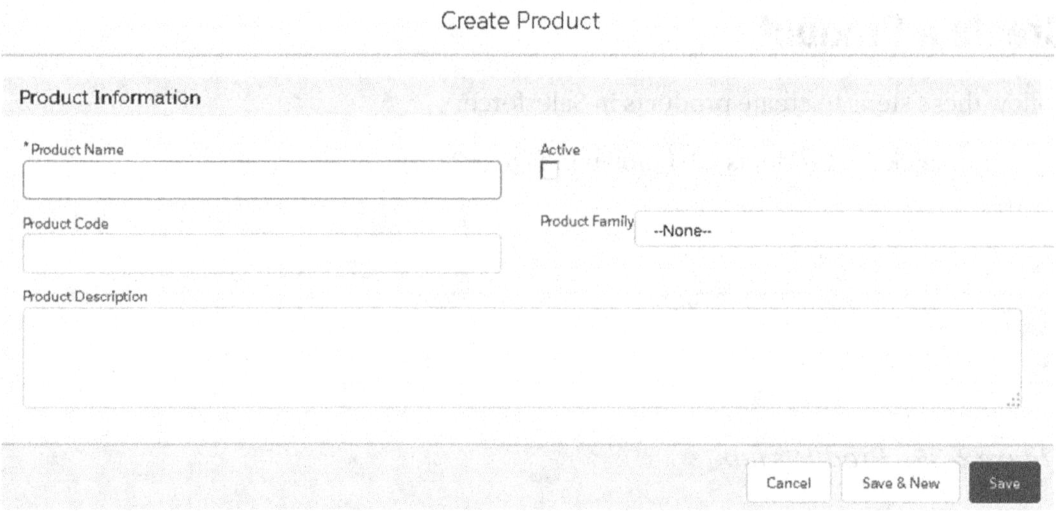

Create Product

Product Information

* Product Name

Active

Product Code

Product Family   --None--

Product Description

Cancel   Save & New   Save

Figure 2-37. *The Create Product edit page includes Product Name, Product Code, Description, Product Family, and Active status*

4. Click the Active check box to activate the product in Salesforce.

5. Click Save.

6. From the Related tab on the Product record, click Add Standard Price (shown in Figure 2-38).

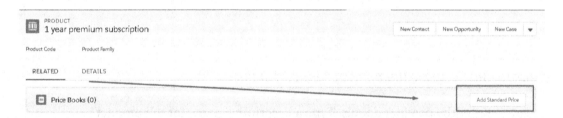

PRODUCT
1 year premium subscription

New Contact   New Opportunity   New Case

Product Code   Product Family

RELATED   DETAILS

Price Books (0)   Add Standard Price

Figure 2-38. *Add Standard Price button*

7. Enter the list price of the product, as shown in Figure 2-39, and associate it with the standard price book if no other price books are being used.

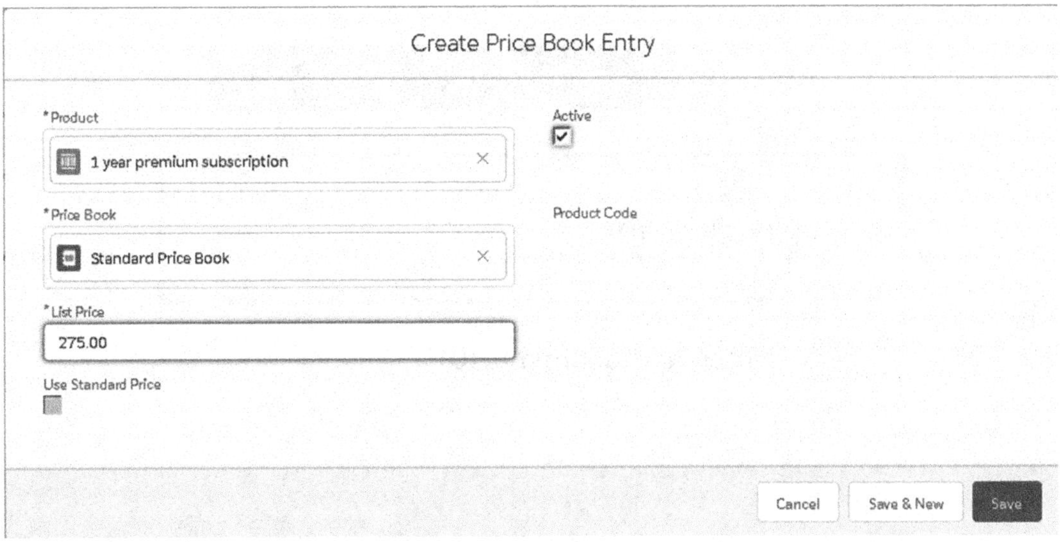

Create Price Book Entry

* Product   Active

☑ 1 year premium subscription   ✕   ☑

* Price Book   Product Code

☑ Standard Price Book   ✕

* List Price

275.00

Use Standard Price
☐

Cancel   Save & New   Save

Figure 2-39. *Price book entry page*

8. Click Save. Salesforce creates the new pricebook entry record.

Note   How are products related with pricebooks? Products must be added to a pricebook in order to be available to an opportunity. Pricebooks can be used to record multiple pricing on a single product. Define prices for wholesalers, distributors, and other customers with Pricebooks.

Opportunity Products

Follow these steps to create opportunity products in Salesforce:

1. From an opportunity record, click the arrow in the Products list shown in Figure 2-40.

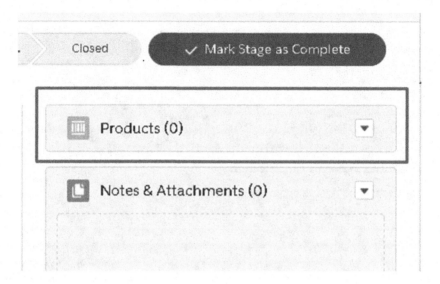

Figure 2-40.   *Products list on an opportunity record*

2.   Click Add Products.

3.   Select the + button next to each product that should be attached.
     See Figure 2-41.

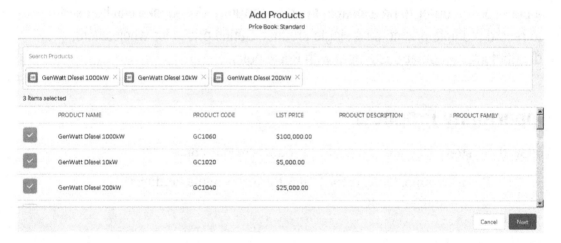

Figure 2-41.   *Product selection page*

4. Click Next.

5. Select the quantity for this particular opportunity and for each
   product, as shown in Figure 2-42.

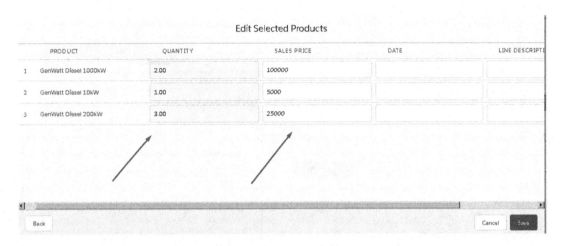

Figure 2-42. *Opportunity product selection*

6. Update the sales price for each product.

7. Enter a date or line description if desired.

8. Click Save.

9. View new opportunity product records successfully attached to
   this opportunity, as shown in Figure 2-43.

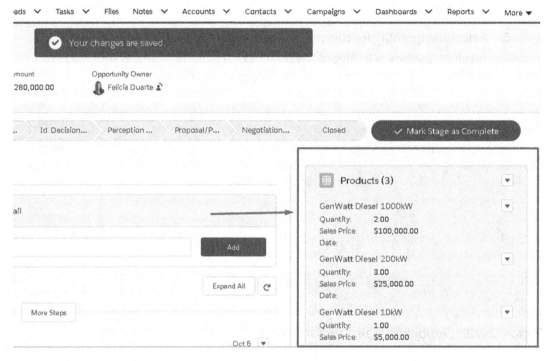

Figure 2-43. *Opportunity home page with new products attached*

Opportunity Record Page

The product panel to the right in Figure 2-43 displays the products associated to the opportunity. Click ▼ next to any product record to edit or delete from the opportunity.

The Stage workspace at the top of the page in Figure 2-43 is an interactive tool, which can be used to help sales agents move along their sales process.

Activity Timeline

Prioritize your day-to-day tasks by setting reminders and assigning tasks in Salesforce. Use activities to create a task, create an event, or log a call. In the Lightning Experience, the Activity timeline replaces the classic Activity History and Open Activities lists, as shown in Figure 2-44.

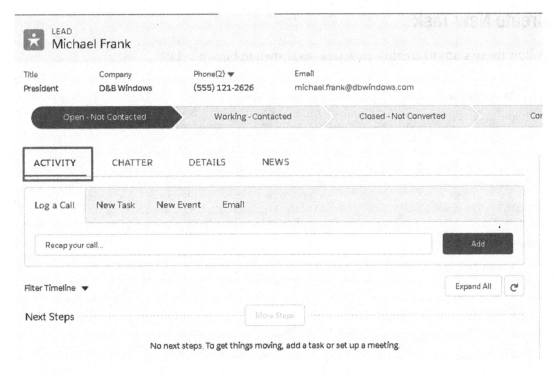

Figure 2-44.   *Activity section within lead record*

Use the comments section of the Log a Call tab to record important call details. Relate the contact to another account or opportunity.

Configuring Activity Feed

You can configure your activity feed by creating new tasks and events.

Create New Task

Follow these steps to create a new task, as shown in Figure 2-45:

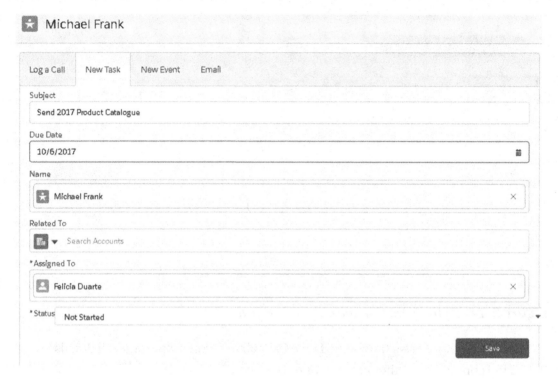

Figure 2-45. *Steps to create a new task*

1. Type the subject of your task.

2. Enter the task due date. The due date will be used to notify when a task is upcoming or overdue.

3. Relate the task to another record in Salesforce in the Related To section. By default, whoever is creating the task is the Assigned To person. Simply change this by clicking the x and selecting the person the task should be assigned to.

4. Select a status. Not Started, In progress, Completed, Waiting on someone else, and Deferred are the standard status values.

5. Click Save. A successful task record will display a message, as shown in Figure 2-46.

Figure 2-46. *Successful task message*

6. The task is saved and recorded in the Next Steps section. Tasks that have been completed are moved and displayed in the Past Activity area, as shown in Figure 2-47.

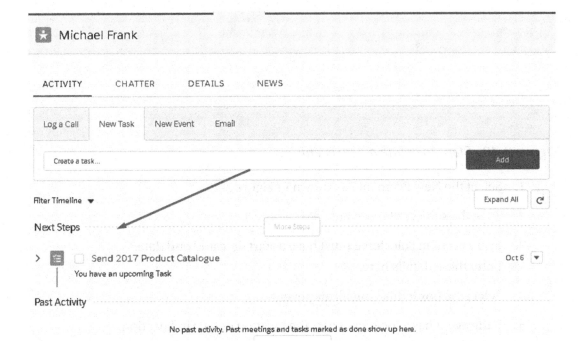

Figure 2-47. *Next Steps section*

Create a New Event

Keep track of any events that are related to your leads or contacts. An event will have a start date and an end date.

Follow the next steps to create a new event for a lead record and refer to Figure 2-48.

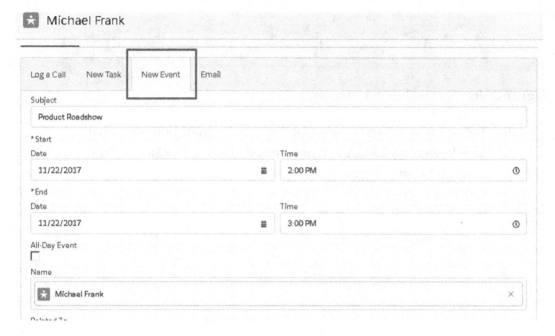

Figure 2-48. *Steps to create a new event*

1. Select the New Event tab, as shown in Figure 2-46.

2. Type the subject of the event.

3. Every event in Salesforce must have a start date and end date. Enter these details here.

4. Select the box if this is an all-day event.

5. If the event has a location, enter the location details in Location. This is optional.

6. If the event is related to an account, search for the related account to associate the two, as shown in Figure 2-49.

Figure 2-49. *Related To and Assigned To fields on the event page*

7. Tasks and events can be assigned to other Salesforce users. Choose who the task should be assigned to, as shown in Figure 2-49.

8. Click Save.

Create a Web-to-Lead Form

With a web-to-lead form, leads can instantly be generated into Salesforce from your web site. For example, create a Contact Us form on your web site to create new lead records in Salesforce. Create custom fields to track specific information from your web site and into Salesforce.

Follow these steps to create a web-to-lead form:

1. Click Setup.

2. Search for *web-to-lead* in the Quick Find section.

3. Click Create Web-to-Lead Form.

4. Standard and Custom fields are displayed in the Available Fields multiselect picklist, as shown in Figure 2-50. Add the fields to the Selected Fields column to display on your web-to-lead form.

Note   Formula fields are not available to be selected.

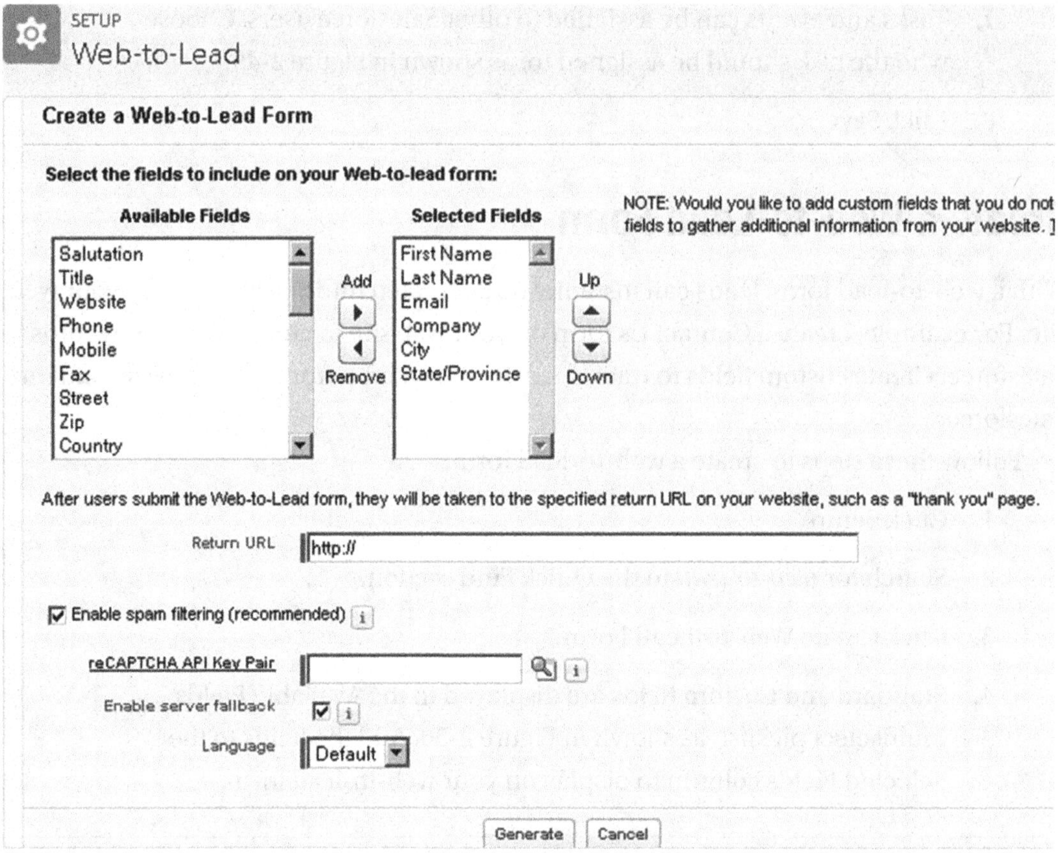

Figure 2-50. *Web-to-Lead setup page*

5.   After users submit a web-to-lead form, they are taken to a specified return URL. Type the return URL here. Note that this is typically a thank-you page.

6.   Select this check box to enable reCaptcha to prevent spam. This is recommended.

7.   To use this feature, go to the Google reCaptcha web site and click Get reCaptcha to register domain. Once this is attained, enter the API key pair here.

8.   If the Google servers are down, select this box to allow all traffic and leads to be generated without reCaptcha.

Note   You can generate up to 500 leads within 24 hours. Any additional leads exceeding this amount are placed in a queue.

Create a Web-to-Lead Autoresponse Rule

Improve your client communication by sending out autoresponse messages to leads captured from your web site. As an example, create an autoresponse rule notifying the client that you received their submission and will reach out within 24 hours.

1. Click the New button shown in Figure 2-51.

Figure 2-51.   *Create a new web-to-lead auto-response rule*

2. Name the auto-response rule shown in Figure 2-52.

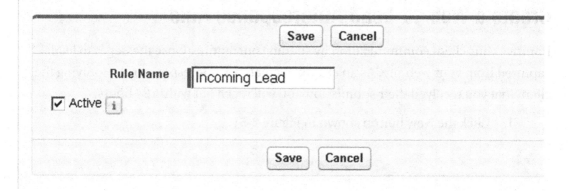

Figure 2-52. Naming the auto-response rule

3. Select Active to activate the rule.

4. Click Save.

5. Select the created rule.

6. Click New in the Rule Entries section.

7. Determine the sort order and set your desired criteria. In this example, I'm creating an auto-response rule for all leads coming from my web site, as shown in Figure 2-53.

Rule Entry Edit
Incoming Lead

Enter the rule entry   [Save] [Save & New] [Cancel]

Step 1: Set the order in which this rule entry will be processed

Sort Order [i] [1]

Step 2: Select the criteria for this rule entry

Run this rule if the following [criteria are met ▼] :

Field	Operator	Value	
Lead: Lead Source ▼	equals ▼	Website	🔍 AND
—None— ▼	—None— ▼		AND
—None— ▼	—None— ▼		AND
—None— ▼	—None— ▼		AND
—None— ▼	—None— ▼		

Add Filter Logic...

Step 3: Specify the name and address to include on the auto-response message From line

Figure 2-53. *Setting the criteria for auto-response rule*

8. Select the criteria for this rule to be triggered. This rule will be triggered when any lead has the source Web.

9. Type the name of the sender.

10. Type the email address of the sender.

11. Select the email template to be used.

12. Click Save. Now any lead that meets the criteria you set will automatically receive an email using the template you chose.

Create a Lead Assignment Rule

Automate your lead routing process by creating a lead assignment rule New leads can automatically be assigned to a user or queue based on the condition that is set.

1. Click Setup.

2. Search for *Lead Assignment Rules* in Quick Find and select it.

3. Click the New button.

4. Give the rule a name and type it here.

5. Select Active to activate this rule; only one rule can be active at a time.

6. Click Save.

7. Select the rule name.

8. Click the New button in the Rule Entry section, as shown in Figure 2-54.

Lead Assignment Rules

Help

Automatically assign leads to users or queues based on criteria you define. You can create multiple rules with different conc one rule can be active at a time.

Click a rule name to add or edit rule entries.

New

Action	Rule Name	Active	Created By	Created On
Rename	Del	Sales Manager		Felicia Duarte	1/24/2017
Rename	Del	Standard	✓	Felicia Duarte	1/22/2017

Figure 2-54. *List of lead assignment rules*

9. Salesforce will evaluate each entry based on the sort order. Set the sort order for this rule.

10. Set the criteria for this rule by selecting the field, the appropriate operator, and the value. In this example, I am creating the rule for all leads coming from the state of California.

11. Determine whether leads that meet this criteria should be assigned to a user or queue. Type the name of the user or queue.

12. Click Save.

Create a Lead Queue

Manage your workload by controlling the way leads are assigned. Leads are bucketed into these queues for group members to view and accept. Lead records remain in queue until a user accepts.

1. From Setup, go to Queues.

2. Click the New button shown in Figure 2-55.

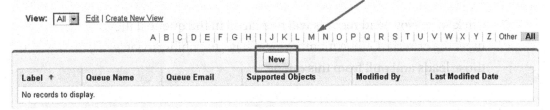

Figure 2-55. *Lead queue*

3. Type the name of the queue.

4. To notify group members that a lead has been added to a queue, enter the queue email and select Send Email to Members.

5. Select Lead and move to Selected Objects.

6. Choose the queue members as shown in Figure 2-56 and move them to Selected Members. You can define the selected members by users, roles, and groups.

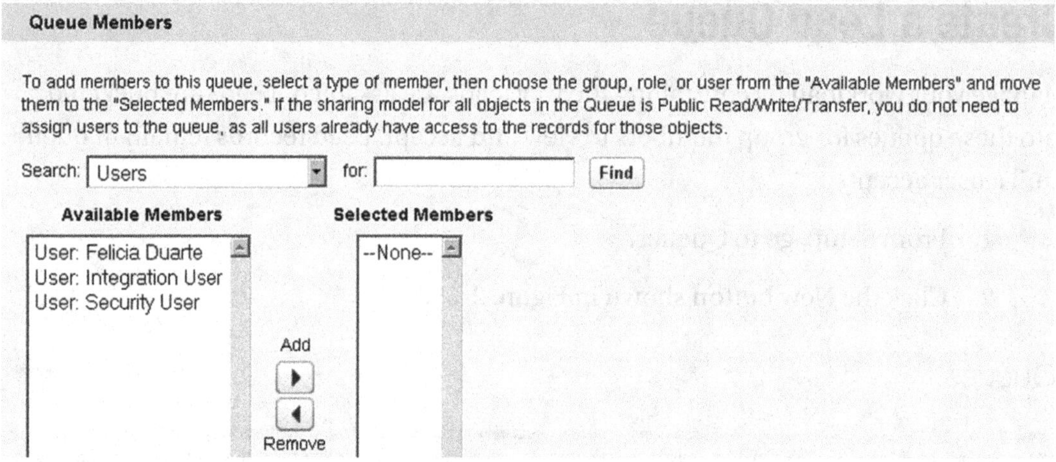

Queue Members

To add members to this queue, select a type of member, then choose the group, role, or user from the "Available Members" and move them to the "Selected Members." If the sharing model for all objects in the Queue is Public Read/Write/Transfer, you do not need to assign users to the queue, as all users already have access to the records for those objects.

Search: Users ▾   for: [   ]   Find

Available Members   **Selected Members**

User: Felicia Duarte   --None--
User: Integration User
User: Security User

Add
▶
◀
Remove

Figure 2-56. Adding members to a queue

7. Click Save. Now lead records will be placed in the queue if they meet the criteria. Queue members will have the ability to view those leads and pull from this queue.

Create a Campaign

Marketing professionals can use this powerful tool to track any marketing initiatives and efforts. Track the response and conversion rates to ultimately calculate return on investment (ROI). Use these metrics to confirm the effectiveness of your marketing efforts. Campaigns can be an effective tool to improve future marketing efforts.

Follow these steps to create a campaign and add campaign members:

1. Select New Campaign from the Campaign tab, as shown in Figure 2-57.

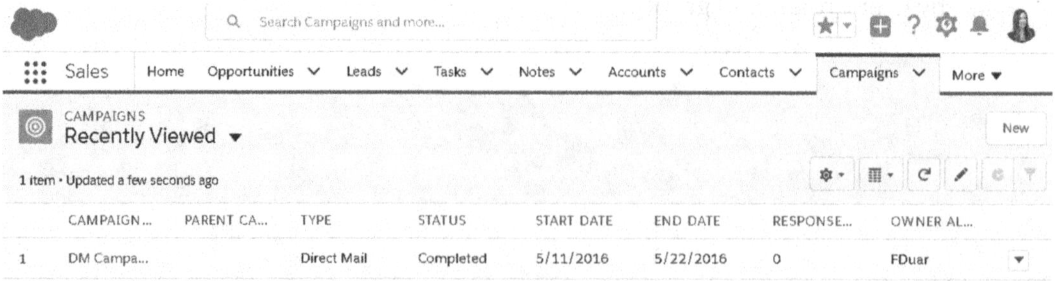

Figure 2-57. Campaigns tab and list view

2. Type the name of your campaign, as shown in Figure 2-58.

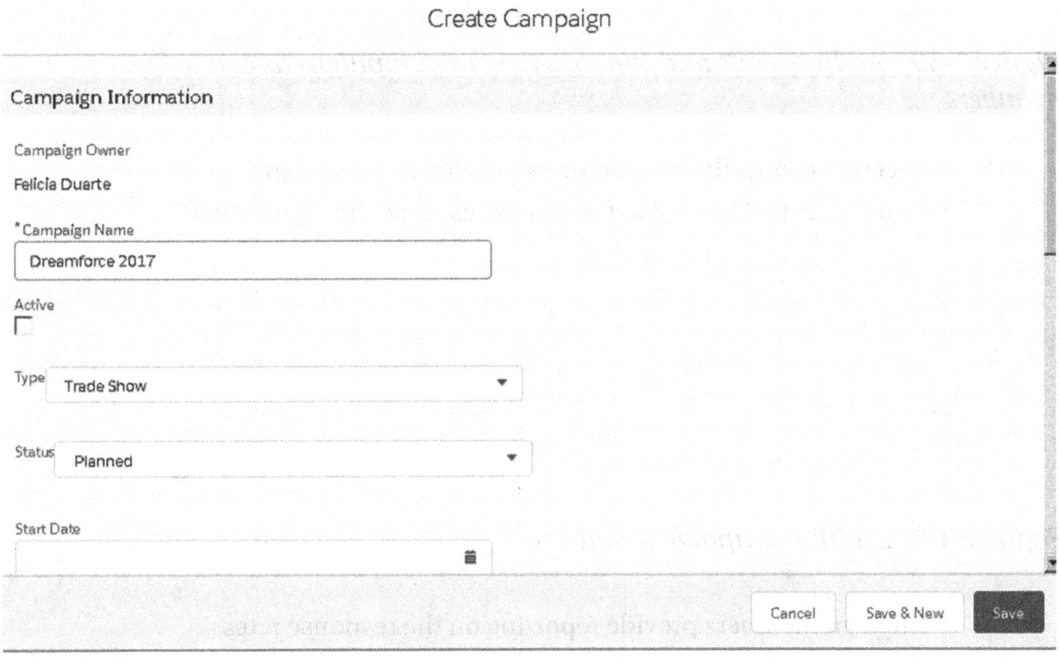

Create Campaign

Figure 2-58. Campaign edit page

3. Fill in the details about your campaign Include the type of campaign, the start date and end date of the campaign, and other important information.

4. Click the Active check box to make the campaign active and current.

5. Click Save.

Once the campaign is active, you'll want to add campaign members. This will tie everything together. Campaign members are the leads and contacts that you associate to any given campaign.

Note that a lead and contact have a many-to-one relationship. This means that they can be associated to many campaigns. Click Add Leads to associate lead records or click Add Contacts to associate contact records (Figure 2-59). These leads and contacts are considered campaign members to your campaign.

Figure 2-59. *Adding leads and contacts to your campaigns as campaign members*

6. Select the records that should be associated as campaign members and select Add to Campaign, as shown in Figure 2-60.

Figure 2-60. *Adding campaign members*

Campaign members provide reporting on the response rates of your campaign. Salesforce tracks these efforts by using these standard values: Sent and Responded.

7. Enter the campaign that this record should be associated with.

8. Define the member status as existing or update the member status as Sent or Responded (see Figure 2-61).

Figure 2-61. *Steps to associate the campaign and status that the selected campaign members should have*

    9.   Click Submit. Salesforce will generate a success message, as shown in Figure 2-62.

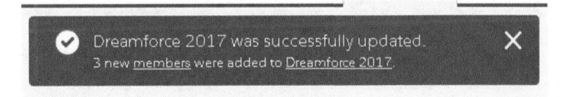

Figure 2-62. *Campaign member success message*

Summary

Sales Cloud provides effective tools to connect your sales and marketing teams. Sales Cloud sets the foundation for your CRM needs and provides insightful information into your opportunity pipeline.

CHAPTER 3

Salesforce Service Cloud

Salesforce Service Cloud allows your customer service representatives and support representatives (users) to manage, track, and resolve customer inquiries and issues. The Service Cloud application uses the Case object to capture all the details needed to help them to resolve the inquiries and issues. Your users can manually create cases for requests via phone and in person or accept cases from multiple channels (e.g., web forms, email, real-time web chat, online communities, and social media outlets). You can allow your users to efficiently manage these channels by setting up case assignment rules. The Salesforce Service Cloud application also allows you to create case escalation rules when an issue needs to be escalated to management. Tracking the various customer inquiries your company brings in could even help you to establish new procedures. It also will help you to understand any weak points within your company. Figure 3-1 shows the internal communication that can take place in Service Cloud. In short, the application can help to resolve issues with customers faster.

© Felicia Duarte, Rachelle Hoffman 2018
F. Duarte, R. Hoffman, *Learn Salesforce Lightning*, https://doi.org/10.1007/978-1-4842-2994-1_3

Figure 3-1. *Internal communication*

Overview of Salesforce Case Management

Salesforce case management allows users to capture the necessary details of the Case object to manage and successfully resolve their case. Users can see important case details in 29 standard fields as well as create their own custom fields. They can keep track of the status of a case with a drop-down field with values such as New, Working, Escalated, and Closed. Users can also access all the necessary connected objects such as the account, contact detail, and product information. Giving users access to the account and contact details will allow them to get a full view of the customer submitting the case. They can assign the case to a High, Medium, or Low priority based on the case submission as well as set up their page layout to best fit their needs and the needs of the company.

Introduction to Standard Case Fields and Related Lists

Salesforce offers a number of standard fields via its Case object that are displayed in Figure 3-2. Before you decide to create a custom field, we recommend that you leverage an existing standard field instead. The majority of Salesforce standard fields have back-end automation applied to them. Because every business is different, you will most likely need custom fields, but why re-create the wheel if it's not necessary?

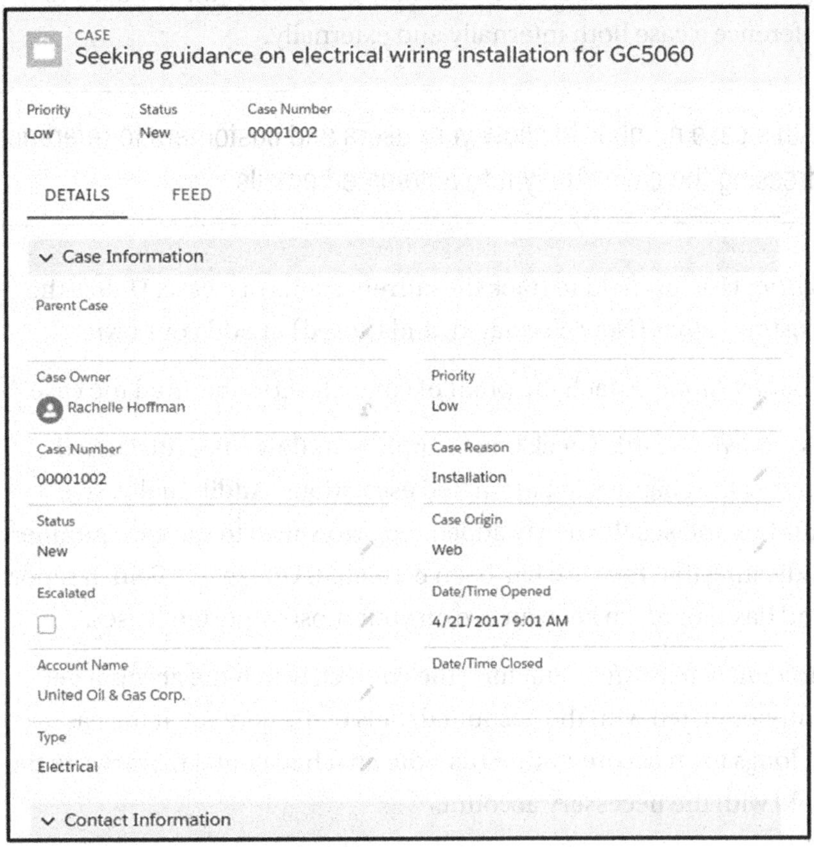

Figure 3-2. *Case information fields*

You will find the following fields in the Case Information section (as shown in Figure 3-2):

- *Parent Case*: Attach a case that currently exists and was the reason for the new case.

Note   If you use this function, it is essential to add the related list "Related Cases" to the case layout to get a full view of all the cases attached to a parent case.

- *Case Owner*: Assign the user who is primarily responsible for managing the case.

- *Case Number*: This is an automatically generated number used to reference a case both internally and externally.

Tip   Use this case number to allow your users and customers to reference it when addressing the case. Apply it to automated emails.

- *Status*: Use this field to track the current status of a case. Utilize the existing values (New, Escalated, and Closed) or add your own.

- *Contact Name*: Attach the point of contact who submitted the case.

- *Escalated*: Use this check box to apply workflow rules (discussed later in the chapter) to automated escalations. Additionally, select this box and see the newly added red arrow next to the case number indicating that the case has been escalated. Utilize this field in reports and dashboards to keep an eye on your most important cases.

- *Account Name*: After attaching the contact, watch the account get autopopulated with the account details of the contact. If the case belongs to an account other than the attached contact, overwrite the field with the necessary account.

- *Priority*: Apply the necessary priority to the case using the standard values of High, Medium, or Low. Utilize this field in reports and dashboards to keep an eye on your most important cases.

- *Type*: Use this field to track the types of cases your teams are managing. Use this field to help determine what FAQs should be developed or updated.

- *Case Reason*: Use this field to track the reasons why a client contacted you. You can also use this field to help update FAQs, internal process, and so much more.

- *Case Origin*: Use this field to track where your cases are coming from, whether it be an online form, email, phone, or in person.

- *Date/Time Opened*: This field is automatically populated with the date and time the case was created.

- *Date/Time Closed*: This field is automatically populated with the date and time the case was closed. Cases can be closed by changing the case status to a closed status or via many other ways (e.g., API, import update, automation rules, etc.).

Note   Salesforce reports come with an Age field that tracks the duration in days. However, this field is not a field that you can put on your case layout. You can create a formula field if you would like your users to see the duration a case has been (or was open for) on the case page layout.

- *Closed When Created*: Users are able to create a new case and close it right away. When this happens the checkbox is marked true for this field and can be used in reports.

Under Contact Information in Figure 3-3, you'll find the following fields:

- *Contact Phone, Contact Mobile, Contact Fax, and Contact Email*: These fields pertain to the contact attached to the case. They are all formula fields that are used to map fields from one object to another. Since these are formula fields, they are locked fields that can't be updated from the Case object. Instead, you'll need to go to the contact record and update the information there.

Under Web Information in Figure 3-3, you'll find the following fields:

- *Web Email, Web Company, Web Name, and Web Phone*: When the web-to-case function is configured (we'll cover this later in the chapter), cases will be automatically created in Salesforce. These fields will be populated with the corresponding data from your web form.

Under Description Information in Figure 3-3, you'll find the following fields:

- *Subject*: Use this field as the incoming subject line of an email when the email-to-case feature is configured or as a quick reference to what the case is about. Notice that this field's data is replicated at the top the page layout as well.

- *Description*: Use this field as the incoming body of an email when the email-to-case feature is configured or as a long description of the case.

- *Internal Comments*: Use this field to create case comments while you are on a call with a client.

- *Created By*: This field is found on every record in Salesforce. It captures who and at what date and time the case was created.

- *Last Modified By*: This field is also found on every record in Salesforce. It captures who and at what date and time the case was last updated or modified.

Tip   Don't worry if these fields aren't enough or don't work for your company. The default positions of some of these fields are easily modified. Salesforce allows up to 500 custom fields on the Case object. You can create fields for text, dates and time, numbers, currency, percents, picklists, multiselect picklists, check boxes, emails, phones, and URLs.

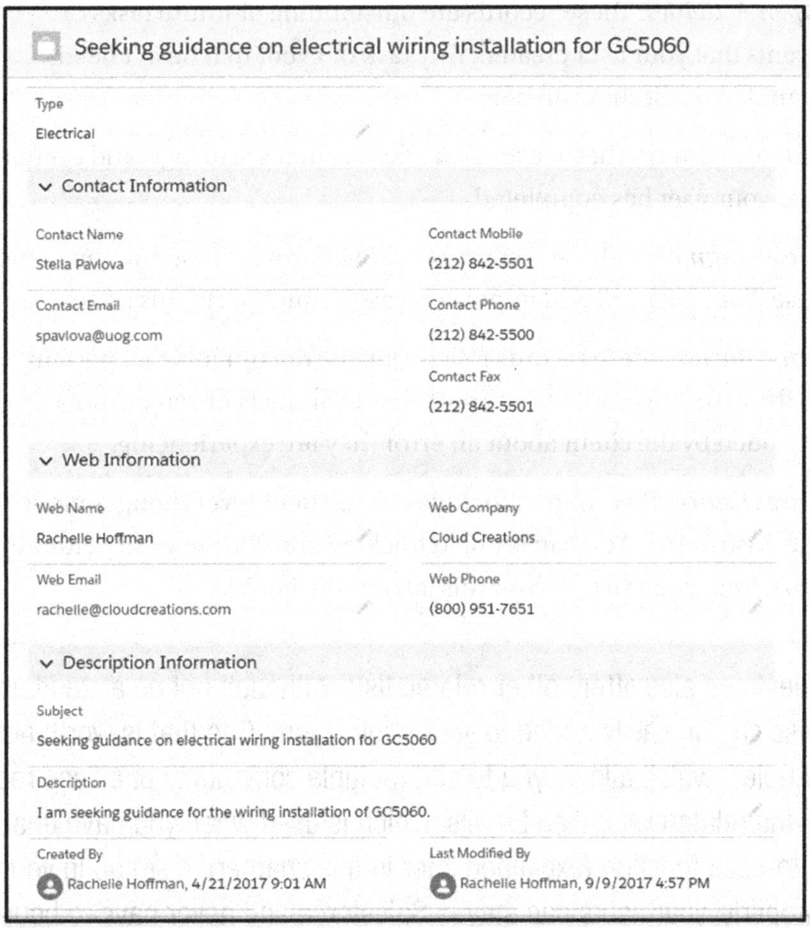

Figure 3-3. *More case fields*

Next, we'll discuss the standard related list found on the Case object.

Figure 3-4 shows the standard Case object related list. A *related list* is another object within your Salesforce organization that is connected to the current object you are viewing. The related list you'll find on the Case object includes the following:

- *Solutions*: This related list houses articles created in another Salesforce object called Solutions. Solutions are used to house content that either can be used to help you user close a case faster or can be used to provide information to the case contact. This object works with another Salesforce product called Knowledge. Solutions and Knowledge are important products because they provide resources to your users that help them move a case forward.

- *Open Activities*: These records are outstanding or future tasks or events that your user created. Any task or event that hasn't been completed will show up here.

- *Activity History*: These records are tasks, emails, call logs, and events that your user has completed.

- *Case Comments*: These records provide information pertaining to the case. Your user will add important case comments to this area.

- *Attachments*: These records reflect outside documents that pertain to the case. This could be current client contracts or screenshots provided by the client about an error they are experiencing.

- *Case History*: This content includes all the field-level changes made to the Case object. You can set field tracking and choose what fields are most important (we'll cover this later in the book).

Note   Salesforce also offers other related lists. Although not on a standard page layout, these can be easily added to your page layout. One that is worth noting is Contact Roles, which allows you to add multiple contacts to one case record. Another is the related list called Emails, which is used when you have enabled the email-to-case function (explained later in this chapter). If set up in your email account properly, your users can stay in Salesforce and never have to bounce between the two (also covered later).

Tip   Salesforce allows you to relate objects to one another. Should your Case object need multiple records of another, you can create a junction object. For instance, if you would like to relate multiple products that are involved in one case, you can do so. Creating custom objects is simpler than you may think.

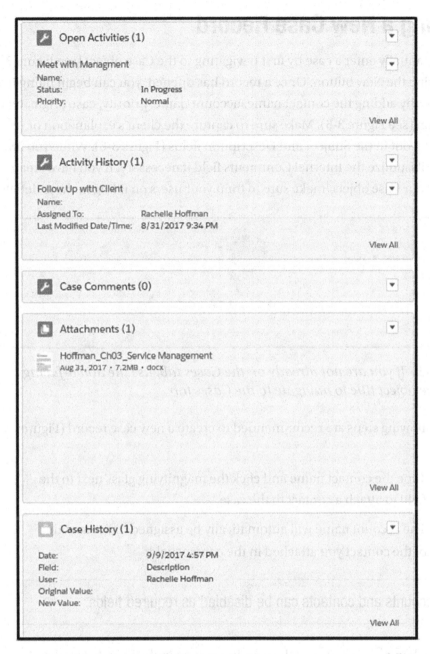

Figure 3-4. *Case layout with standard related lists*

Creating a New Case Record

You can manually enter a case by first navigating to the Case object (see Figure 3-5) and then clicking the New button. Once a record has opened, you can begin filling in the case details by adding the contact name, account name, priority, case origin, type, and case reason (see Figure 3-6). Make sure to capture the client's explanation or reasoning for reaching out in the Subject and Description fields (Figure 3-6). While you are adding these details, utilize the Internal Comments field if necessary. If you have created custom fields for your Case object, make sure to train your users on filling in these details as well.

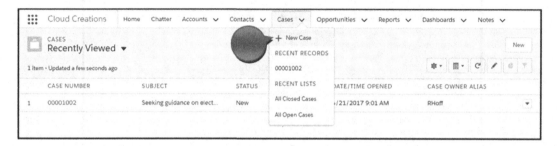

Figure 3-5. *If you are not already on the Cases tab, use the down-facing arrow next to the object title to navigate to the Cases tab*

The following steps are recommended to create a new case record (Figures 3-6 and 3-7):

1. Type the contact name and click the magnifying glass next to the field to attach a contact to the case.

2. The account name will automatically be assigned to the account of the contact you attached in the contact field.

Tip Accounts and contacts can be disabled as required fields.

---

3. Change the priority of the case by clicking in the field. Select the appropriate value from the provided values.

4. Select the case origin by clicking into the field and select the appropriate value. Notice the * next to this field. This means that it is required.

5. Select the type and case reason by clicking into the field and selecting the appropriate value.

6. Fill out any custom fields appropriately if necessary at this time.

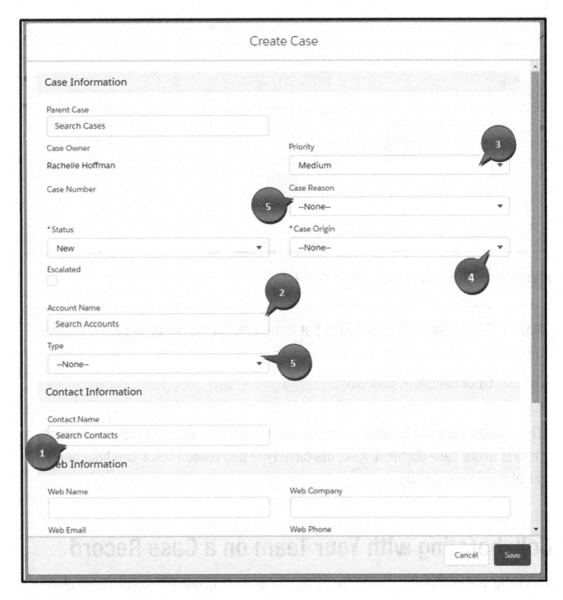

Figure 3-6. *Creating a case, steps 1 to 6*

7. Type in the subject of the case.

8. Type in the description of the case.

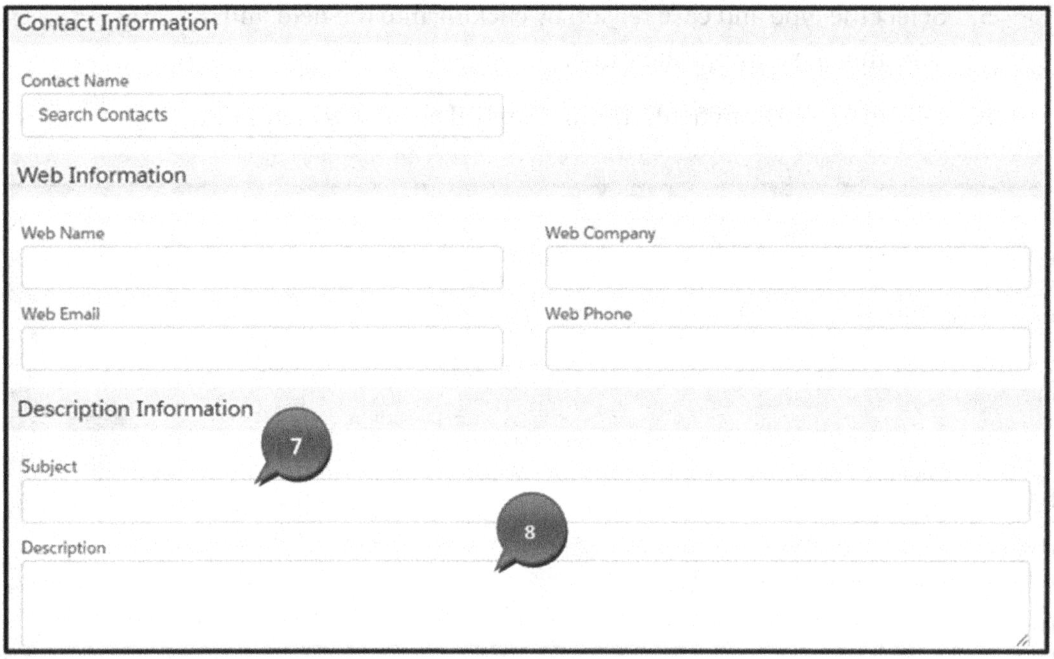

Figure 3-7. *Creating a case, steps 7 and 8*

Note   The Subject and Description fields are used in the email-to-case functions.

9.   Once complete, click Save.

Tip   Utilize the case Date/Time Opened and Date/Time Closed fields to generate reports about case duration. Also, the case type and reason fields can help define client and internal FAQs.

Collaborating with Your Team on a Case Record

Managing and efficiently closing cases can take more than one person being involved from your team. Users can utilize the case feed found in their case record to quickly communicate with others on your team. They can also direct a message to any Salesforce user who has access to the case record.

To mention a comment to a user, you use the @ symbol followed by the user's name and, once the name populates below the text area, click the hyperlinked name. You'll also see that every action is tracked in the case feed for a complete view of the case and what happened throughout its duration. The feed filters on the left side of the case record help you to quickly navigate to case's feed-related items. Feed details will display from the oldest at the bottom to the newest created at the top. This gives you a quick view of the latest conversations or work done on the case. Figure 3-8 shows the functions of the case feed.

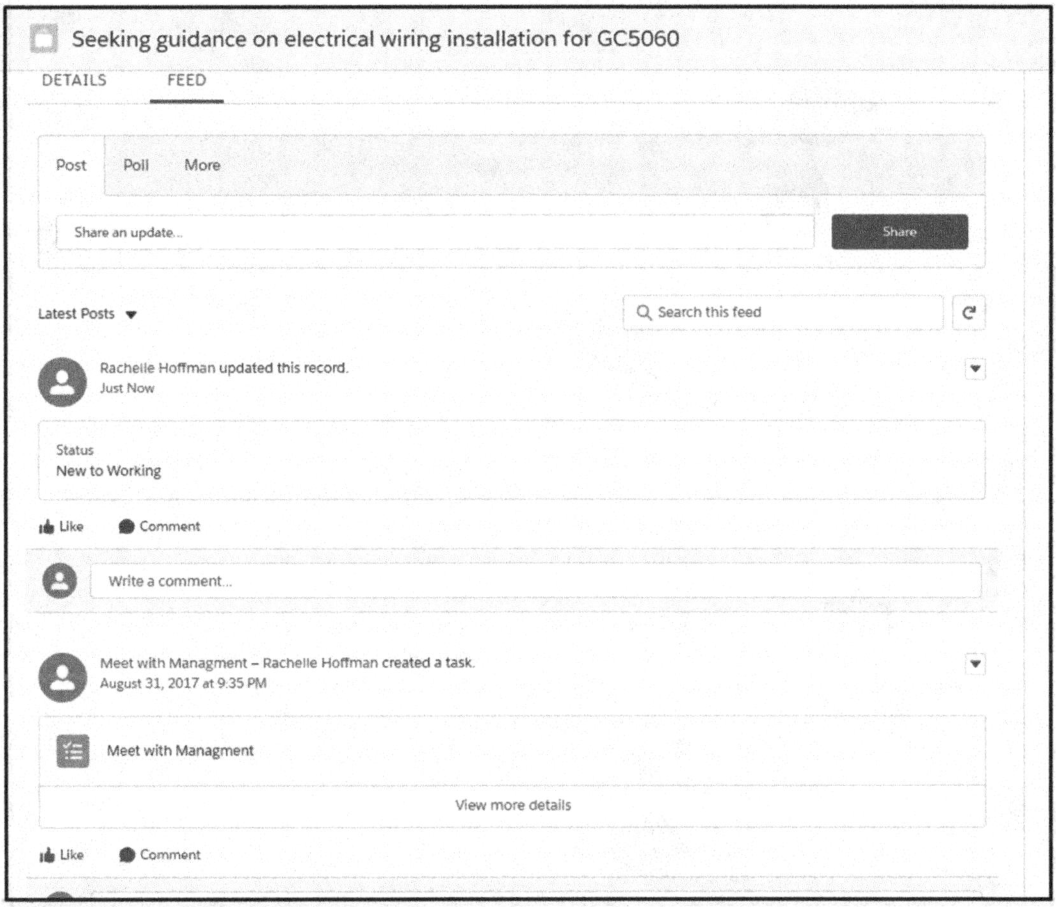

Figure 3-8. *Case feed*

To collaborate with your team, follow these steps:

1. Access the case feed by clicking the tab Feed.

2. Utilize the post area to communicate with your team on the case.

3. Utilize the case feed to track all conversations throughout the case duration.

4. The case feed captures changes made to the case status.

5. The case feed also tracks activities such as the Log a Call activity and other general tasks (see Figure 3-9).

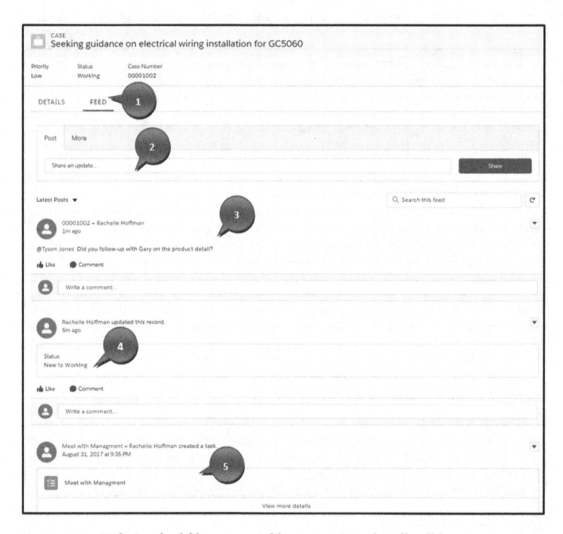

Figure 3-9. *Utilizing feed filters to quickly navigate to the all call logs, case notes, status changes, and task and events*

Case Automation

Salesforce offers the ability to automate functions such as automatically assigning a case to a queue or to a specific user. Salesforce also allows you to create rules to auto-respond to your clients related to a case based on specific criteria. You can also configure case escalation rules based on criteria that will automatically assign the case to an escalated case. Along with this case escalation, you can apply automated notifications to be sent when this criterion is met. You can also route cases from your email or from a web form. You are also able to adjust some support settings that allow you to further customize your case automation. Figure 3-10 shows a case queue.

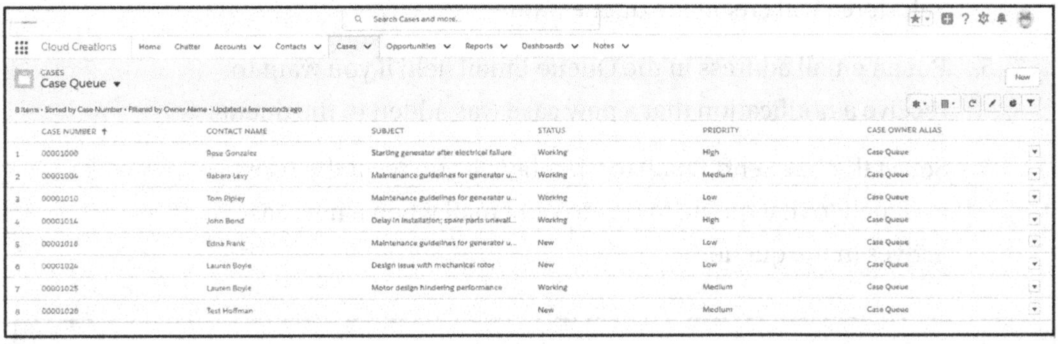

Figure 3-10. *Case queue*

Creating Case Queues

A case can be sent to a queue in many ways. You can automatically assign a case to a queue when it created or throughout the life of the case because a change to the case record can send it to a queue. You can think of a queue as a holding tank. This holding tank will allow you to give multiple users access to it and give them the option of accepting new cases. Instead of assigning a case to a specific owner, you can assign it to a queue using the case assignment rules. In Figures 3-11 through 3-14, you'll learn how to create a queue in Salesforce. The steps are as follows:

1. Navigate to the Setup menu by clicking the settings cog icon in the upper-right corner of the Salesforce window.

2. Using your search area, enter **Queue**. Click Queues under Users.

3. Click the New button.

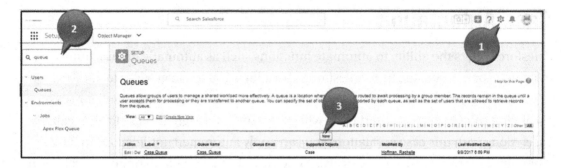

Figure 3-11. *Creating a case queue*

4.   Create a user-facing label for the queue and hit your Tab key.
     Salesforce will create the queue name.

5.   Put an email address in the Queue Email field if you want to
     receive a notification that a new case was added to the queue.

6.   Select the box Send Email to Members if you want the users
     assigned to that queue to receive an email when a new case
     arrives in the queue.

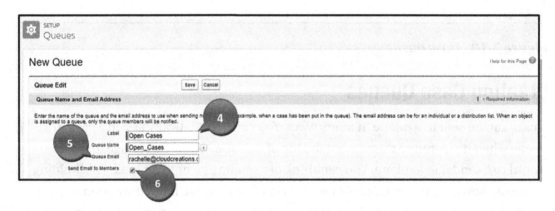

Figure 3-12. *Naming your queue and setting notification options*

7.   Select the Case object and click the arrow to move it to the
     Selected Objects section.

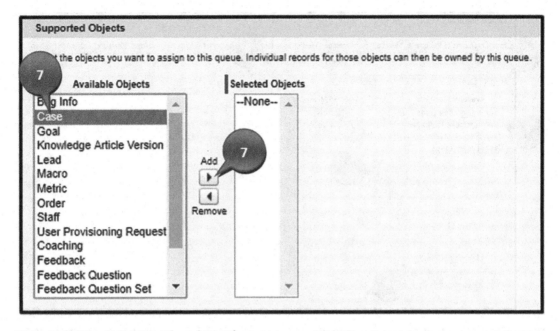

Figure 3-13. *Selecting the object for your queue*

8. Using the search area, select in the drop-down whether you want to search for a specific user, public group, role, or role and subordinates.

Note   Selecting the option Roles and Subordinates gives access to the specific queue to a specific role and all that fall under the role. For instance, if your CEO sits at the top of your role hierarchy and you give the CEO access using this function, it gives all below the CEO role access as well.

---

9. Select the specific user, public group, role, or role and subordinates and use the right-facing arrow to move it into the Selected Members area.

10. Click Save.

119

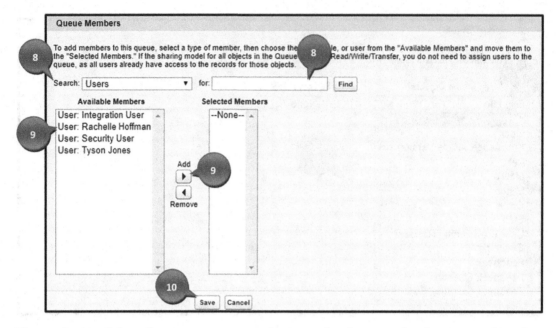

Figure 3-14. *Select the users, groups, roles, or roles that need to have access to this queue.*

Tip   Queues can be used for more than just cases. You can set up lead queues and set up lead assignment rules just like you can on cases.

Creating Case Assignment Rules

Now that you have created your first queue, it's time to automatically assign cases to that queue or to a specific owner. You can create case assignment rules based on specific criteria in the case and related records to the case. For instance, you can create an assignment rule to automatically assign all cases that came in for a specific account or contact to a specific user. Or you can assign a case to a queue based on the case origin, case reason, case type, or any other field found in the case record. Some companies create queues for VIP or platinum clients and only allow their most experienced users to handle these cases. Figures 3-15 through 3-20 show you this process. The step-by-step process is as follows:

1. Navigate to the Setup menu by clicking the settings cog icon in the upper-right corner of the Salesforce window.

2. Using your search area, enter **Case Assignment**. Click Case Assignment under Service.

3. Click New to start the case assignment rule.

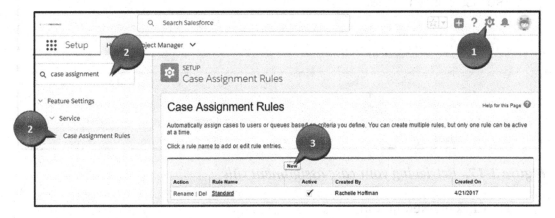

Figure 3-15. *Accessing case assignment rules*

4. Name the rule and click Save. You can activate the rule now by checking the Active check box or hold off and activate it later.

5. Click Save.

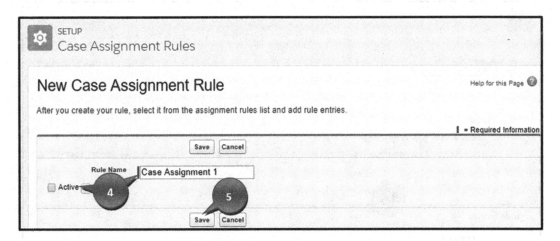

Figure 3-16. *Creating a case assignment name and activating it*

After saving the rule name, it will return you to the case assignment area. Click the rule name you just created.

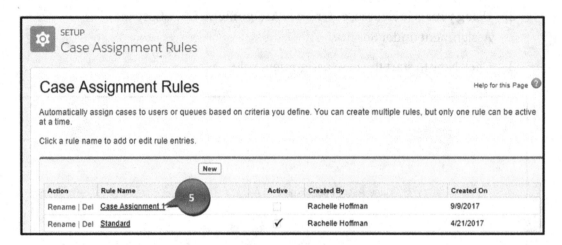

Figure 3-17. *Retrieving your case assignment rule*

6. Click the New button.

Note   In Figure 3-18 notice the Active box above Modified By. This is where you will activate the rule after you have completed it using the Active check box.

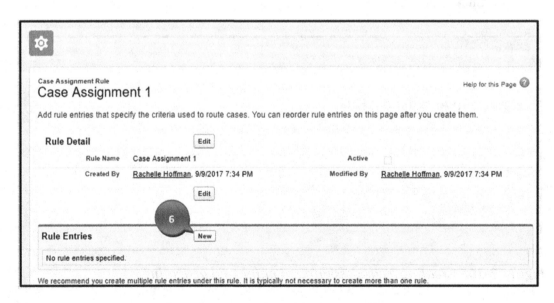

Figure 3-18. *Creating the rule criteria for your case assignment*

7. If this is your first case rule assignment, type the number **1** into the Sort Order field. If you have configured many rules, the Sort Order field tells Salesforce which rules to run first. Once a rule runs and assigns the case, it will not run other rules on the same case. Assign the sorting to all your rules according to importance.

8. In step 2 you create the rule criteria. The rule criteria tells Salesforce that if the criteria you enter here is true, then it assigns the case to the specified location (steps 9 and 10).

    a. To start this process, you'll first need to click None in the field column. Here you will select the field that Salesforce should evaluate for the rule. This can be the case type, case reason, case origin, account, contact information, or any field criteria found in the case, account, or contact.

    b. Choose the appropriate operator. For instance, if you want every case type that equals a specific value to be auto-assigned to specific users, you would choose the operator "equals" and select those values.

    c. Choose or enter the appropriate value or outcome in which the case will auto-assign.

    d. You can also configure your filter logic by clicking Add Filter Logic. This allows you to change the logic from being "all" the field criteria (using "and") to "or." For example, you can say if the case type is Problem OR the case origin is Email. The standard setup would make that logic sentence be "If the case type is Problem AND the case origin is Email."

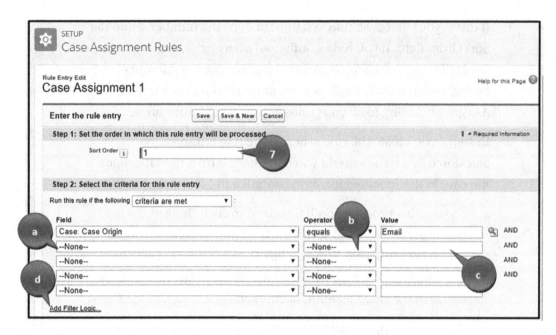

Figure 3-19. *Setting up the field criteria for the case assignment rule*

9. Choose to assign the case to a specific user or to the queue you set up in the previous section.

10. Select an email template that you would like to autosend to the user or queue.

11. Click Save or click Save and New to set up another case assignment.

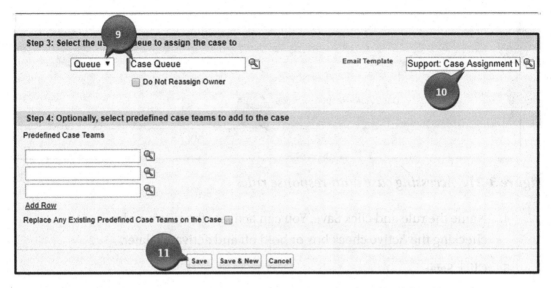

Figure 3-20. *Assigning the specific user or queue and send them a notification*

Note   Step 4 provides a functionality that is not a Lightning component and would have to be set up in Classic.

Creating Case Auto-Response Rules

Case auto-response rules allow you automate communication with your client based on field-level change. For instance, if you want an email sent to your client when the status of the case changes from one value to another, you can do that. Any field-level change from a value to another can activate this email send or another automation. Figures 3-21 through 3-26 will walk you through creating case auto-response rules.

1. Navigate to the Setup menu by clicking the settings cog icon in the upper-right corner of the Salesforce window.

2. Using your search area, enter **Case Auto-Response**. Click Case Auto-Response Rules under Service.

3. Click New to start the Case Auto-Response rule.

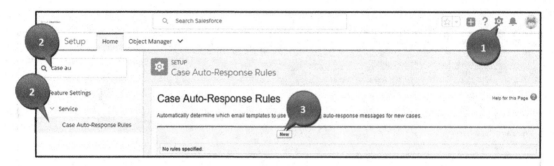

Figure 3-21. *Accessing case auto-response rules*

4. Name the rule and click Save. You can activate the rule now by checking the Active check box or hold off and activate it later.

5. Click Save.

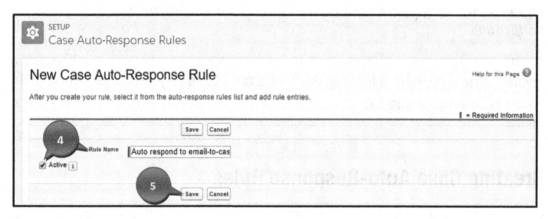

Figure 3-22. *Naming your case auto-response rule*

6. After saving the rule name, it will return you to the case assignment area. Click the rule name you just created.

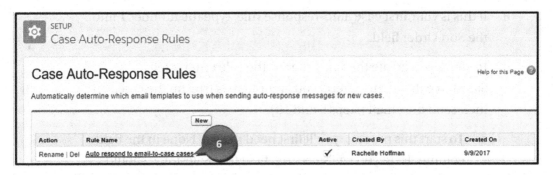

Figure 3-23. *Retrieving your case auto-response rule*

7. Click the New button.

Note   In Figure 3-24, notice the Active check box above the Modified By field. This is where you can activate the rule after you have completed it using the Active check box.

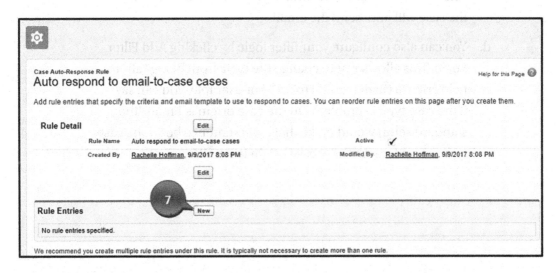

Figure 3-24. *Creating your new rule criteria for the case auto-response rule*

8. If this is your first case auto-response rule, type the number **1** into the Sort Order field.

9. In step 2 you create the rule criteria. The rule criteria tells Salesforce that if the criteria you enter here is true on the case, then send the email (steps 9 and 10).

    a. To start this process, you'll first need to click None in the field column. Here you will select the field that Salesforce should evaluate for the rule. This can be the case type, case reason, case organ, account, contact information, or any field criteria found in the case, account, or contact.

    b. Choose the appropriate operator. For instance, if you want every case type that equals a specific value to automate the email, you would choose the operator "equals" and select those values.

    c. Choose or enter the appropriate value or outcome in which the case will auto send the email.

    d. You can also configure your filter logic by clicking Add Filter Logic. This allows you to change the logic from being "all" the field criteria (using "and") to "or." For example, you can say if the case type is Problem OR the case origin is Email. The standard setup would make that logic sentence be "If the case type is Problem AND the case origin is Email."

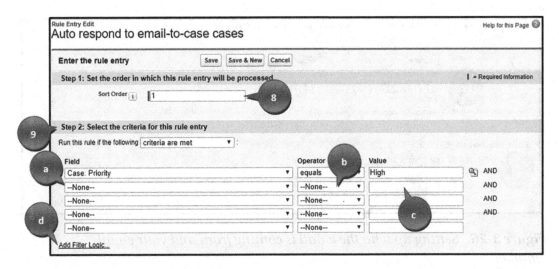

Figure 3-25. *Creating the criteria for your case auto-response rule*

10. In step 3, you'll need to provide the name of who the email is coming from.

11. Enter the sender's email address in the Email Address field.

12. Provide a reply-to address should the client want to respond to the email.

Note   You can only use one of your user's emails or an email that you set up as an organization-wide email.

---

13. Assign the email template that you want to be sent for this auto-response rule.

14. Once steps 1 through 4 are complete, click Save.

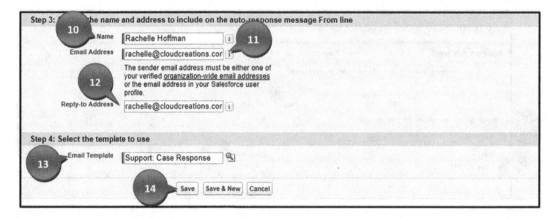

Figure 3-26. *Setting up who the email is coming from and your email template*

Creating Case Escalation Rules

Case escalation rules allow you to create automation for when a case will get escalated and what actions will take place thereafter. Like the other rules that you have created in the previous section, you'll be able to determine when the case gets escalated based on field-level criteria of the case. Once the field-level criteria are met, then you can set actions such as sending a notification email, reassigning the case to another user, and notifying that user. Figures 3-27 through 3-34 show the setup. The steps include the following:

1. Navigate to the Setup menu by clicking the settings cog icon in the upper-right corner of the Salesforce window.

2. Using your search area, enter **Escalation Rules**. Click Escalation Rules under Service.

3. Click New to start the escalation rule.

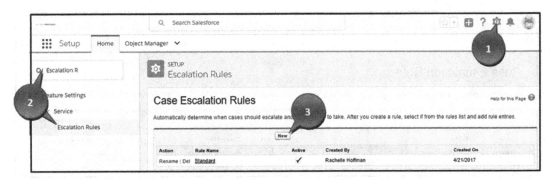

Figure 3-27. *Navigating to the case escalation rules*

4. Name the rule and click Save. You can activate the rule now by selecting the Active check box or hold off and activate it later.

5. Click Save.

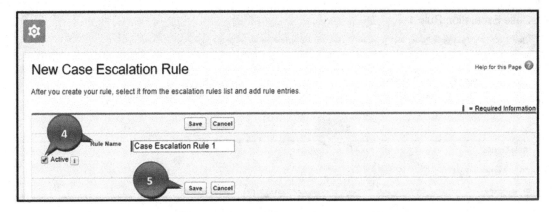

Figure 3-28. *Creating your name for your case escalation rule*

6. After saving the rule name, it will return you to the case assignment area. Click the rule name you just created.

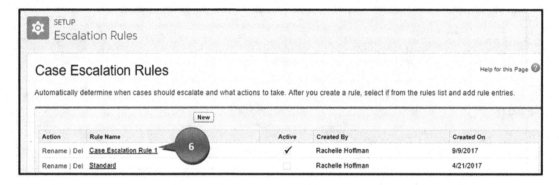

Figure 3-29. *Retrieving your case escalation rule*

7.   Click the New button.

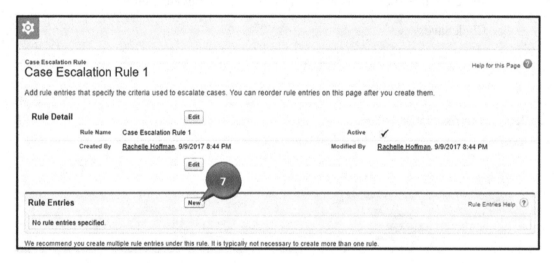

Figure 3-30. *Creating the criteria for your case escalation rule*

Note   In Figure 3-30, notice the Active check box; this is where you will activate the rule after you have completed it using the Active check box.

---

8.   If this is your first case escalation rule, type the number **1** into the Sort Order field. If you have configured many, the Sort Order field tells Salesforce which rule to run first. Once a rule runs and executes the action, it will not run other rules on the same case. Assign the sorting to all your rules according to importance.

9. In step 2 you create the rule criteria. The rule criteria tells
    Salesforce that if the criteria you enter here is true on the case,
    then it will send the email (steps 9 and 10).

    a. To start this process, you'll first need to click None in the field
        column. Here you will select the field that Salesforce should
        evaluate for the rule. This can be the case type, case reason,
        case organ, account, contact information, or any field criteria
        found in the case, account, or contact.

    b. Choose the appropriate operator. For instance, if you want
        every case type that equals a specific value to automate the
        email, you would choose the operator "equals" and select
        those values.

    c. Choose or enter the appropriate value or outcome in which
        the case will autosend the email.

    d. You can also configure your filter logic by clicking Add Filter
        Logic. This allows you to change the logic from being "all" the
        field criteria (using "and") to "or." For example, you can say
        if the case type is Problem OR the case origin is Email. The
        standard setup would make that logic sentence be "If the case
        type is Problem AND the case origin is Email."

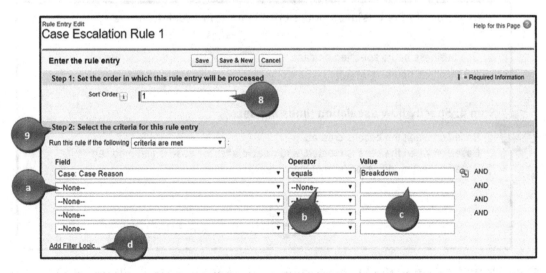

Figure 3-31. *Creating your rule criteria for the case escalation rule*

10.   In step 3 you can choose a business hour to set for this escalation.

Note   To choose business hours to set, you to need to have created this in Salesforce. In the Setup menu, search for *business hours* for more information. By default, the business hours are set for 24 hours 7 days a week.

---

11.   In step 4 you select how escalation times will be determined.

    a.   You can select when the case is created, which will evaluate the criteria only once when the case is created.

    b.   You can select when the case is created and disable it after the case is first modified. This option will check your case's criteria after the first time the case is modified (usually this is after a user has started to handle it).

    c.   You can select the last modification time of the case. This will check the criteria of the case every time a change is made to it. This will allow the escalation rule to be applied when the case is modified.

12.   Click Save.

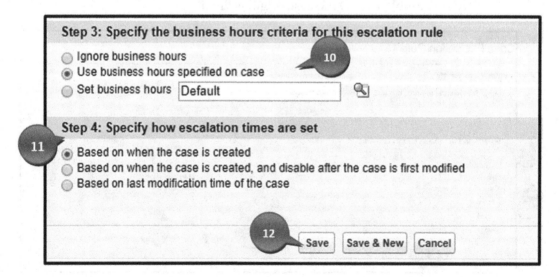

Figure 3-32. *Selecting the business hours and when the case escalation rule should run*

13.   Click the New button to start the creation of your actions.

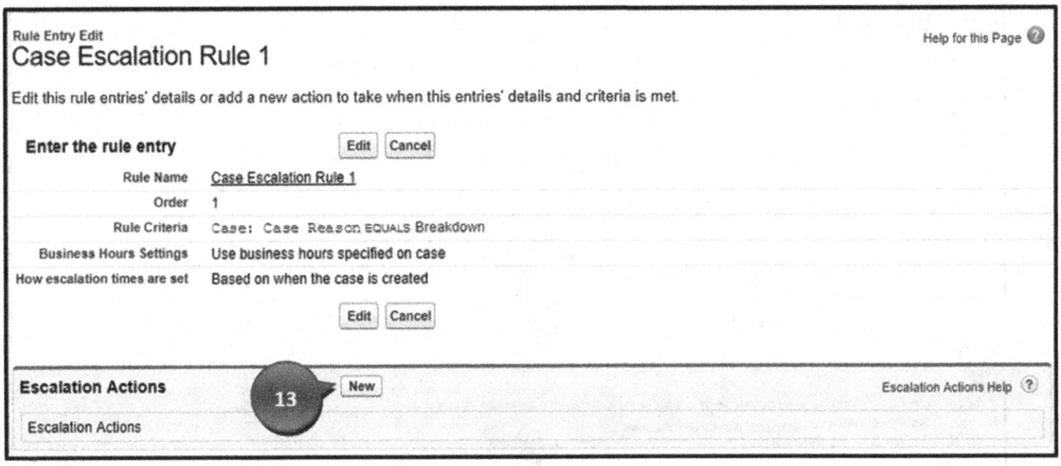

Figure 3-33.   *Creating your escalation rule action*

14.   For the Age Over field, you determine the number of hours that a case with matching criteria can be open before it escalates. You can change the drop-down to show single minutes or adjust it for 30-minute increments.

15.   Under "Choose one or more of the following actions," you can do the following:

a.   Choose to have the case reassigned to another user or a queue. In the field next to "Auto-reassign cases to," choose an email template that will get sent to that user or the users belonging to that queue.

b.   Choose who will get notified that a case has escalated and select the template that should notify the user. Usually, this is an individual in management.

c.   If you are not choosing to reassign the case, you can at this time notify the current owner of the case that it has escalated.

d.   In the Additional Emails field, choose in addition to the previous setting if anyone else should receive a notice of the case escalating.

16.   When you have completed your action, click the Save button.

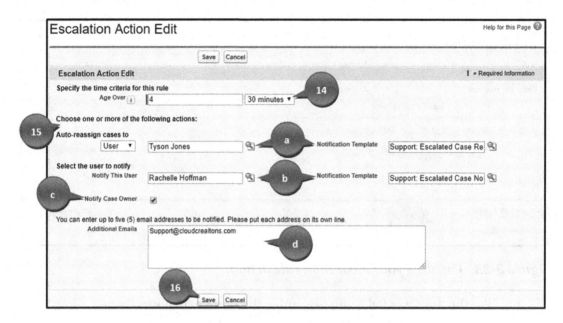

Figure 3-34. *Setting up the actions on your case escalation rule*

Tip   You can create one escalation rule with multiple actions, such as if you want a particular case to be escalated after two hours of meeting the rule criteria. Then if the case still isn't closed four hours after that and you want to escalate it again, you could set this up. All you would need to do is create another action.

Setting Up Email-to-Case

Email-to-case is a function that allows you to automatically have a case created based on an email being sent to a specific email address. For instance, if you have a support group that manages tech questions about your products, you can publicize an email and allow clients to submit requests that will automatically be routed to Salesforce and create a case for you. Figures 3-35 through 3-42 will walk you through this setup.

1. Navigate to the Setup menu by clicking the settings cog icon in the upper-right corner of the Salesforce window.

2. Using your search area, enter **Email-**. Click Email-to-Case under Service.

3. Click the Edit button.

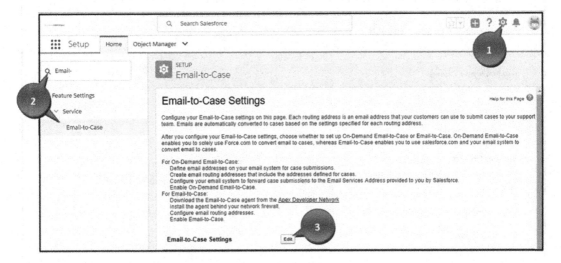

Figure 3-35. *Navigating to the email-to-case setup*

4. Select the boxes Enable Email-to-Case and Enable HTML Email.

5. Click the Save button.

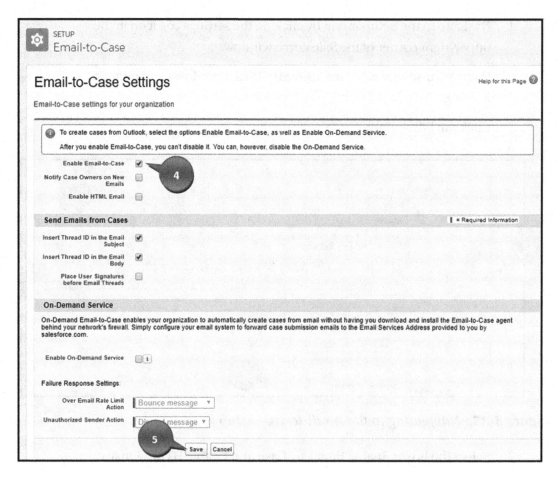

Figure 3-36. *Enabling the email-to-case function*

6. Click the New button.

Email-to-Case Settings   [Edit]

(i) To create cases from Outlook, select the options Enable Email-to-Case, as well as Enable On-Demand Service.

After you enable Email-to-Case, you can't disable it. You can, however, disable the On-Demand Service.

Enable Email-to-Case	✓
Notify Case Owners on New Emails	☐
Enable HTML Email	☐

Send Emails from Cases

Insert Thread ID in the Email Subject	✓
Insert Thread ID in the Email Body	✓
Place User Signatures before Email Threads	☐

On-Demand Service

On-Demand Email-to-Case enables your organization to automatically create cases from email without having you download and install the Email-to-Case agent behind your network's firewall. Simply configure your email system to forward case submission emails to the Email Services Address provided to you by salesforce.com.

Enable On-Demand Service	☐ [i]

Failure Response Settings:

Over Email Rate Limit Action	Bounce message
Unauthorized Sender Action	Discard message

Routing Addresses ⑥   [New] [Email2Case ▼]

No email addresses defined

Figure 3-37. *Creating a new routing address for the email-to-case setup*

7. Enter the email's routing name. Usually, this is the name of the email.

8. Enter the actual routing email address.

9. You can choose to save an email's header and set who you will accept them from. However, because these are usually images, it will take up 15KB of your organization's storage. Most users do not enable this option.

10. Under Task Settings, you can create a task along with the case being created when it comes in.

11. Under Case Setting, set the priority of the case and the case origin.

12. Click Save or click Save & New to set up more email routing addresses.

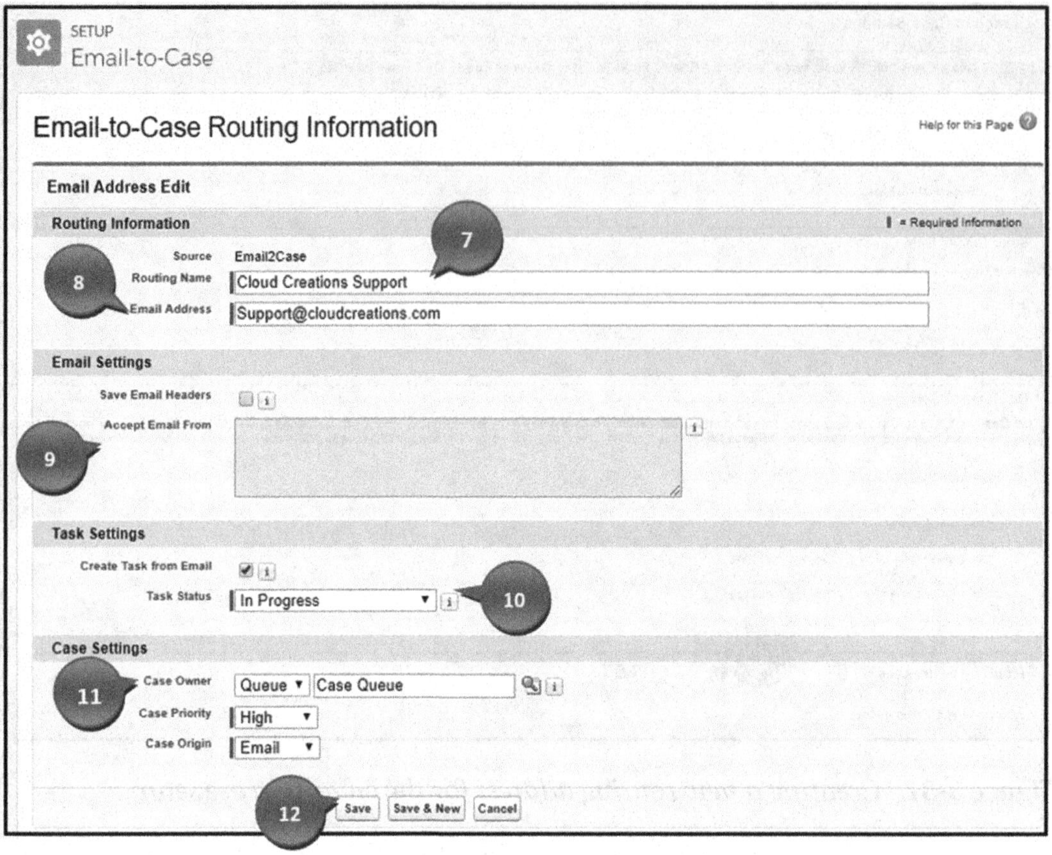

Figure 3-38. *Setting up your routing address for the email-to-case function*

13.   An email will be sent automatically to the routing address that you entered in step 8. If you don't receive an email within a couple hours, make sure to check your spam or other firewall settings your company may have or click the Resend link shown in Figure 3-39.

Figure 3-39. *If you don't receive the verification email, you can use this Resend link to resend the email*

14.   The email you receive should look like the example in Figure 3-40.
You'll need to click the link within the email to verify that this is a
working email address. After clicking the link, you'll be taken to
another Salesforce screen; click the Continue button, as shown in
Figure 3-41.

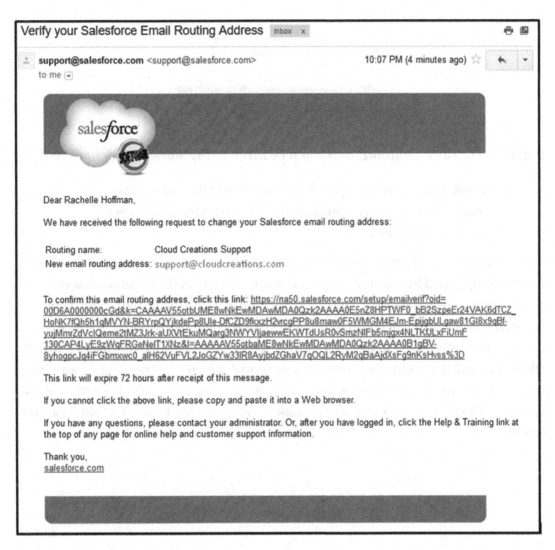

Figure 3-40. *Email verification sent*

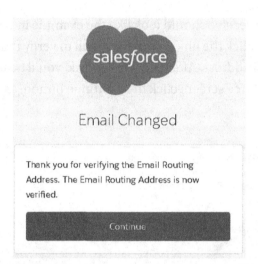

Figure 3-41. *Click Continue, and you'll be taken to the Salesforce login page*

15.   Lastly, you'll need to apply some email forwarding rules on your email inbox to forward emails to the e-mail service address that Salesforce provides.

Creating the email forwarding rule is what utilizes the on-demand email-to-case functions supported by Salesforce. By forwarding all your emails to the email service address provided by Salesforce, you can give your users a one-stop application with Salesforce. When an email is sent into Salesforce, the client receives a reply with a unique case thread found in the body and the subject line of the email. This case thread allows an email that comes back into the same email account and per your forwarding rules gets sent into Salesforce to be attached to the existing case. This allows your users to stay in Salesforce while they address support case inquiries. Figure 3-42 shows a case thread.

Figure 3-42. *This case thread allows your client email to get attached to the appropriate case.*

Note   The email-to-case function has some limitations. First, you can only receive attachments up to 10MB. Second, this option only allows up to 5,000 email messages a day. For workarounds, see the Setup area to have Salesforce deal with bounced messages. Finally, if the case thread is not included in an email, a new case will be created.

Tip   You would want to use the email-to-case option if your case inquiries are generally over 25MB. Also, the email-to-case setup will automatically identify contacts and replies to the case. The on-demand feature allows for a much more custom solution. It allows for custom field mapping, and its setup is fairly simple.

Setting Up Web-to-Case

The web-to-case function in Salesforce allows you to embed HTML code into your preexisting web site or web form. The majority of clients that have used this function embed the HTML code into a Contact Us form found on support-related web pages on their web sites. This function, like that of the email-to-case function, allows automatically generated cases to make it into Salesforce. Follow the steps shown in Figures 3-43 through 3-48.

1.   Navigate to the Setup menu by clicking the settings cog icon in the upper-right corner of the Salesforce window.

2.   Using your search area, enter **Web-to-case**. Click Web-to-Case under Service.

3.   The check box Enable Web-to-Case should be select, as shown in Figure 3-43.

4.   Set the default Case Origin option to Web or any other option that describes where this case is coming from.

5.   Attach a response template that you want your client to receive upon submitting their case.

6.   Hide Record Information will hide the record information in the email that is sent.

Note   If you want to create an email template for this, go to Setup, search for *Email Template*, and under the Email section you'll find Email Template.

---

7.   Add an email signature if you choose to otherwise create it in the email template.

8.   Click Save.

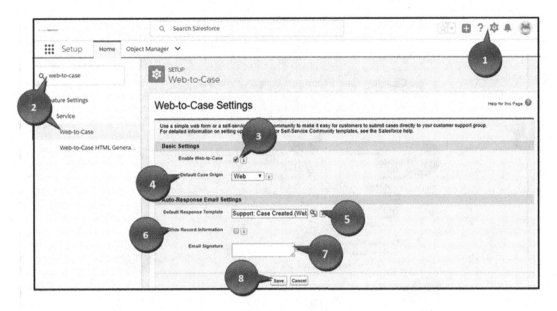

Figure 3-43. *Creating the web-to-case function*

Now that you have enabled the function, you can generate the HTML code to embed on your web site. Figures 3-44 through 3-45 show you how it's done.

1. On the left side in the Setup menu you should see Web-to-Case HTML Genera.... If not, you can search for *web-to-case HTML*. Click the phrase.

2. In the Available Fields area, select fields to be included on your web form.

3. Move the field from Available Fields to Selected.

4. In the URL field, enter the URL that you want your client to be returned to after submitting their web form.

5. The Enable Spam Filtering option will require the Captcha API key to be created (this requires developer work and will not be explained in this book). To set this up, you'll need to navigate to Salesforce Classic.

6. Click the Generate button.

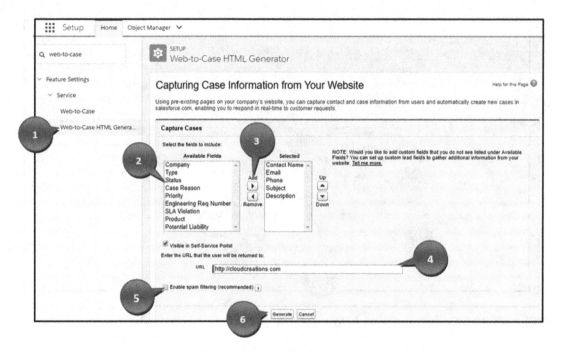

Figure 3-44. *Setting up the web-to-case HTML generator*

7.   Copy this HTML code and send it to your web site manager.

8.   Click Finished when done.

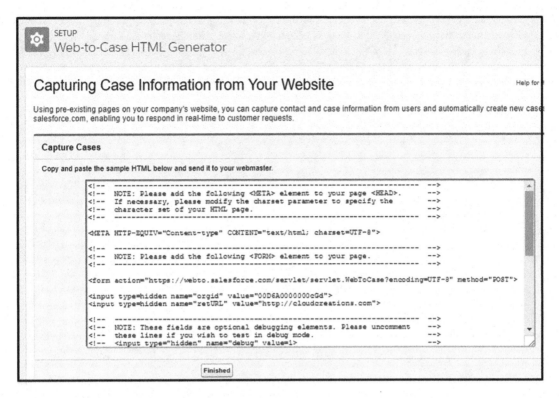

Figure 3-45. *The HTML that is generated*

Summary

With Salesforce Service Cloud, you can tailor the experience to your organization's needs or utilize the great standard functionalities that come with your purchase. Whichever path you choose, you can assure yourself that setup is the least of your worries.

CHAPTER 4

Lightning Apps

The AppExchange marketplace comprises a suite of apps, Lightning components, and consulting resources. Salesforce customers can install add-on applications to their Salesforce organization. You can search across thousands of apps to find prebuilt solutions for business needs. The marketplace is also the place to search across thousands of registered Salesforce consultants (shown in Figure 4-1).

Figure 4-1. *Blaze new trails with the AppExchange*

Apps

Increase productivity by installing prebuilt packages, called *apps*, which provide custom solutions for every role and industry. Visit the AppExchange web site at `http://appexchange.salesforce.com`. Here you can sort and filter in numerous ways including by popularity and rating.

To pick the right app, we recommend identifying your business challenges, budget, and time frame.

149

© Felicia Duarte, Rachelle Hoffman 2018
F. Duarte, R. Hoffman, *Learn Salesforce Lightning*, https://doi.org/10.1007/978-1-4842-2994-1_4

Discover the AppExchange Marketplace

You should take the time to explore the business app store in Salesforce, otherwise known as the AppExchange marketplace. There are more than 3,000 apps and components that can be used to extend the power of Salesforce. Follow these steps:

1. From the App Launcher, click Visit AppExchange, as shown in Figure 4-2. Or, from Setup, search for *AppExchange marketplace* in the Quick Find area.

Figure 4-2. *Visit the AppExchange from the App Launcher*

2. Click AppExchange Website, as shown in Figure 4-3.

Figure 4-3. *Click AppExchange Website to navigate to the complete database of apps and components*

This marketplace contains apps and components for end users to install and download into their Salesforce organization. In addition, you have access to thousands of reviews about these apps, components, and consultants. It's complete transparency at your fingertips.

On your home page, shown in Figure 4-4, apps can be searched and filtered by various categories. You'll find a wide array of apps! They range from point solutions to full-blown integration and automation. There are free apps, and there are paid apps. The good news is that Salesforce makes it easy to find what you are looking for.

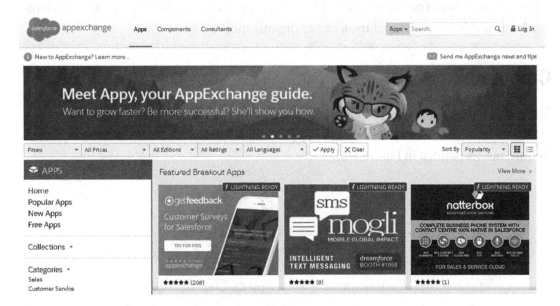

Figure 4-4. *The AppExchange home page*

Choose an App

Choosing the right app can seem overwhelming with the number of solutions available. So, it's important to have a strategy in this decision-making process.

1. Start by defining your business challenges. Identify your company goals and objectives. Once you've determined what they are, search and review a handful of solution options in the Salesforce marketplace.

2. Once you've narrowed down a handful of prospective solutions, evaluate the solutions and vendors. Consider the ease of use, support options, total cost, reviews, the ease of administration, and solution match. Use this information to help make a decision.

3. If available, request a demo or trial, or install the app into your sandbox for user testing and acceptance.

Price

One important factor is cost. There are apps in Salesforce that are free, but there are others that have a cost associated with them. While some apps display their total cost, others require you to contact them to find out the price. Some of these payment options can be monthly, annually, per user, or per organization.

Compatibility

Make sure to check the compatibility of the solution. You can find the compatibility information in the details section of the app under Requirements and Other System Requirements (shown in Figure 4-5).

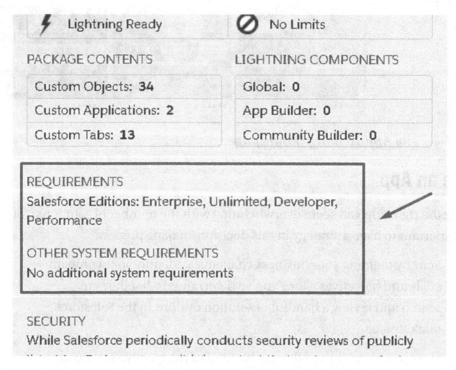

Figure 4-5. *Requirements and Other System Requirements sections in the app details*

App Home Page

The home page of an app provides an overview, details, reviews, and provider information (shown in Figure 4-6).

Figure 4-6. *Home page of an application*

The page also contains this information:

- *Highlights*: The highlights bar located at the top of the application page, shown in Figure 4-7, displays key components of the app. This typically includes Lightning readiness, organization compatibility, and limitations.

153

Figure 4-7. *Highlights bar*

- *Cost*: The cost is located on the left side of the home page. If the app is free, the app will state Free. If there is a cost associated with the app, it will state Paid.

- *Overview*: Click the Overview tab shown in Figure 4-8 for a brief description of the app. Some apps contain links to their web site or include video demos here. It is recommended that you watch any videos for further insight into the app's capabilities. You can also find detailed pricing information, the release date, and screenshots in this area.

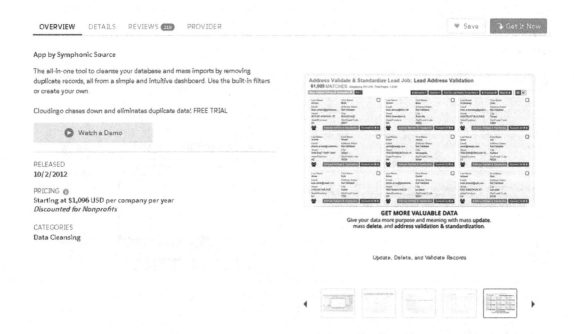

Figure 4-8. *Overview tab for app*

- *Details*: Click the Details tab shown in Figure 4-9 to gather more insightful details. This typically includes any technical specifics, software requirements, a supported feature list, data sheets, and security-related information.

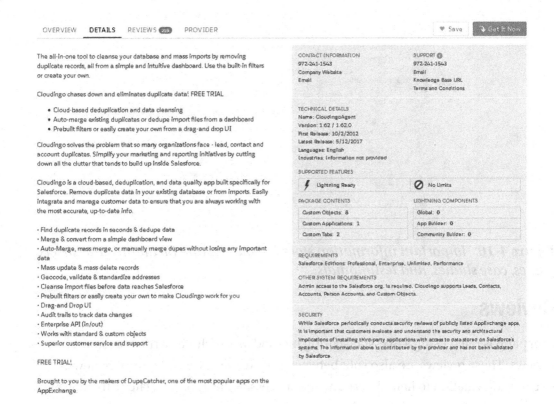

Figure 4-9. *Details tab*

To reach the app provider directly, contact information is displayed at the top-right corner of the page.

Tip   For an app that requires extensive setup, consider the support options available for each app.

At the bottom of the Details tab are documents including data sheets, customization guides, case studies, and customer testimonials provided by the app company, as shown in Figure 4-10.

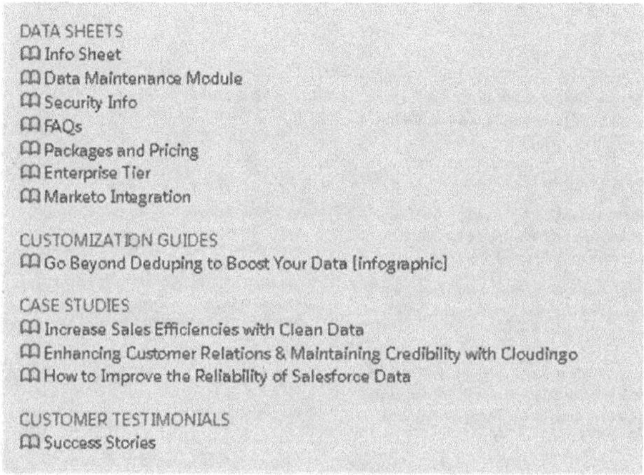

DATA SHEETS
- Info Sheet
- Data Maintenance Module
- Security Info
- FAQs
- Packages and Pricing
- Enterprise Tier
- Marketo Integration

CUSTOMIZATION GUIDES
- Go Beyond Deduping to Boost Your Data [Infographic]

CASE STUDIES
- Increase Sales Efficiencies with Clean Data
- Enhancing Customer Relations & Maintaining Credibility with Cloudingo
- How to Improve the Reliability of Salesforce Data

CUSTOMER TESTIMONIALS
- Success Stories

Figure 4-10. *Important information stored about the app including data sheets, guides, case studies, and testimonials*

Reviews

Every app is rated using a five-star scoring method and includes written customer reviews. These reviews are also split between positive reviews and critical reviews. Use this information to help determine the success of the app. Navigate to the reviews section on the Reviews tab to read customer feedback (shown in Figure 4-11).

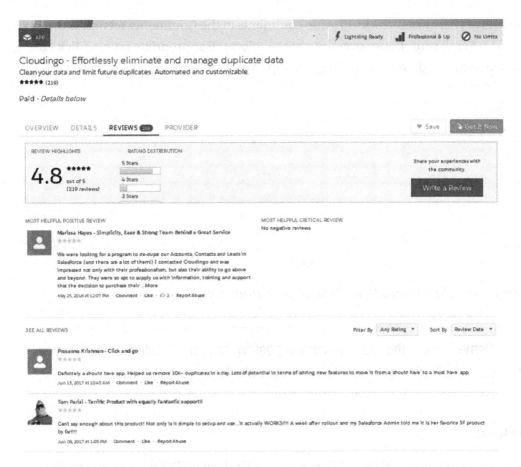

Figure 4-11. *The Reviews tab includes positive and critical reviews*

To write a review, a user must be authenticated. To write a review, click Write a Review in the Review Highlights section, as shown in Figure 4-12.

Figure 4-12. *Click this button to write a review*

Next, give your review a title. Provide comments in the Comments section shown in Figure 4-13. Scroll your mouse over the stars to select the appropriate rating. Click Post Review when finished. Note that it may take up to an hour for your review to post.

Figure 4-13. *Information to include in your app review*

Note   Come back to this page to write a positive or critical review of an app you have installed. This brings more value to the Salesforce community.

Provider

This tab holds more details about the app provider. Find out additional apps the provider has created that may be relevant to your business needs. Additional details include headquarter location, web site, employee count, and year founded, as shown in Figure 4-14.

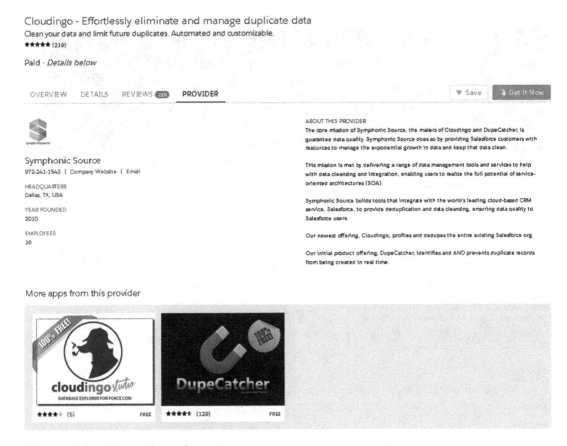

Figure 4-14. *Provider tab*

Install an App

Apps can be installed directly into your production or sandbox environment. Production environments are where your active users are using Salesforce with live data. The sandbox is your testing environment. These can be production or development environments used for testing applications. It is recommended that you install here first to see how it will interact with your existing setup.

An app can also be installed for a specific group of users or all users.

To install an app, follow these steps:

1. Do some research and select the app to be installed.

2. Click the Get It Now button, as shown in Figure 4-15.

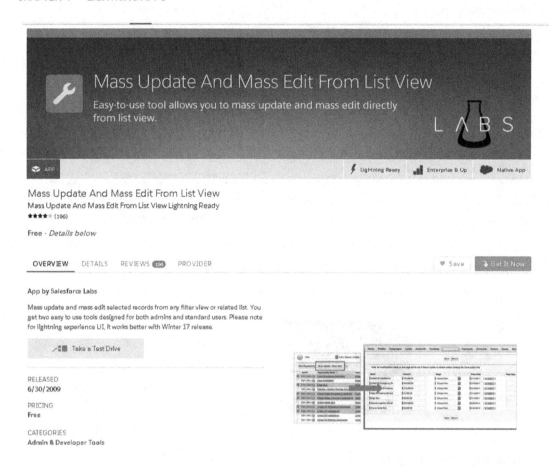

Figure 4-15. *Get It Now button on the home page*

3. Log in using your Salesforce credentials.

4. Select the appropriate installation method, as shown in Figure 4-16.

    •   Click "Install in production" to install into a live, production environment.

    •   Click Install in Sandbox to install into the sandbox test environment.

Figure 4-16. *Choosing to install into production or the sandbox*

5. Review the package components, version, expiration, and subscription cost for the app that will be installed. Review the terms and conditions.

6. Select "I have read and agreed to the terms and conditions," as shown in Figure 4-17. Click Confirm and Install.

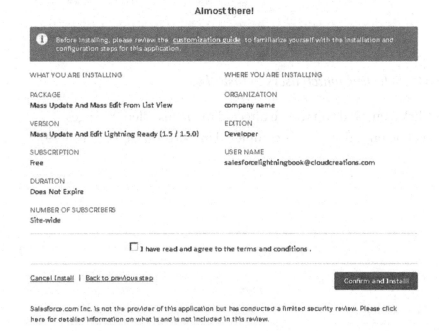

Figure 4-17. *Last step before installing*

7. Identify the users who should have access to this app. Select the appropriate option from the following list: Install to Admins Only, All Users, or Specific Profiles.

Note   You can open access to this app to other users after the install.

8. Click Install, as shown in Figure 4-18.

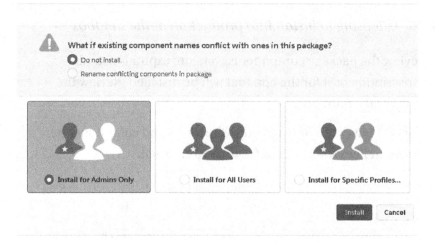

Figure 4-18.   *Selecting which users to install to*

9. Click Done and you will be directed to the Installed Packages
   section once the app has completed installation (see Figure 4-19).

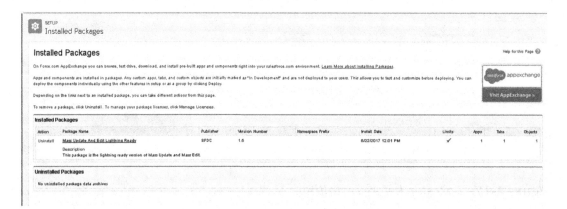

Figure 4-19.   *Details on installed and uninstalled packages*

Installed Packages

Installed apps create a package of components and dependencies. This includes custom objects, Visualforce pages, and Apex classes and code. The installed app can come in the form of a managed or unmanaged package.

- A *managed package* contains restrictions to the components installed.

- An *unmanaged package* has more flexibility and allows development on top of any components installed.

To uninstall an app, navigate to the Installed Packages area in Setup and click Uninstall.

To find details on any installed apps, including all components and dependencies, click the name of the package, as shown in Figure 4-20. The details will appear, as shown in Figure 4-21.

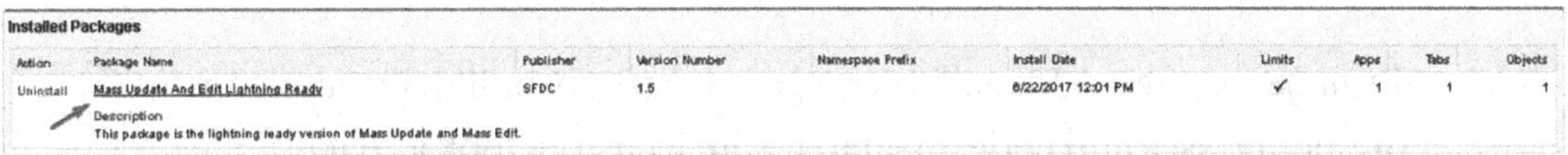

Figure 4-20. *Package name*

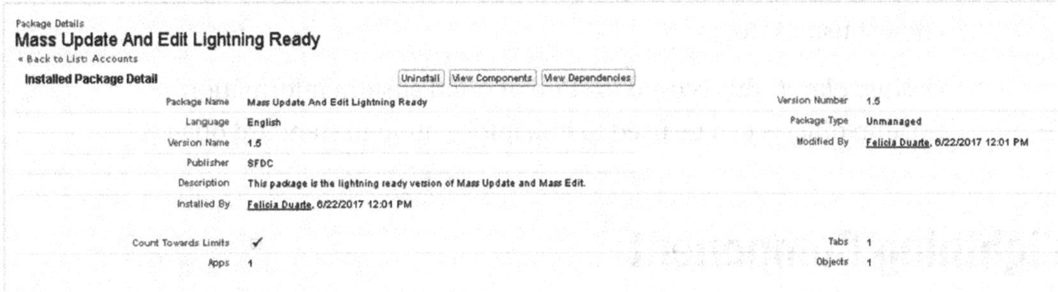

Figure 4-21. *Package details*

Click View Components for the complete breakdown, by type, of everything installed, as shown in Figure 4-22.

Action	Name	Parent Object	Type
	MassEditContact		Visualforce Page
	MassEditCase		Visualforce Page
	MassEditProduct		Visualforce Page
	MassEditOpp		Visualforce Page
	MassEditLead		Visualforce Page
	LEXSelection		Visualforce Component
	MassEditContract		Visualforce Page
	MassEditCampaign		Visualforce Page
	MassEditAsset		Visualforce Page
	MassEditAccount		Visualforce Page
	About Mass Update And Mass Edit Vf		Visualforce Page
	Mass Update And Mass Edit		App
	All	abc	List View
	MassUpdateSimpleController:Test		Apex Class
	MassUpdater		Apex Class
	MassEditExtensionTest		Apex Class
	MassUpdateSimpleController		Apex Class
	MassEditExtension		Apex Class
	abc		Custom Object

Figure 4-22. Viewing your package components

- *Visualforce page*: A Visualforce page is a custom-built page made up of Apex classes and code, used to create a custom look and feel.

- *Apex class*: An Apex class is part of a unique Salesforce programming language that gives developers and app builders the capability to create business logic.

- *Custom object*: This is used to store or build custom information. Custom objects can be used to link information to standard objects.

Lightning Component

Lightning components are reusable containers of prebuilt tools and elements. These components can be added to your pages to ramp up the productiveness of your end users. As mentioned earlier in the book, components can easily be dragged and dropped into your desired page. Salesforce makes this easy to do without a developer and without code. Discover these tools by searching through the marketplace, as shown in Figure 4-23.

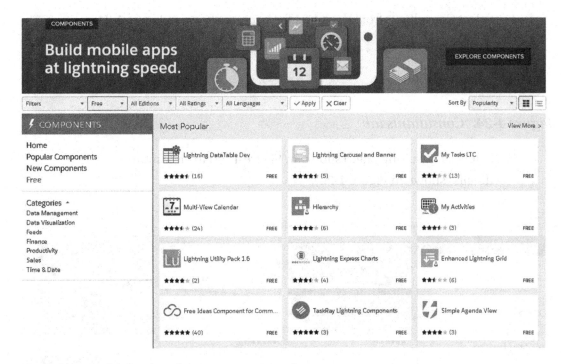

Figure 4-23. Lightning Components search page

To download a component, follow the same steps used to download an app.

Find a Consultant

Consultants are registered and often certified Salesforce partners. They help make up the Salesforce ecosystem by providing custom Salesforce solutions and implementations. Consultants typically provide Salesforce training, implementation solutions, quick-start packages, data migration, and more.

Your Salesforce account executive will often recommend a Salesforce consulting partner. Typically a discovery or scoping call with a consultant follows, and a quote with timeframe, deliverables, and cost is provided.

Similar to app browsing, browse through a list of consultants and sort by the type of service, specialization, tier, territory, and more.

1.   Select Consultants from the top of the page, as shown in Figure 4-24.

Figure 4-24. *Consultants tab*

2.   Select a consulting page (shown in Figure 4-25) to view more
details (shown in Figure 4-26).

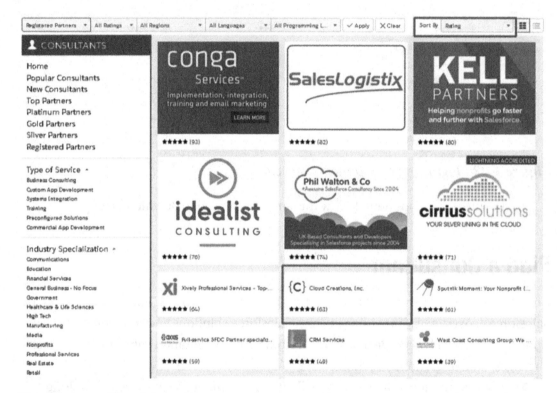

Figure 4-25. *Cloud Creations, consulting company*

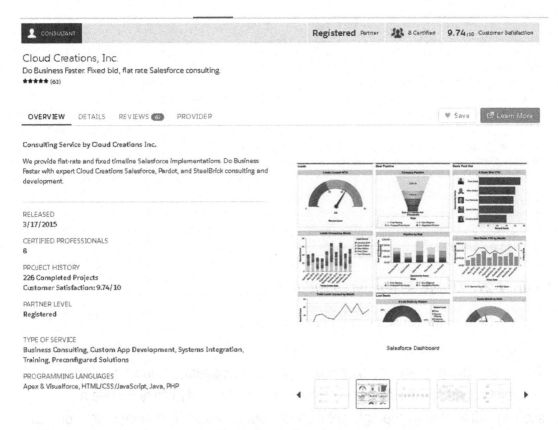

Figure 4-26. *Cloud Creations consultant detail page*

3. Find more details about this prospective consultant, including the number of projects completed, satisfactory ratings, geographic focus, and more on this page (shown in Figure 4-27). You can also find the consultant's contact information here to contact them for services.

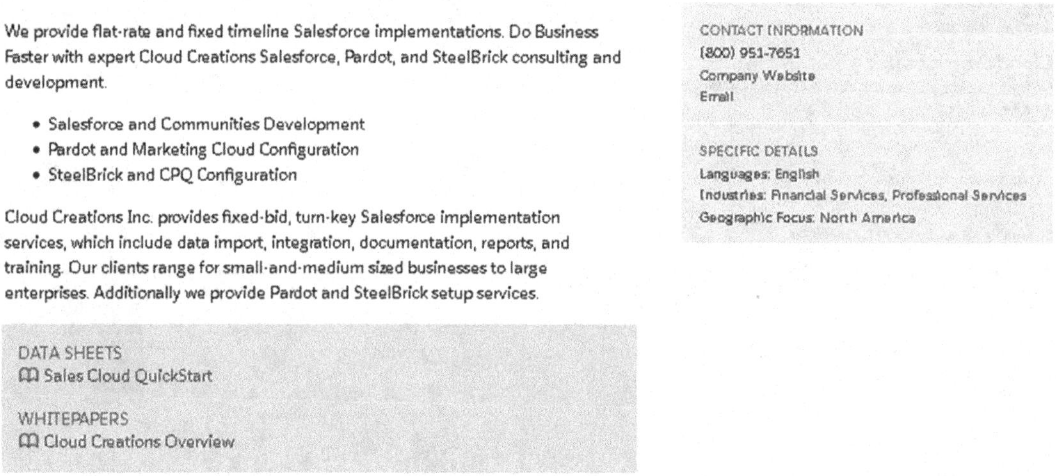

We provide flat-rate and fixed timeline Salesforce implementations. Do Business Faster with expert Cloud Creations Salesforce, Pardot, and SteelBrick consulting and development.

- Salesforce and Communities Development
- Pardot and Marketing Cloud Configuration
- SteelBrick and CPQ Configuration

Cloud Creations Inc. provides fixed-bid, turn-key Salesforce implementation services, which include data import, integration, documentation, reports, and training. Our clients range for small-and-medium sized businesses to large enterprises. Additionally we provide Pardot and SteelBrick setup services.

CONTACT INFORMATION
(800) 951-7651
Company Website
Email

SPECIFIC DETAILS
Languages: English
Industries: Financial Services, Professional Services
Geographic Focus: North America

DATA SHEETS
📖 Sales Cloud QuickStart

WHITEPAPERS
📖 Cloud Creations Overview

Figure 4-27. *Details section on consultant*

4. Contact the consultant and request a quote.

Tip   Consultants often employ a mix of project managers, business analysts, developers, and specialists. Hourly rates vary widely and typically include a scoping call to identify the right solution for your business. The more detail you can give your potential consultant, the more accurate the cost estimate will be.

Summary

The AppExchange marketplace consists of the Salesforce ecosystem of app partners and consultants. It is a growing market and is expected to make big changes in the near future. Visit the AppExchange marketplace to maximize your Salesforce setup.

CHAPTER 5

Lightning Reports and Dashboards

Salesforce reports and dashboards give you necessary insight into the data that you
have collected in Salesforce. Every custom field and the majority of standard fields in
any Salesforce object can be used in a Salesforce report. Salesforce dashboards help
you to display this data in 11 different visual charts and tables. One report can be used
in several dashboard components; however, a dashboard component can use only one
report. A dashboard can display up to 20 dashboard components. Figure 5-1 shows the
report that comes standard on your user's home page in Lightning.

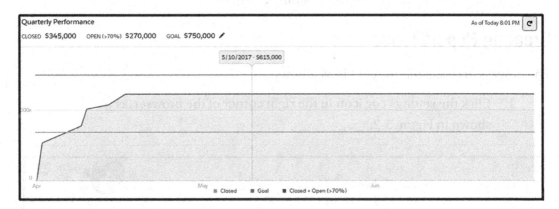

Figure 5-1. *The home screen of opportunity performance by quarter in Salesforce*

© Felicia Duarte, Rachelle Hoffman 2018
F. Duarte, R. Hoffman, *Learn Salesforce Lightning*, https://doi.org/10.1007/978-1-4842-2994-1_5

Understanding Reports and Report Features

Reports allow you to see your data based on specific criteria that you define. Once you have defined your criteria, you can group your data, create a chart for easy viewing, filter your data further, and store the report for later use in report folders. In these next couple of sections, we'll cover some of the functions available in the report builder that are necessary to understand, and then we'll jump into building your report.

Report Types

Report types allow you to define what objects and fields are available to you when creating a report. You can create report types based on a relationship with an object to a related object. A good example of this type of relationship is accounts and their related opportunities. Your opportunities would be the primary object, and the account would be the related. Don't worry, you don't need to create report types to start using Salesforce reports because out of the box Salesforce has set up the standard objects for you. However, if you find a field missing on a report or you can't find a custom object related to another, you'll want to continue reading. Or if the standard-use report types don't work for your business, you can customize your own!

Creating Report Types

The process to create report types is as follows:

1. Click the settings cog icon in the right corner of the browser, as shown in Figure 5-2.

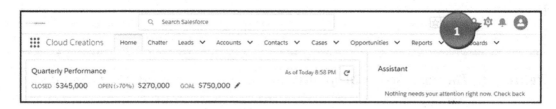

Figure 5-2. *Navigating to the Setup menu*

2. In the Quick Find box, search for *report types* (do not press Enter) and select the yellow highlighted phrase Report Types, as shown in Figure 5-3.

Figure 5-3. *Accessing the report types*

Tip Salesforce offers help on most of its administrative processes. If you are seeing "What is a Custom Report Type?" instead, feel free to read this content too and then click Continue. You can also click "Don't show me this page again" to disable this window in the future, as shown in Figure 5-4.

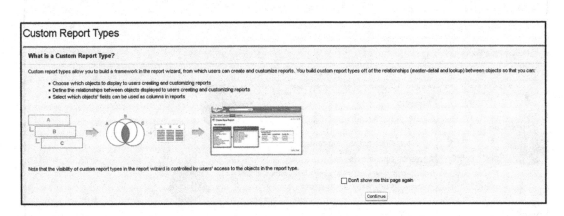

Figure 5-4. *Custom Report Types help page*

3. Click New Custom Report Type, as shown in Figure 5-5.

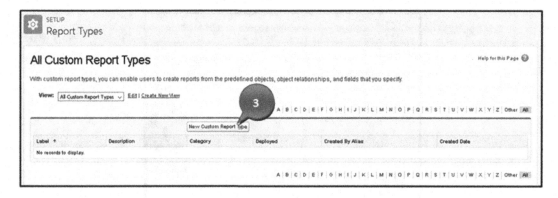

Figure 5-5. *Creating a new custom report type*

    4.   Select the primary object from the drop-down field that your
report should have, as shown in Figure 5-6.

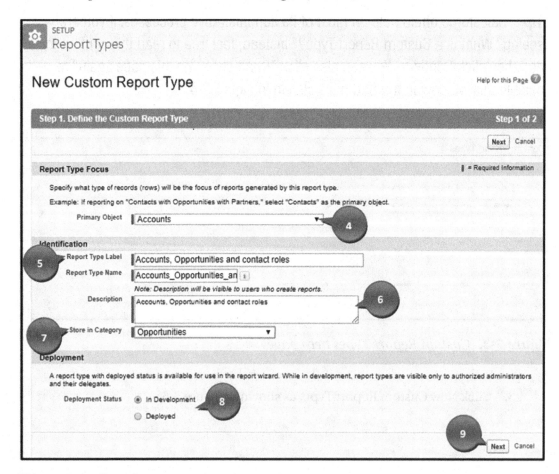

Figure 5-6. *Creating a customer report type*

5. Label your report type. This label will be displayed to your users when they are selecting the report type for the report builder. After you have finished your name, hit your Tab key, and Salesforce will automatically create the report type name.

6. Type a description for the report type. This will be visible to users who use this report type.

7. Select the category where this report type should be stored. For example, if the report type created was an opportunity and contact report, you should put it in the Opportunity folder. If the report type was a combination of multiple objects, you can choose to store it in one of those object's folders.

8. Select what status this report type should be in. Selecting the In Development radio button will hide this report type for all users except administrators or those with delegated permissions. Selecting the Deployed status will make this report type visible to all users who have access to the report builder. You can always come back and select the Deployed option when you have finished and tested your report type.

9. Click Next.

10. Select "Click to relate another object," as shown in Figure 5-7.

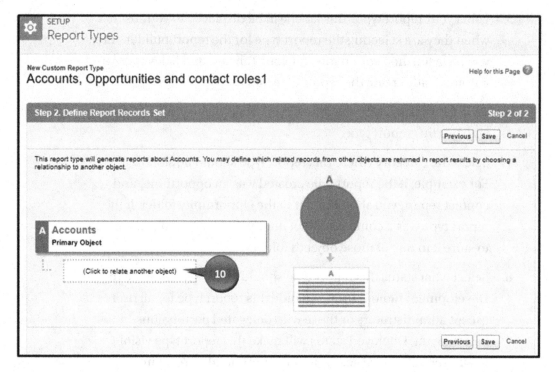

Figure 5-7. *Relating another object for your custom report type*

11. Click the Select Object drop-down to choose your related object
     for this report type, as shown in Figure 5-8.

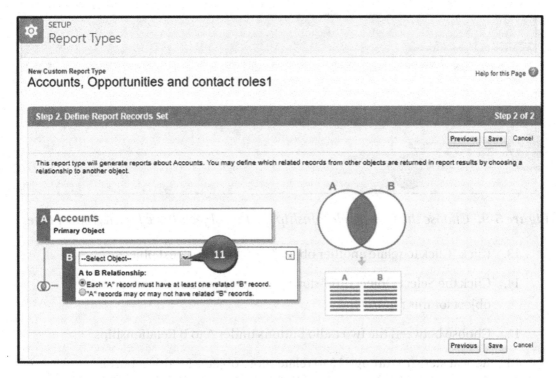

Figure 5-8. *Relating another object to your customer report type*

Note If you are not seeing the object you want to relate to this object, it means that there is no connection between these objects. To create a connection, you'll need to create a lookup field on the related object to the primary object. Before data will populate this report, that field on your records will have to be filled with a primary object record. Building custom objects and fields is simpler than you think. We don't cover how to do that in this book, but Salesforce offers great "trailheads" on this topic. Go to https://trailhead.salesforce.com to find your trailhead and further your education.

---

12.   In Figure 5-9, you'll have two choices shown under A to B Relationships. The option "each 'A' record must have at least one related 'B' record" will only show B records where at least one A is related to it. For example, all contacts that are related to accounts will show, but if you have a contact that has no relation to an account, it won't show. The option "'A' record may or may not have related to 'B' records" will show all B records whether or not they are related to your A record.

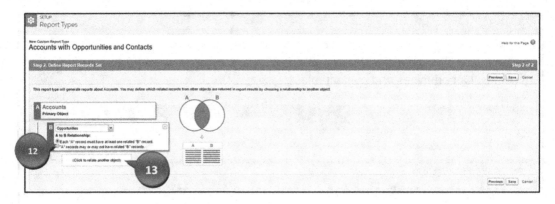

Figure 5-9. *Choose the type of relationship the two objects have for this report type.*

13. Click "Click to relate another object" to select your next object.

14. Click the Select Object drop-down to choose your next related object for this report type.

15. Choose between the two radio buttons under A to B Relationships.

16. Repeat steps 13 through 15 to relate more objects for this report if necessary.

17. Click Save, as shown in Figure 5-10.

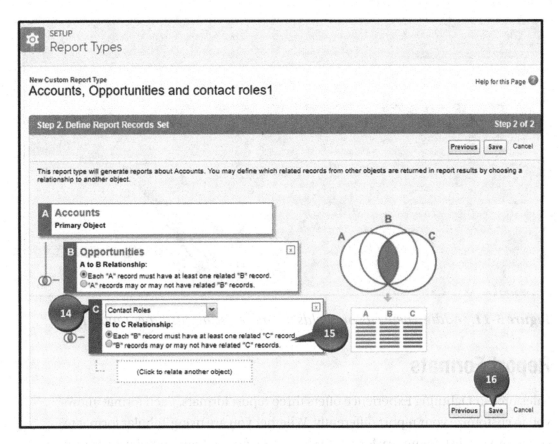

Figure 5-10. *Relating another object to your custom report type*

Note   If you add new fields to your objects after creating a custom report type, you'll have to add the new fields to the report type. You can do this by going to Setup, clicking your report type name, and clicking Edit Layout under "Fields Available for reports." This is shown in Figure 5-11.

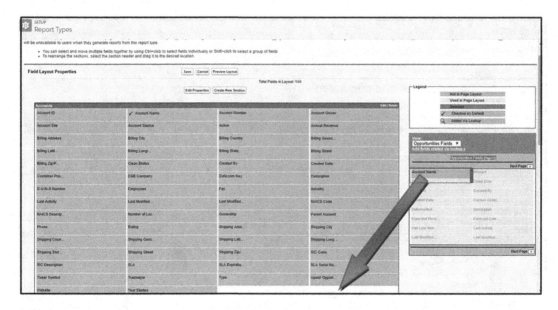

Figure 5-11. *Adding new custom fields to your existing customer report types*

Report Formats

Salesforce in Lightning Experience offers three report formats. Each format allows you to customize your report differently. Whether you are using Tabular format to generate a call list, Summary format to show data grouped horizontally, or Matrix format to summarize your data by both rows and columns, Salesforce has the proper format for you. You also have an additional report format, Joined reports, that you can use; however, you need to switch to Salesforce Classic to build and view these types of reports. Each report format has its strengths; let's look into these a little further. Figure 5-12 shows where you can make this adjustment between report formats.

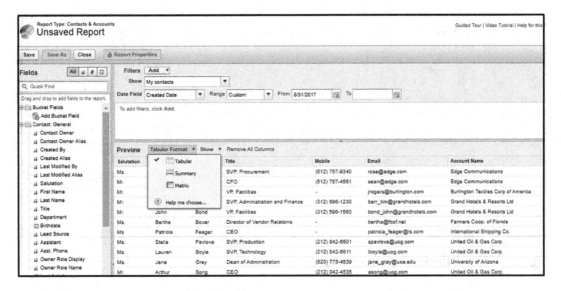

Figure 5-12. *Switching report formats*

Tabular Report Formats

The Tabular format reports are easily comparable to a flat file like a spreadsheet. This report format contains columns as the different data points and rows with your actual records. These reports are best used for creating a list of records like a call list or to list records with one grand total. This report format can't be grouped, and you can't display the information in a chart or use it in a dashboard component unless you use a row limit filter (see Figure 5-33). Most clients will use a Tabular report format to see a grand total of their sales with specific criteria set. For instance, if you want to run a quick report on all the sales your team generated for a quarter, you could use a tabular report. Figure 5-13 shows what a call list tabular report would look like.

REPORT
Cloud Creations Contact List

Total Records
20

ACCOUNT OWNER	ACCOUNT NAME ↑	SALUTATION	FIRST NAME	LAST NAME	MOBILE	EMAIL
Rachelle Hoffman	Burlington Textiles Corp of America	Mr.	Jack	Rogers	-	jrogers@burlington.com
Rachelle Hoffman	Dickenson plc	Mr	Andy	Young	(785) 265-5350	a_young@dickenson.com
Rachelle Hoffman	Edge Communications	Ms.	Rose	Gonzalez	(512) 757-9340	rose@edge.com
Rachelle Hoffman	Edge Communications	Mr.	Sean	Forbes	(512) 757-4561	sean@edge.com
Rachelle Hoffman	Express Logistics and Transport	Ms.	Babara	Levy	(503) 421-5451	b.levy@expressl&t.net
Rachelle Hoffman	Express Logistics and Transport	Mr.	Josh	Davis	(503) 421-4387	j.davis@expressl&t.net
Rachelle Hoffman	GenePoint	Ms.	Edna	Frank	(650) 867-7686	efrank@genepoint.com
Rachelle Hoffman	Grand Hotels & Resorts Ltd	Mr.	Tim	Barr	(312) 596-1230	barr_tim@grandhotels.com
Rachelle Hoffman	Grand Hotels & Resorts Ltd	Mr.	John	Bond	(312) 596-1563	bond_john@grandhotels.com

Figure 5-13. *Tabular report example*

Summary Report Format

The Summary report format is the most widely used report format in Salesforce. This type of report format allows you to group and summarize your data for up to three levels. Within these groups, you can summarize on the column and obtain the subtotal for that particular grouping and at the end of your report the grand total. You can use formulas in this report to further define your report. You can use this type of report format to show how your sales users are stacked against each other by grouping on opportunity owner. You can also use this report to determine who in your company holds the highest record count by also grouping on users of that record. Or you can build a report to group the different type of contacts you have by title. This format can also be used and represented on a dashboard and in charts. When you leave your report ungrouped, it will display in a Tabular format. Figure 5-14 shows a report that clients would use to see how much new business is coming in versus how much business is coming from current clients. You can also see that it is grouped by the user to show how each user is stacking up against the other.

				AMOUNT
REPORT — Cloud Creations Opps by Type and User				
Total Records **10**	Total Amount **$2,375,000.00**			
TYPE ↑	OPPORTUNITY OWNER ↑	ACCOUNT NAME	OPPORTUNITY NAME	Sum
Existing Customer - Upgrade (5 records)	Rachelle Hoffman (5 records)	GenePoint	GenePoint SLA	$30,000.00
		Grand Hotels & Resorts Ltd	Grand Hotels Generator Installations	$350,000.00
		United Oil & Gas Corp.	United Oil Standby Generators	$120,000.00
		United Oil & Gas Corp.	United Oil SLA	$120,000.00
		United Oil & Gas Corp.	United Oil Installations	$235,000.00
	Subtotal			$855,000.00
Subtotal				$855,000.00
New Customer (5 records)	Rachelle Hoffman (5 records)	GenePoint	GenePoint Standby Generator	$85,000.00
		Edge Communications	Edge Emergency Generator	$75,000.00
		Burlington Textiles Corp of America	Burlington Textiles Weaving Plant Generator	$235,000.00
		Grand Hotels & Resorts Ltd	Grand Hotels Emergency Generators	$210,000.00
		United Oil & Gas Corp.	United Oil Refinery Generators	$915,000.00
	Subtotal			$1,520,000.00
Subtotal				$1,520,000.00
GRAND TOTAL (10 RECORDS)				$2,375,000.00

Figure 5-14. *Summary report example*

Matrix Report Format

The Matrix report format allows you to group your data by both columns and rows. This allows for a cross examination of your data. Just like the Summary report format, on the groups you create in the Matrix format you can see subtotals, record counts, and grand totals as well as see them by row or column, as shown in Figure 5-15. Use this type of report to show how well products perform over date ranges by grouping your columns by date and your rows by opportunity products. Or use this report to determine how well your users are performing over time. Use this report to compare your incoming case origin against your case reasons. This type of report can also be used in dashboard components as well as charts. Additionally, you can use formulas to further calculate your data. If your groupings or criteria display no results, this format report will be downgraded to Summary format.

REPORT
Cloud Creations Opportunity Type

Total Records: 31   Total Total Price: $5,760,000.00

TYPE	STAGE	JANUARY 2017 COUNT	JANUARY 2017 TOTAL PRICE Sum	FEBRUARY 2017 COUNT	FEBRUARY 2017 TOTAL PRICE Sum	MARCH 2017 COUNT	MARCH 2017 TOTAL PRICE Sum	APRIL 2017 COUNT	APRIL 2017 TOTAL PRICE Sum	Total COUNT	Total TOTAL PRICE Sum
.	Prospecting	0	$0.00	1	$100,000.00	0	$0.00	0	$0.00	1	$100,000.00
	Id. Decision Makers	0	$0.00	0	$0.00	0	$0.00	1	$60,000.00	1	$60,000.00
	Subtotal	0	$0.00	1	$100,000.00	0	$0.00	1	$60,000.00	2	$160,000.00
Existing Customer - Upgrade	Needs Analysis	0	$0.00	0	$0.00	1	$675,000.00	0	$0.00	1	$675,000.00
	Value Proposition	1	$80,000.00	0	$0.00	0	$0.00	1	$250,000.00	2	$330,000.00
	Id. Decision Makers	1	$15,000.00	0	$0.00	0	$0.00	0	$0.00	1	$15,000.00
	Perception Analysis	1	$120,000.00	0	$0.00	0	$0.00	0	$0.00	1	$120,000.00
	Proposal/Price Quote	1	$100,000.00	0	$0.00	0	$0.00	1	$270,000.00	2	$370,000.00
	Negotiation/Review	0	$0.00	2	$395,000.00	0	$0.00	0	$0.00	2	$395,000.00
	Closed Won	3	$240,000.00	4	$995,000.00	1	$350,000.00	3	$270,000.00	11	$1,855,000.00
	Subtotal	7	$555,000.00	6	$1,390,000.00	2	$1,025,000.00	5	$790,000.00	20	$3,760,000.00
Existing Customer - Replacement	Id. Decision Makers	0	$0.00	0	$0.00	0	$0.00	1	$35,000.00	1	$35,000.00
	Subtotal	0	$0.00	0	$0.00	0	$0.00	1	$35,000.00	1	$35,000.00
New Customer	Qualification	0	$0.00	1	$15,000.00	0	$0.00	0	$0.00	1	$15,000.00
	Closed Won	2	$270,000.00	2	$320,000.00	2	$1,125,000.00	1	$75,000.00	7	$1,790,000.00
	Subtotal	2	$270,000.00	3	$335,000.00	2	$1,125,000.00	1	$75,000.00	8	$1,805,000.00
	Total	9	$825,000.00	10	$1,825,000.00	4	$2,150,000.00	8	$960,000.00	31	$5,760,000.00

Figure 5-15. *Matrix report example*

Report Filters

While in the report builder it will be necessary to understand the use of report filters that Salesforce has to offer. You can utilize up to five filter features to help customize your reports further. Filters allow you to get a closer look at your data and make it more specific for your reporting needs.

Standard Filters

Standard filters in the report builder of Salesforce will differ for some objects. Since the data you are collecting across accounts and contacts is different from that of opportunities or cases, you'll see these standard report filters change based on the report type. Let's take a look at each report type and their standard filters.

Accounts, Contacts, and Leads

Accounts, contacts, and leads all share similar standard report filters. Like most things to learn in Salesforce, if you understand the components of one object, those sometimes will translate into other objects. For the accounts, contacts, and leads, you'll find they share similar attributes.

- *All accounts*: This report filter allows you to choose if you see all accounts regardless of the owner, only contacts you own, only the accounts you own, or your team's accounts, as shown in Figure 5-16. If you have security set in place with role hierarchies or sharing rules, your users will only be able to see the accounts, contacts, and leads they are set up to see.

Figure 5-16. *Account filter for ownership of records*

- *All leads*: This report filter for leads is similar; you have the option to see the leads you own, your team's leads, and user-owned leads (compared to queue owned), queue-owned leads, and all leads, as shown in Figure 5-17.

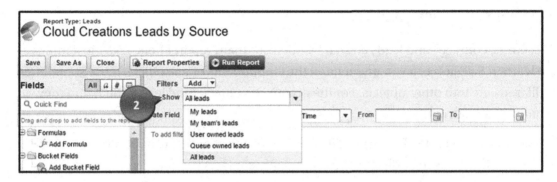

Figure 5-17. *Lead filter for the ownership of records*

- For the accounts, contacts, and leads, you can choose from any date field within that report type to filter from as well as use Salesforce smart dates. Smart dates allow you to choose dates that will update to the relative time every time you run your report. For instance, you can choose from the drop-down This Week or Current Calendar Year or use your own custom date range in the From and To fields, as shown in Figure 5-18.

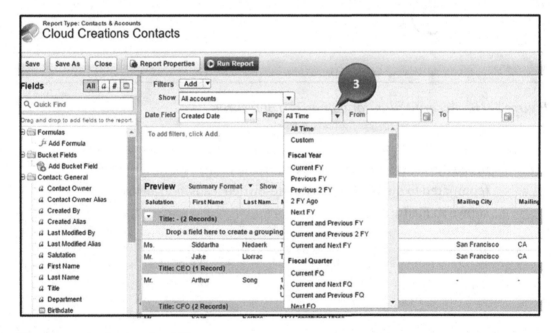

Figure 5-18. *Smart date filters*

Note If these smart dates don't work for your report, see "Field Filters" for more ideas.

Opportunities' Standard Filter Fields

Opportunities' standard filter fields are unique to their report type, so let's look at them.

- Similar to accounts, contacts, and leads, opportunities have a standard report filter that allows you to choose all opportunities regardless of who owns them, your team's opportunities, and your opportunities, as shown in Figure 5-19. If you have security set in place with role hierarchies or sharing rules, your users will only be able to see the opportunities they are set up to see.

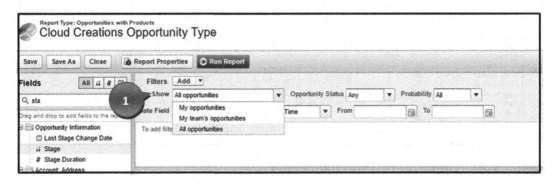

Figure 5-19. *Opportunity ownership filter*

- The Opportunity Status filter allows you to see any opportunity whether it is closed, open or won, and all opportunities with any status, as shown in Figure 5-20.

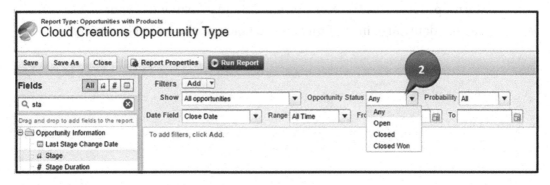

Figure 5-20. *Opportunity status filter*

- Opportunity Probability allows you to filter based on the Probability field (which is associated with this stage). You can choose options such as greater than 90 percent to get a better picture of what is in your pipeline that will most likely close, as shown in Figure 5-21.

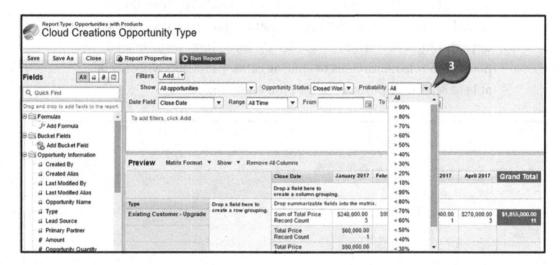

Figure 5-21. *Opportunity Probability filter*

- The opportunity Date Field filter works just like the one for accounts, contacts, and leads. You can choose from any date field within that report type to filter from as well as use Salesforce smart dates. Smart dates allow you to choose dates that will update to the relative time every time you run your report. For instance, you can choose from the drop-down This Week or Current Calendar Year or use your own custom date range in the From and To fields, as shown in Figure 5-22.

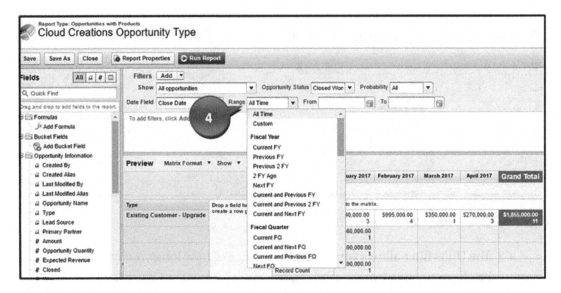

Figure 5-22. *Opportunity smart date filters*

Case Filters

Case filters have some similarities to other objects standard filters and some that are unique to this report type.

- The Show filter on cases allows you to see all your cases, all cases regardless of who owns them, user-owned cases (opposed to queue owned), queue-owned cases, your case team's cases, or role-based team's cases, as shown in Figure 5-23. If you have security set in place with role hierarchies or sharing rules, your users will only be able to see the cases they are set up to see.

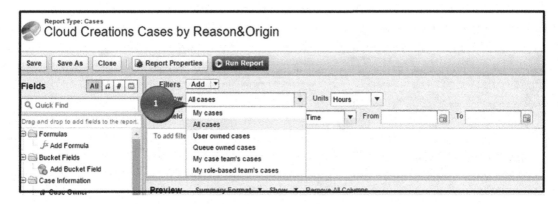

Figure 5-23. *Case ownership filter*

- The Units filter allows you to display the age of how long your case has been open in minutes, hours, or days, as shown in Figure 5-24.

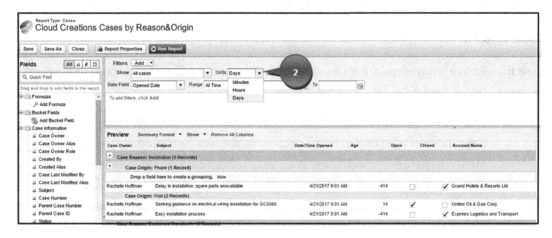

Figure 5-24. *Case units filter*

- The case Date Field filter works just like the one for accounts, contacts, leads, and opportunities. You can choose from any date field within that report type to filter from as well use Salesforce smart dates, as shown in Figure 5-25. Smart dates allow you to choose dates that will update to the relative time every time you run your report. For instance, you can choose from the drop-down This Week or Current Calendar Year or use your own custom date range in the From and To fields.

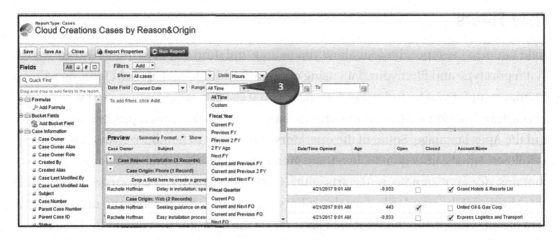

Figure 5-25. *Case smart date filter*

Campaigns

Campaigns have only one option for standard filtering.

- The Show filter allows you to filter by a specific campaign and provides a lookup field to find it, as shown in Figure 5-26. It also allows you to see all of your active campaigns, campaigns you own, all active campaigns regardless of who owns them, and all campaigns.

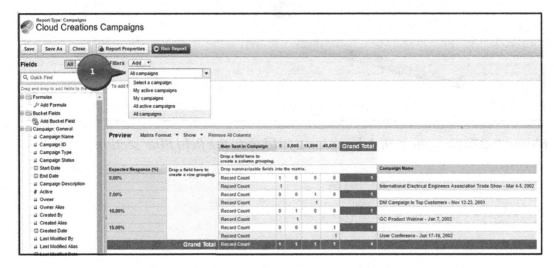

Figure 5-26. *Campaigns' ownership filter*

Field Filters

Field filters in the report builder allow you to drag and drop any field found within that report type and filter your data using operators and values. This field filtering will be important for you to understand because you'll see this same feature used widely throughout Salesforce. You can find this in list views, workflow rules, process builders, and the Apex language. Some of the operators you'll want to familiarize yourself with are as follows: equals, not equal to, less than, greater than, less or equal, greater or equal, contains, does not contain, and starts with. Here is also where you can customize smart dates further if the standard smart date filters don't work for you. Drag and drop the date field of your choice into the filter field section, set the operator to "equals," and use a phrase like Next N Days (replace "N" with your desired number) or Last N Months.

1. Take your field from the left-side Fields section and drag it to the filters section, as shown in Figure 5-27.

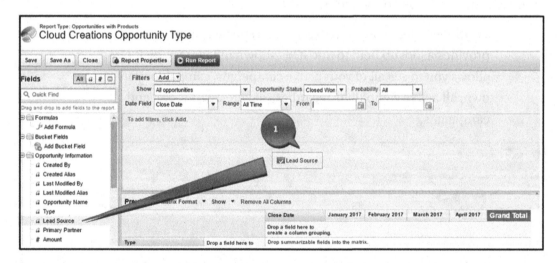

Figure 5-27. *Dragging and dropping a field onto the field filter section*

2. Choose the operator appropriate for your filter, as shown in
    Figure 5-28.

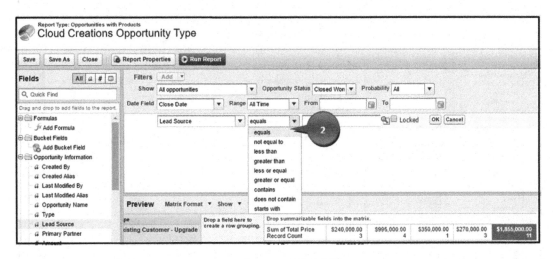

Figure 5-28. *Selecting an operator for your field filter*

3. If the field filter chosen is a picklist field, you can click the lookup
    icon. If the field is another data type, you can enter the value
    necessary.

4. For picklist fields only, you'll check the values that your filter
    should include.

5. For picklist fields only, click Insert Selected to add these values to
    your filter, as shown in Figure 5-29.

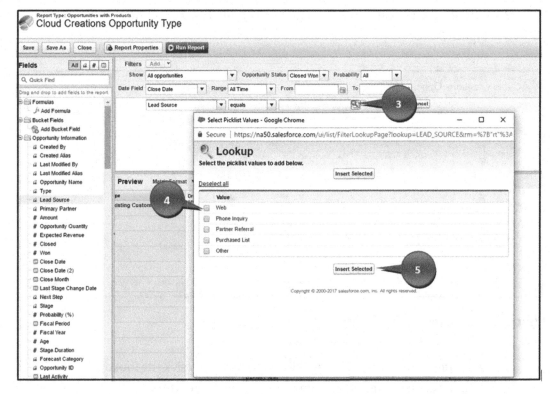

Figure 5-29. *Selecting the field value of a picklist field*

6.   Click OK to finalize your field filter, as shown in Figure 5-30.

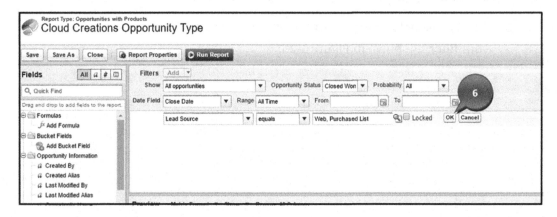

Figure 5-30. *Completing your field filter*

Note Notice the Locked check box next to the OK button in Figure 5-30. This check box, if selected, allows you to lock the filter on your report so it can't be changed unless the user has the permission to modify reports. Figure 5-31 shows how it is locked.

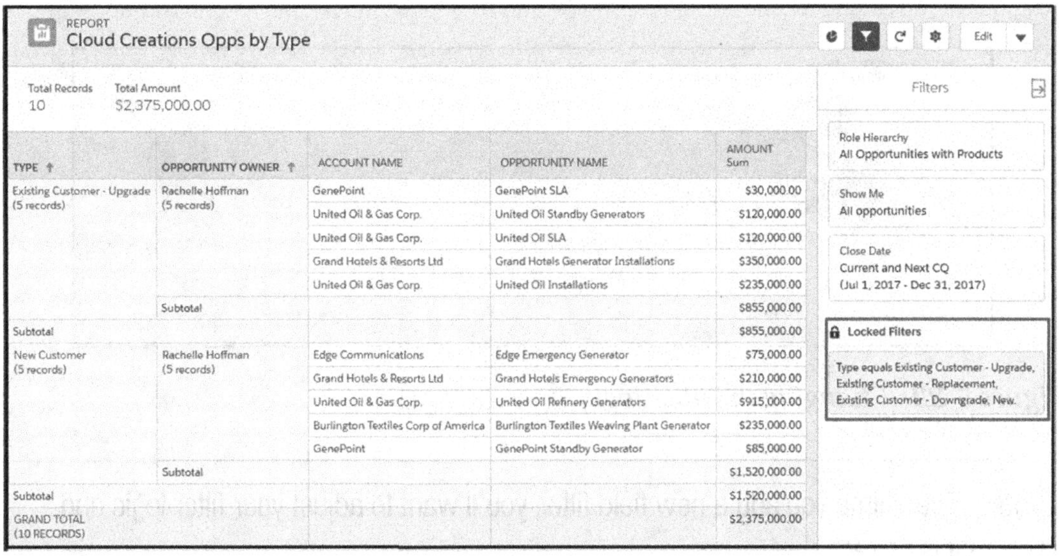

TYPE	OPPORTUNITY OWNER	ACCOUNT NAME	OPPORTUNITY NAME	AMOUNT Sum
Existing Customer - Upgrade (5 records)	Rachelle Hoffman (5 records)	GenePoint	GenePoint SLA	$30,000.00
		United Oil & Gas Corp.	United Oil Standby Generators	$120,000.00
		United Oil & Gas Corp.	United Oil SLA	$120,000.00
		Grand Hotels & Resorts Ltd	Grand Hotels Generator Installations	$350,000.00
		United Oil & Gas Corp.	United Oil Installations	$235,000.00
	Subtotal			$855,000.00
Subtotal				$855,000.00
New Customer (5 records)	Rachelle Hoffman (5 records)	Edge Communications	Edge Emergency Generator	$75,000.00
		Grand Hotels & Resorts Ltd	Grand Hotels Emergency Generators	$210,000.00
		United Oil & Gas Corp.	United Oil Refinery Generators	$915,000.00
		Burlington Textiles Corp of America	Burlington Textiles Weaving Plant Generator	$235,000.00
		GenePoint	GenePoint Standby Generator	$85,000.00
	Subtotal			$1,520,000.00
Subtotal				$1,520,000.00
GRAND TOTAL (10 RECORDS)				$2,375,000.00

***Figure 5-31.** Locked field filters*

Filter Logic

After you have set up at least one field filter, filter logic will allow you to apply "and," "or," or "not" statements on how the fields are evaluated. You can create a complex statement of as many field filters that are necessary for your report. If you use filter logic, you do have to include all your field filters in the statement. You can use parentheses to group logic together to further define your report. The default filter logic places AND into the logic, meaning "1 AND 2 AND 3," and so on. This tells the report to only include records that meet all three of the criteria that you've set up (or however many you've set up) into the report.

1. Click the Add button next to Filters and choose Filter Logic.

2. Create your statement. You'll use the number next to the field filter to define what field filter needs to be placed with an "and" or "or" statement. The statements that you'll use will look like "(1 OR 2) AND 3 AND 4." Another example would be "1 AND 2 AND 3 AND 4 AND (5 OR 6 OR 7)."

3. Click OK to complete your filter logic, as shown in Figure 5-32.

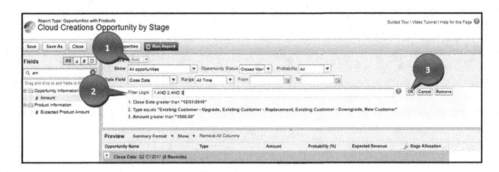

Figure 5-32. *Changing the filter logic*

Note   Every time you add a new field filter, you'll want to adjust your filter logic and ensure it is correct.

Cross Filter

Cross filters in Salesforce allow you to apply conditions on objects related to the current object you are reporting from. You can use cross filters by applying "with" or "without" conditions on the related objects. After you use your cross filter, further define your field filter via that related cross filter. An example of this would be filtering all opportunities without follow-up activities. Or use the cross filter to set up filtering on opportunities without products to determine what opportunities still need to be completed. Another example of using cross filters would be to determine whether an account or contact has had any interaction with your sales team. You can set this up by creating an account or contact report and adding the cross filter logic of "without" activities. This will give you a list of all the accounts or contacts that need to be reached out to or checked in on. To set this up, create at least one field filter and follow these steps:

1. Click the Add button next to Filters and choose Cross Filter.

2. Select the primary object that you want to use to relate other objects to.

3. Define whether you want to see these related objects with the word "with" or choose "without."

4. Select the related object you would like to see or not see.

5. Click the Add Related Object filter, select the operator along with the value, and click OK, as shown in Figure 5-33.

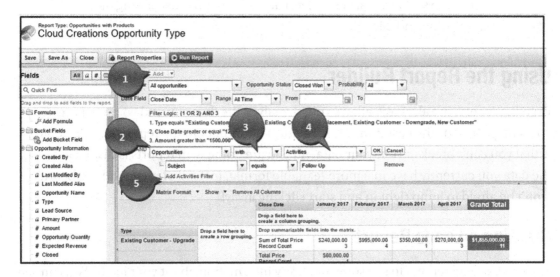

Figure 5-33. *Setting up a cross filter*

Row Limit

Row limit filters are used with Tabular reports and allow you to display your report in a table or chart on a dashboard if you limit the number of rows it returns and sort by a field. To create this, follow these steps:

1. Click the Add button and choose Row Limit, as shown in Figure 5-34.

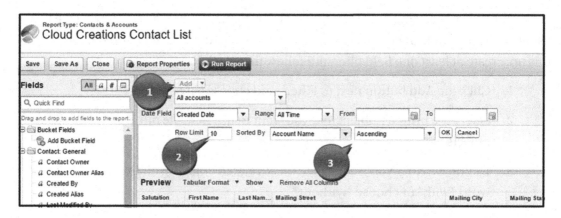

Figure 5-34. *Setting up the row limit*

2. Define the row limit.

3. Choose to sort by a particular field and whether it is ascending or descending and click OK.

Using the Report Builder

Creating reports in Salesforce allows you to analyze the data you and your user are collecting. Perhaps the best thing about being a newcomer to the reports in Salesforce is that you can't break or ruin your data. All you are doing with reports is displaying the data you currently have in a more readable format, instead of in individual records. Don't be afraid to jump right in and start clicking away!

Creating a Leads Report

You can use lead reports to see some or all key information about your leads. You can see how many leads you have, what lead source is working from your marketing team, the number of leads that are being handled by a user versus the ones that are in a queue, and so much more! One of the many business problems that can be resolved with generating lead reports is considering which lead source is working compared to ones that are not. You can build a report on converted leads and group the report by the lead source, as shown in Figure 5-35.

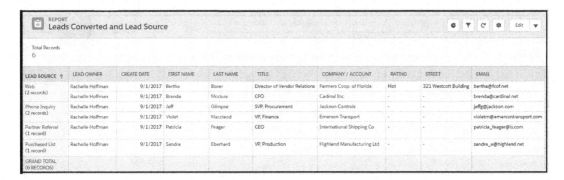

Figure 5-35. *Leads report example*

To create a lead report, follow these steps:

1. Navigate to the Reports tab and click Reports, as shown in Figure 5-36.

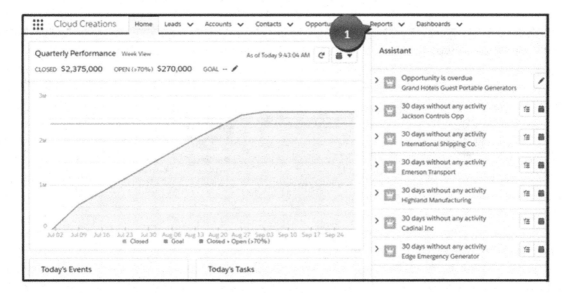

Figure 5-36. *Navigating to the Reports tab*

2. Click New Report, as shown in Figure 5-37.

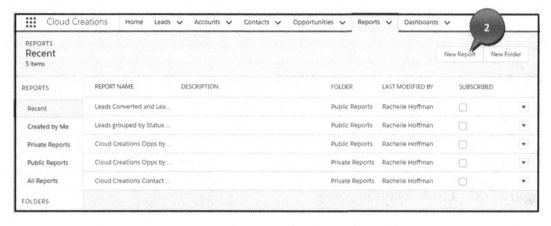

Figure 5-37. *Click the New Report button to start a new report*

3. In the Quick Find, type **Leads** or click Leads and click Create, as shown in Figure 5-38.

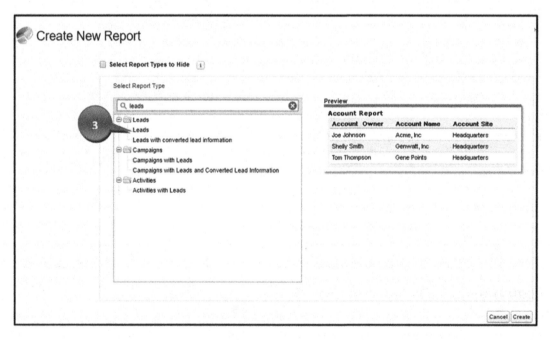

Figure 5-38. *Finding the report type to use*

4. Click and hold the name of the field you would like to move into your reports and drag it to the column where you would like it to be placed. Continue to drag and drop as many fields as necessary for the report. Once finished, click Save, as shown in Figure 5-39.

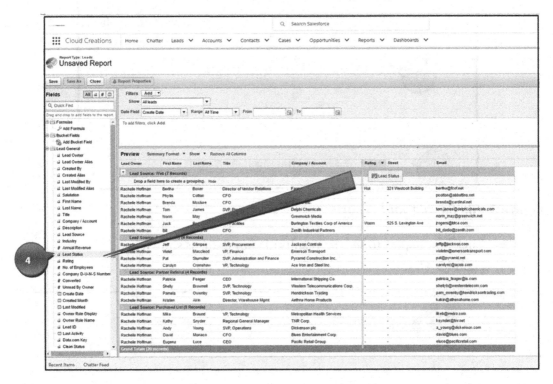

Figure 5-39. *Dragging and dropping a new field into your report*

5. Name your report and press your Tab key for Salesforce to automatically enter a value in the Report Unique Name field.

6. Enter a description that will be displayed to users.

7. Select the report folder where your report should be stored.

8. Click Save, as shown in Figure 5-40.

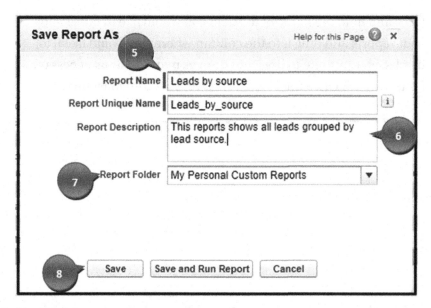

Figure 5-40. *Saving your report*

9. Click Run Report to see the results of your data, as shown in Figure 5-41.

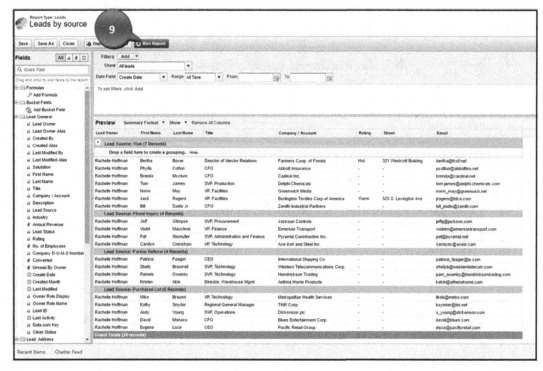

Figure 5-41. *Running your report to see your results*

Creating Contacts and Accounts Report

You can create a contacts and accounts report to display all your contact details. Use this report for a call list, mail merges, viewing newly created contacts and accounts, or any other business needs. Business-to-business (B2B) organizations can benefit from the use of account reports if they want to determine the types of industries they work with. You can generate a report that shows you how many businesses you are engaging with in each industry. This would help you to determine where you should focus your marketing efforts. You can see what this report would look like in Figure 5-42.

INDUSTRY ↑	ACCOUNT OWNER	ACCOUNT NAME	TYPE	RATING	LAST ACTIVITY	LAST MODIFIED DATE	BILLING STATE/PROVINCE
Agriculture (1 record)	Rachelle Hoffman	Farmers Coop. of Florida	-	Hot		9/3/2017	FL
Apparel (1 record)	Rachelle Hoffman	Burlington Textiles Corp of America	Customer - Direct	Warm		9/1/2017	NC
Biotechnology (1 record)	Rachelle Hoffman	GenePoint	Customer - Channel	Cold		9/1/2017	CA
Construction (1 record)	Rachelle Hoffman	Pyramid Construction Inc.	Customer - Channel	-		9/1/2017	-
Consulting (1 record)	Rachelle Hoffman	Dickenson plc	Customer - Channel	-		9/1/2017	KS
Education (1 record)	Rachelle Hoffman	University of Arizona	Customer - Direct	Warm		9/1/2017	AZ
Electronics (1 record)	Rachelle Hoffman	Edge Communications	Customer - Direct	Hot		9/1/2017	TX
Energy (3 records)	Rachelle Hoffman	United Oil & Gas Corp.	Customer - Direct	Hot		9/1/2017	NY
	Rachelle Hoffman	United Oil & Gas, Singapore	Customer - Direct	-		9/1/2017	Singapore
	Rachelle Hoffman	United Oil & Gas, UK	Customer - Direct	-		9/1/2017	UK
Hospitality (1 record)	Rachelle Hoffman	Grand Hotels & Resorts Ltd	Customer - Direct	Warm		9/1/2017	IL
Transportation (1 record)	Rachelle Hoffman	Express Logistics and Transport	Customer - Channel	Cold		9/1/2017	OR

Figure 5-42. *Accounts and contacts report example*

To create a contacts and accounts report:

1. Navigate to the Reports tab and click Reports; once you see your report folders, click New Reports in the right corner.

2. In the Quick Find area, type **Contact**. Or, click Accounts, click Contacts & Accounts, and click Create, as shown in Figure 5-43.

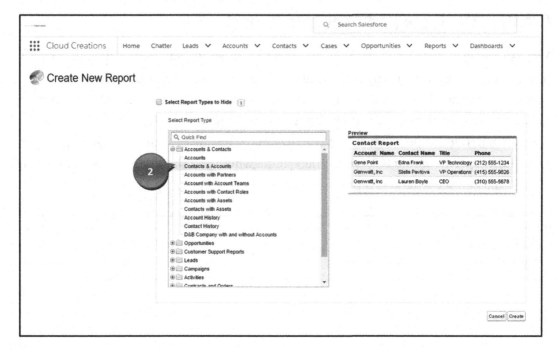

Figure 5-43. *Selecting the report type for your report*

3. Click and hold the name of the field you want to move into your reports and drag it to the column where you would like it to be placed. Continue to drag and drop as many fields as necessary for the report. Once finished, click Save, as shown in Figure 5-44.

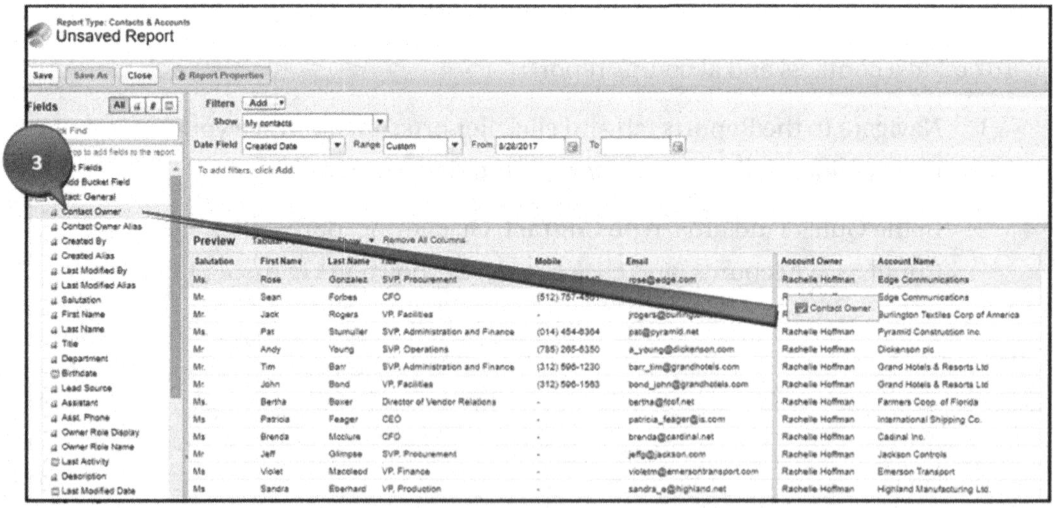

Figure 5-44. *Dragging and dropping a field into your report*

4. Name your report and click your Tab key for Salesforce to automatically enter a value in the Report Unique Name field.

5. Enter a description that will be displayed to users.

6. Select the report folder where your report should be stored.

7. Click Save, as shown in Figure 5-45.

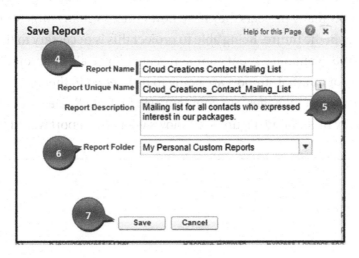

Figure 5-45. *Saving your report*

8. Click Run Report to see the results of your data, as shown in Figure 5-46.

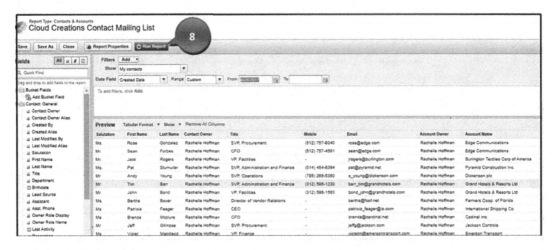

Figure 5-46. *Running your report to see the results*

Creating an Opportunity Report

You can create an opportunity report and opportunity with products report to display the sales your company has generated. Use these report types to display what is in the pipeline, what has dropped out of the pipeline, and all sales that your team has successfully won. Most businesses will generate opportunity reports to help project what efforts may be needed in the future. For instance, project management companies need to project how many projects they have now and how many projects may be closing or starting in the future. Being able to project this is necessary to the operations of the business. Project management companies need to be able to project how many project managers or internal support are going to be needed in the upcoming months. To project this, a project management company will look at all sales with a 90 percent or higher opportunity probability. Figure 5-47 shows what this report would look like.

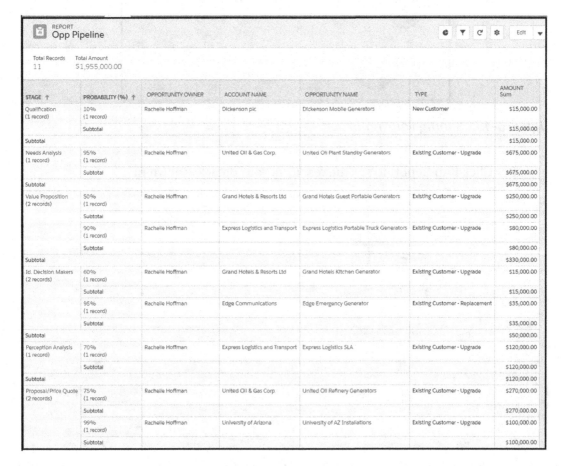

Figure 5-47. *Opportunity report example*

To create an opportunity report, follow these steps:

1. Navigate to the Reports tab and click Reports; once you see your report folders, click New Reports in the right corner.

2. In the Quick Find area, type **Opportunity**. Or, click Opportunity and click Create, as shown in Figure 5-48.

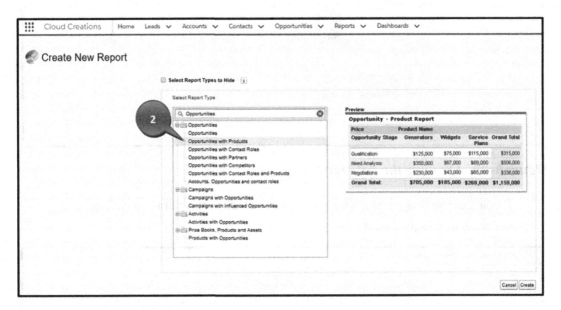

Figure 5-48. *Selecting the report type for your report*

3. Click Show and select Details, as shown in Figure 5-49.

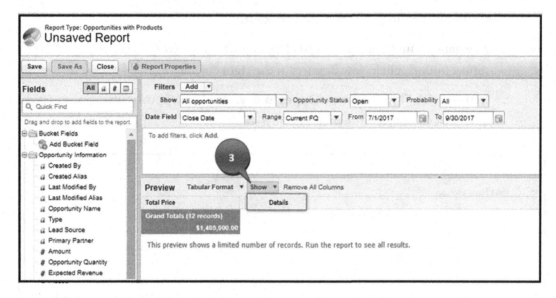

Figure 5-49. *Showing the details on a report*

4. Select the proper filters for your report to show the data desired, as shown in Figure 5-50.

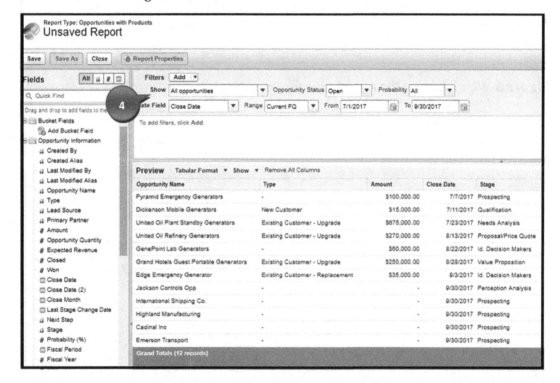

Figure 5-50. *Setting up the report field filters for your report*

5.   Click and hold the name of the field you would like to move into
     your reports and drag it to the column where you would like it to
     be placed. Continue to drag and drop as many fields as necessary
     for the report. Once finished, click Save, as shown in Figure 5-51.

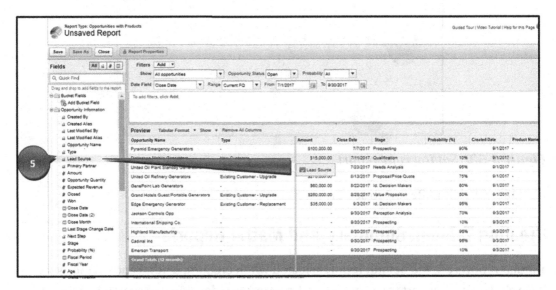

Figure 5-51.   *Dragging and dropping a field into your report*

6.   Name your report and press your Tab key for Salesforce to
     automatically enter a value in the Report Unique Name field.

7.   Enter a description that will be displayed to users.

8.   Select the report folder where your report should be stored.

9.   Click Save, as shown in Figure 5-52.

Figure 5-52. *Saving your report*

10.   Click Run Report to see the results of your data.

Creating Tabular, Summary, and Matrix Reports

Tabular reports are the default report selected when creating a new report. Once you
have chosen your report type and are in the report builder, you can switch between all
three report formats. If switching from the Summary or Matrix report format to Tabular,
you'll want to take the fields you grouped and move them to a column; otherwise,
you'll lose them and have to bring them back to the report once in Tabular format.
When switching from a Matrix report to a Summary report, be aware that you may lose
groupings here as well if you have set up four groupings on the Matrix report; Summary
reports can handle only up to three groupings. Let's look at creating Tabular, Summary,
and Matrix reports.

1.   Navigate to the Reports tab and click Reports; once you see your
report folders, click New Reports in the right corner.

2.   Choose the report type of your choice and click Create, as shown
in Figure 5-53.

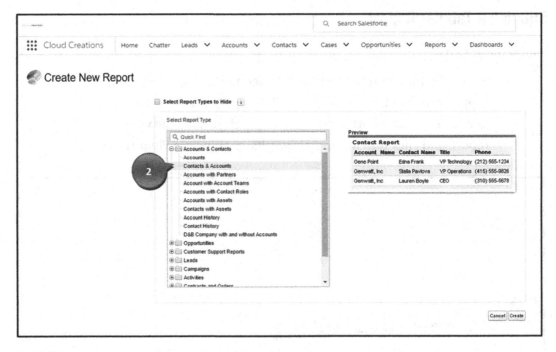

Figure 5-53. *Selecting the report type for your report*

3. In the Preview pane of the report builder, choose the drop-down
   that displays Tabular Format and switch to the report format of
   your choice, as shown in Figure 5-54.

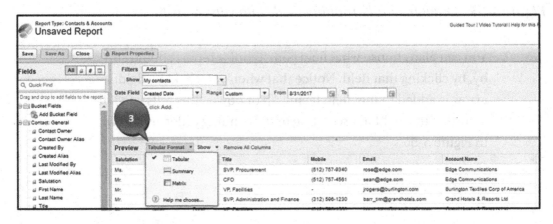

Figure 5-54. *Changing report formats*

Building a Tabular Report

Follow these steps:

1. To build a Tabular report, there is no need to change the format drop-down. Just begin dragging and dropping your fields as needed for your report. Once finished, click Save, name your report, and click Run to see your results, as shown in Figure 5-55.

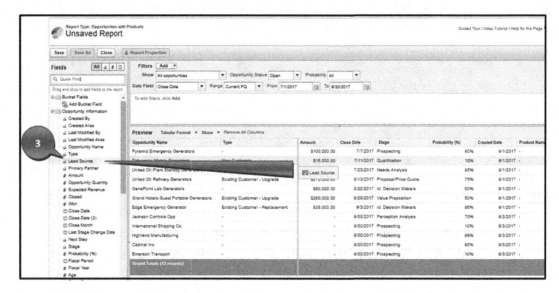

Figure 5-55. *Dragging and dropping fields into your report*

2. You can also choose what field your Tabular report should sort by, by clicking that field. Notice that when you click the field, an arrow is added to that field facing up or down. This tells you if it is sorting this field in ascending or descending order, as shown in Figure 5-56.

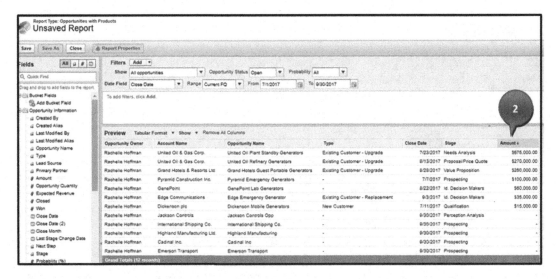

Figure 5-56. *Sorting by a field in your reports*

Note   You can sort any report type like this.

Building a Summary Report

Follow these steps:

1. Once you are in the report builder, change the format to the Summary format, as shown in Figure 5-57.

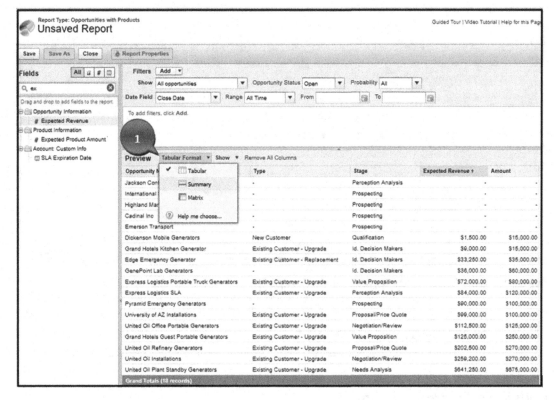

Figure 5-57. *Changing your report format to the Summary report format*

2. Add groupings to your report by dragging and dropping a field into the area "Drop a field here to create a grouping," as shown in Figure 5-58.

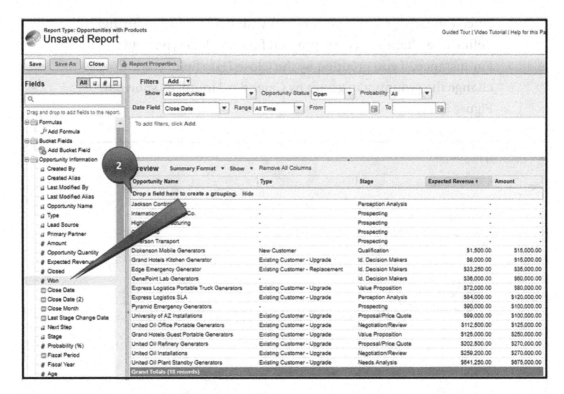

Figure 5-58. *Dragging and dropping fields into the grouping section of the report*

Note   You can add up to three groupings here, and this feature is also available in the Matrix report format.

---

3. Once you have grouped your report with fields, you can further
   define how these fields are grouped for date data type fields.
   For instance, if you grouped by the Close Date field, you can
   change the grouping to group by Calendar Month, as shown in
   Figure 5-59.

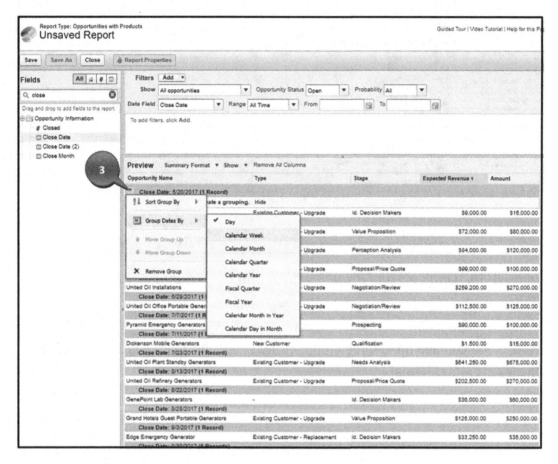

Figure 5-59. *Defining how your report is grouped*

4. Continue building your report by dragging and dropping fields
   into places of your choice. Save and name the report and run!

Building a Matrix Format Report

Follow these steps:

1. Once you are in the report builder, change the Tabular Format drop-down to Matrix, as shown in Figure 5-60.

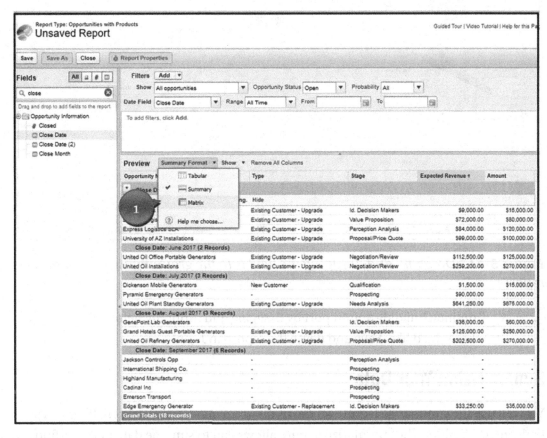

Figure 5-60. *Switching your report format to a Matrix report format*

2. Notice for this report type you have two areas for grouping: at the columns level and at the row level. Drag and drop the field of your choice onto either of these grouping areas. You can add two groups on the column grouping level and on the row grouping level, as shown in Figure 5-61.

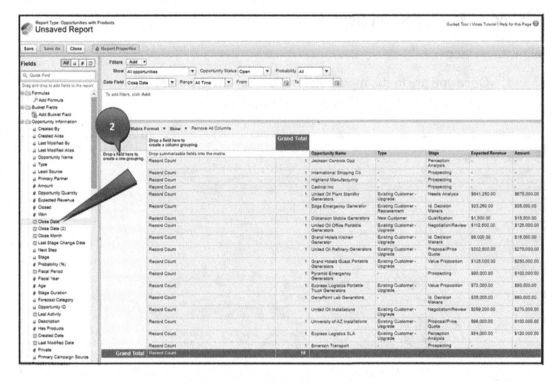

Figure 5-61. *Dragging and dropping the field into the grouping sections of the report*

3. Continue building your report by dragging and dropping fields where you'd like. Save and name the report and run!

Summarizing Your Data

You can use the summarize feature on the number, currency, or percent field data types in the report builder. The summarize feature allows you to sum the data in a row, find the average of data in a row, find the minimum of the data in a row, or find the maximum of the data in a row. Use this feature in an opportunity report to find the average age of an opportunity or case. Or use this feature to simply give you the sum of your amount fields on opportunities. When you use this feature in a summary or matrix report, it will summarize on all grouping levels and give you the grand total.

1. Once in your report builder, click the down-facing arrow next to the field you want to summarize, as shown in Figure 5-62.

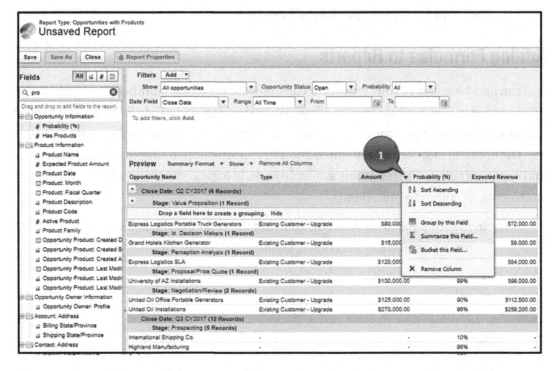

Figure 5-62. *Summarizing a field*

2. Choose to sum, find the average, find the max, or find the min and click Apply, as shown in Figure 5-63.

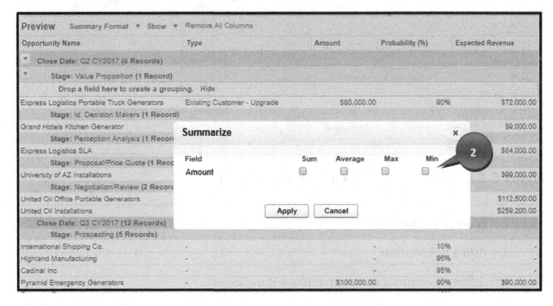

Figure 5-63. *Choosing how you want to summarize a field*

3.   Don't forget to save and run your report.

Adding Formulas to Reports

You can add formulas to your reports to calculate the currency, number, or percent fields from an object. The formula feature allows you to leverage your field formats, summarize field data, use basic operators, use complex functions, and use logic statements.

The operators for formulas include addition, subtraction, multiplication, division, and exponentiation. The functions available include logical statements, mathematical statements, or summary statements.

1.   In the left pane, drag Add Formula into the report and place it in a column position of your choice, as shown in Figure 5-64.

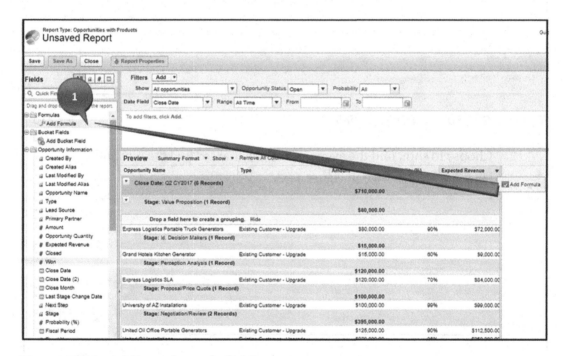

Figure 5-64. *Adding a formula field to your report*

2.   Name your formula.

3.   Add a description.

4.   Adjust the format or decimal place if necessary.

5.   Choose what level to run this formula on.

6. Create your formula using the operators or functions necessary.

Note   Formulas are for the advanced user. We will not be covering the various aspects of what formulas to use in this book. However, Salesforce offers free support, and there are great forums that can offer help as well.

---

7. Click Check Syntax for complex formulas to ensure there are no errors.

8. Click OK to add the formula, as shown in Figure 5-65.

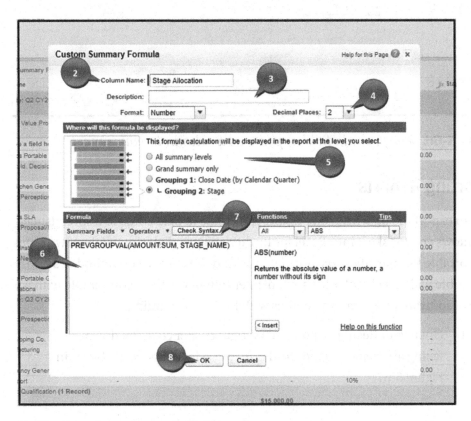

Figure 5-65.   *Creating a formula field on your report*

9. The formula field appears as a column on the report, as shown in Figure 5-66.

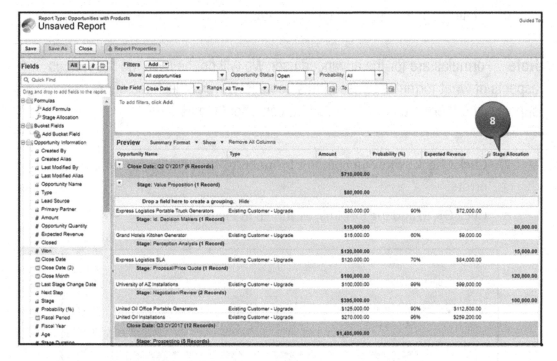

Figure 5-66. *The formula field appears as a column in your report*

Exporting Reports

You can export the data from any report you create in Salesforce to a spreadsheet.
This allows you to take it into Excel for further analysis. Salesforce offers two types
of exportable formats: the Excel format .xls and the comma-delimited .csv. XLS is
compatible with Excel and most spreadsheet software. CSV is compatible with a wider
range of software programs and comes with limited formatting.

1. Open your desired report; in the right corner click the down-
   facing arrow next to the word *Edit* and select Export, as shown in
   Figure 5-67.

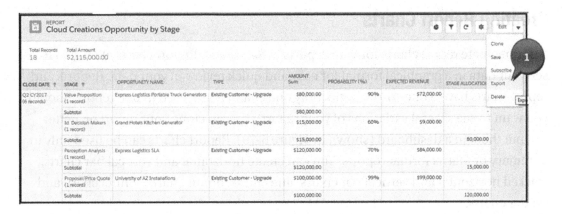

Figure 5-67. *Exporting a report*

2. Choose the format that supports your company software and select Export, as shown in Figure 5-68.

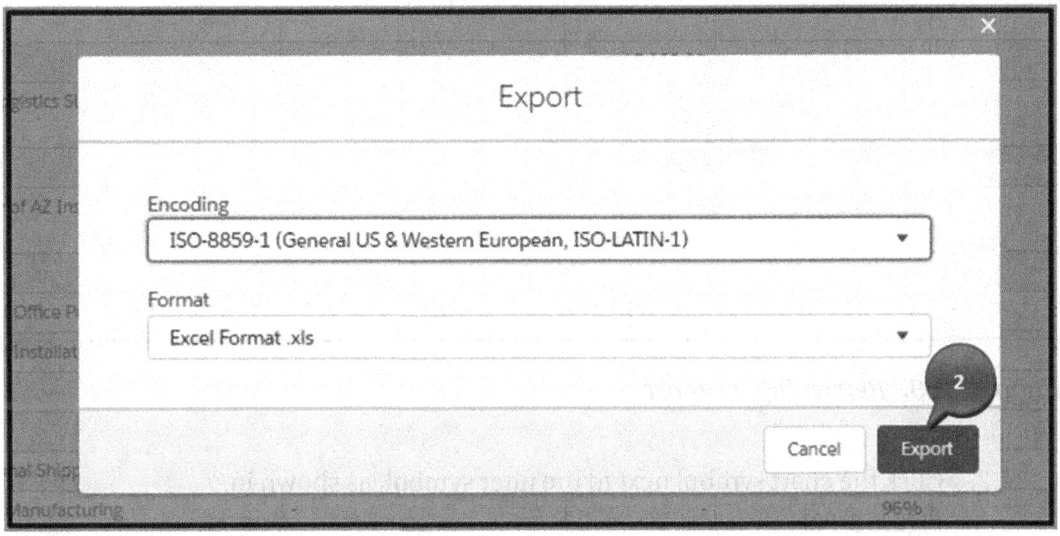

Figure 5-68. *Selecting the export format and exporting the data*

Creating Report Charts

You can create report charts for your reports in Salesforce. Report charts allow you to see your data in a graphical format for easy and quick review of your data. Reports and report charts have a one-to-one ratio: only one chart can be used in one report. Should you want to see several variations of your report, you can clone your report or, better yet, put them in a dashboard (shown in Figure 5-79). Report charts can be used only in Summary or Matrix format reports. You can create horizontal and vertical bar charts, stacked horizontal and vertical bar charts, line charts, donut charts, funnel chart, and scatter charts.

1. Go to your Reports tab and select the report of your choice, as shown in Figure 5-69.

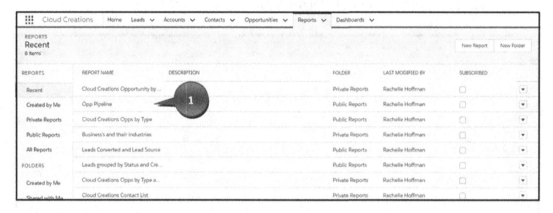

Figure 5-69. *Retrieving a report*

2. Click the chart symbol next to the filter symbol, as shown in Figure 5-70.

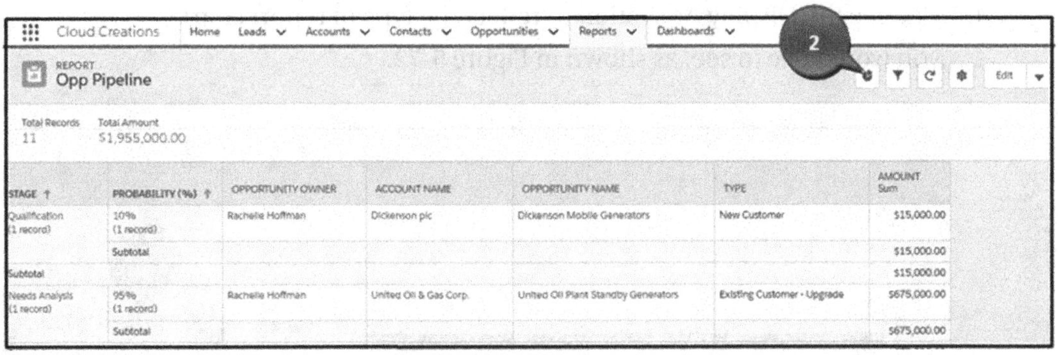

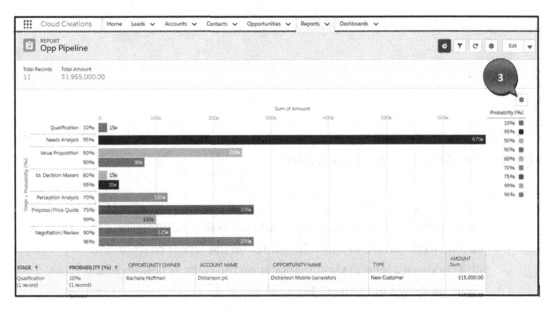

Figure 5-70. *Clicking the chart icon*

3. Based on your report and how your data is put together, Salesforce will display a recommended report. You can change this if needed; click the settings cog icon, as shown in Figure 5-71.

Figure 5-71. *Selecting the Setup icon for the chart*

4. Change the Display As section to reflect the type of report chart you would like to see, as shown in Figure 5-72.

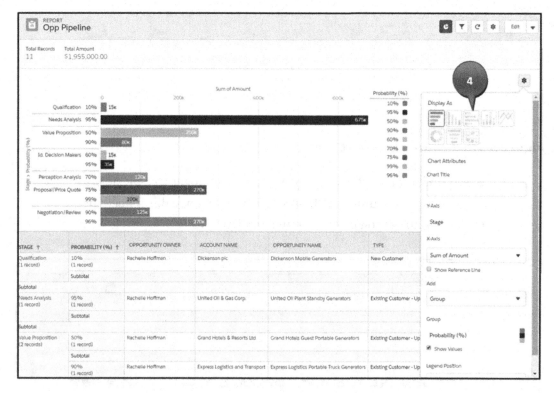

Figure 5-72. *Choosing the type of chart*

5. Adjust the chart attributes within the chart editor; add a chart title, change the *x*-axis to another field, add items like a dimension or second axis, choose to show the values on the report chart or not, and choose if a legend should appear on the right or bottom of the chart, as shown in Figure 5-73.

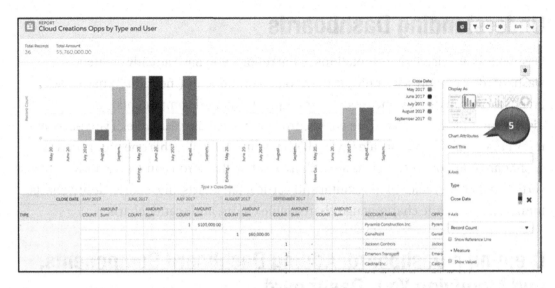

Figure 5-73. *Customizing your report chart attributes*

Note   Some features are available only on specific report charts.

After you have configured your report chart, don't forget to save your work and see your results, as in Figure 5-74.

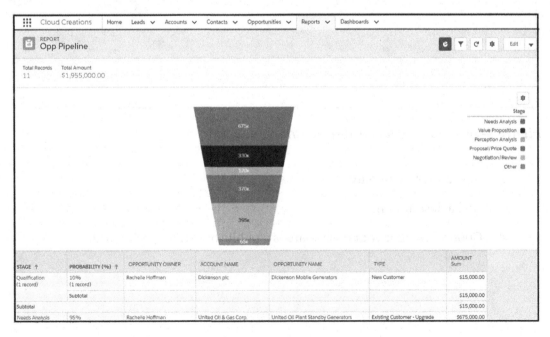

Figure 5-74. *Finishing result of a report chart*

Understanding Dashboards

Dashboards are visual representations of the reports you have already created. Dashboards can represent multiple dashboard components (individual charts and graphs). You can display one report in multiple dashboard components; you can't display multiple reports into one dashboard component. For example, if you have one report that represents your sales by each user, you can display this one report in two dashboard components, such as a pie chart and bar chart. You can create horizontal and vertical bar charts, stacked horizontal and vertical bar charts, line charts, donut charts, funnel charts, metric charts, gauge charts, table charts, and scatter charts.

Creating a Dashboard, Adding Dashboard Components, and Modifying Your Dashboard

Follow these steps:

1. Click your Dashboards tab and click New Dashboard, as shown in Figure 5-75.

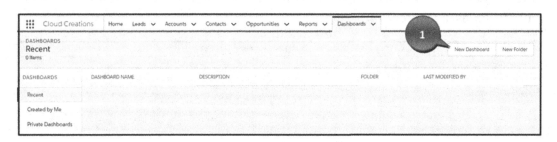

Figure 5-75. *Creating a new dashboard*

2. Name your dashboard.

3. Add a description.

4. Choose whether your dashboard is a public or private dashboard.

5.   Click Create, as shown in Figure 5-76.

Figure 5-76.   *Naming and creating your dashboard*

6.   Click Component in the upper-right corner to add a report you've
     already created to the dashboard, as shown in Figure 5-77.

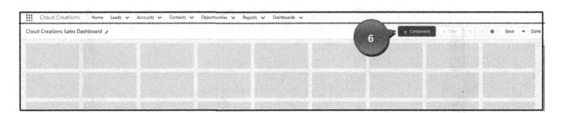

Figure 5-77.   *Adding a new report and chart component to your dashboard*

7.   Search the report you want to add to the dashboard, as shown in
     Figure 5-78.

Figure 5-78. *Finding the report for your dashboard component*

8. Choose the chart you want to display your data in and modify any attributes to better display your data. Once finished, click Add, as shown in Figure 5-79.

Figure 5-79. *Creating the chart to go with your report on your dashboard*

Note   As you make changes to these attributes, watch the preview of the report to see how these changes affect the display.

9. Click the dashboard report and drag the corners out to make your report bigger, or click the dashboard and move the report to another location on the dashboard, as shown in Figure 5-80.

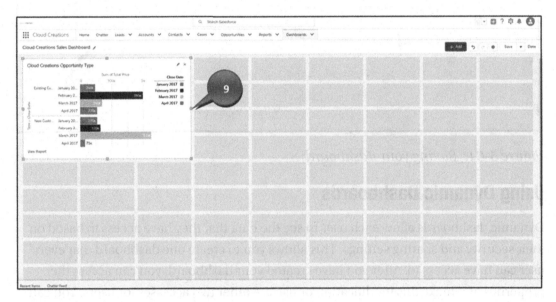

Figure 5-80. *Modifying the size of your report and chart*

10. Continue steps 6 to 9 until you are satisfied with your dashboard.

11. Click Save when you complete or to save your work, as shown in Figure 5-81.

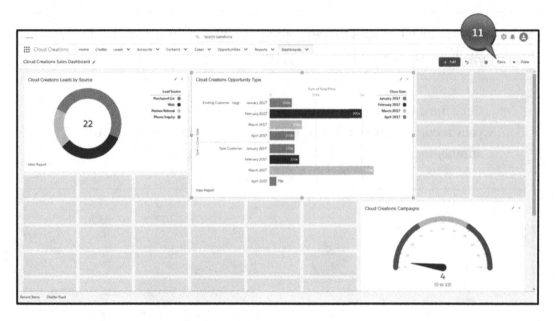

Figure 5-81. *Saving your dashboard*

Using Dynamic Dashboards

Dynamic dashboards allow each user to see the data that they have access to based on their security and sharing settings. This allows you to create one dashboard that every user can have access to. After you have created your dashboard, you can access the properties and make this modification or use the other two accesses for users. You can set a dashboard to be viewed as Me, which allows dashboard readers to see data in the dashboard according to your access to the data. You can select the option "A specified user," which allows users to see data based on the selected user's access. Lastly, you can use the "The logged in user," which allows users to see data based on their access. Additionally, you can prevent users from changing how the dashboard is viewed by deselecting "Allow Dashboard views to change this (dynamic dashboard)." Businesses choose a dynamic dashboard over a nondynamic one when they are trying to prevent users from seeing data that they shouldn't. For instance, a business may have many sales users. With these sales users, there are many territories. If you don't want the salesperson responsible for California to see the sales data for New York, you could use the option "The logged in user." (Granted, you must have set up your security to prevent this from happening, which is covered in Chapter 9.) If having the user's data restricted is not an issue for your company, you can leave the settings as is. Let's take a look at how you can modify this:

1. Click the settings cog icon in the right corner of the dashboard, as shown in Figure 5-82.

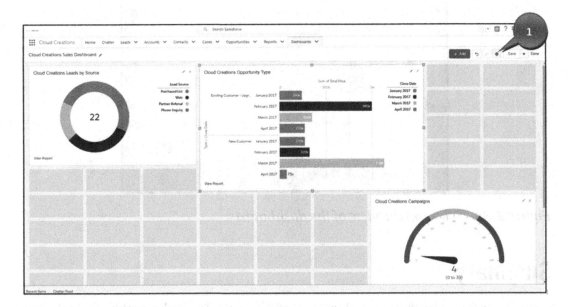

Figure 5-82. *Creating a dynamic dashboard*

2. Select what view you would like to set the dashboard as.

3. Select or deselect if the user should be able to change this.

4. Click Save, as shown in Figure 5-83.

Figure 5-83. *Selecting the view of the dashboard*

Summary

One of the greatest benefits of having Salesforce as your client relationship management tool is the reports that can be generated from the data collected. Being able to calculate your return on investment (ROI) or how your sales team is doing will help you in the months and years of your business to come. The best thing about reports and dashboards is that you can't mess your data up using them. Don't be afraid to click around and play with them. You are only translating data; you can't mess it up!

CHAPTER 6

Collaborating

Salesforce offers many collaboration tools. One valuable collaboration tool offered is called Chatter. This tool and its capabilities can be found on a significant number of standard objects and all custom objects in Salesforce. It allows your users to communicate with each other via internal messaging. You can even allow your users to share files such as Word and PowerPoint files with each other and your customers using content deliveries. Do you need to share your Salesforce records with another Salesforce organization? You can use Lightning Connect and sync data to the other Salesforce organization. You can enable *topics*, which allow your users to interact on specific topics with each other. We can't forget about the Salesforce mobile app, Salesforce, that allows your users to be on-the-go for iPhone and Android users. Figure 6-1 shows the Chatter object.

Figure 6-1. *Chatter tool*

© Felicia Duarte, Rachelle Hoffman 2018
F. Duarte, R. Hoffman, *Learn Salesforce Lightning*, https://doi.org/10.1007/978-1-4842-2994-1_6

Understanding Chatter

Salesforce Chatter is an essential tool that can be used to help you collaborate internally with co-workers and externally with clients. You can use the Chatter feature post, which allows you to post messages to other users or post messages on a record itself about that record. Give your employees the ability to post a question that needs an answer to your management team. Or collect information from your employees via an anonymous poll. Chatter has a number of great built-in tools that can be used in various ways. Let's look into some of these tools further.

Sidebar

The sidebar on the Chatter tab gives you quick access to Chatter features (Figure 6-2). Use the What I Follow link to quickly see all Chatter posts corresponding to all the records that users follow in Salesforce (more on this feature in a bit). Use the To Me link to see any post that a user directed at you using the @ symbol or any post that was left on your profile from another user. Use Bookmarked to see any post you have bookmarked. The Company Highlights quick-access link uses Einstein's artificial intelligence (AI) to bring you all the trending topics in your organization. The Streams quick-access link allows you to create quick-access links to records. Use this section to see all accounts, cases, contacts, and more that you follow. Recent Groups allows you to create and see the latest groups you have followed.

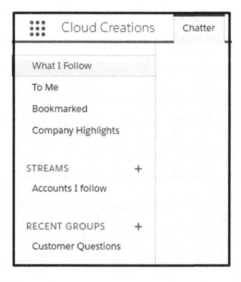

Figure 6-2. *Chatter sidebar*

Following in Chatter

Following is a powerful tool available in Salesforce. You can follow anything from people to groups to records. Following allows you to see all the relevant content and interactions that have happened to the record you choose to follow. Following in Chatter is comparable to following someone on Twitter. Want to see everything your training instructor is posting on Salesforce? Go to their profile and click the + Follow button. If you have a stream set up for that object, you can choose to add this record to the stream or to just use What I Follow. If you are viewing your Chatter feed, hover over the name of another user and use the Follow button here. Find the Follow button at the top of any record, as shown in Figure 6-3. Following brings the content and posts into your Chatter feed and allows you to interact right from your feed.

Figure 6-3. *Following in Chatter*

Bookmarking a Post

You can bookmark a post just like you would bookmark a web site. If you want to save this post for later use and have it appear in your Bookmarked quick-access list in Chatter, all you'll need to do is click the down-facing arrow to the right of the post and click Bookmark (Figure 6-4). Notice that a yellow triangle with a star appears next to the arrow. Remove the bookmark the same way except choose Remove Bookmark in the drop-down.

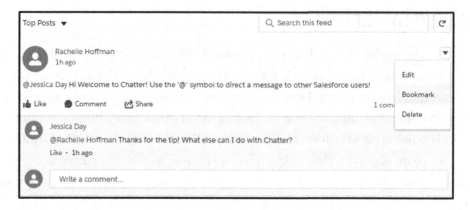

Figure 6-4. *Bookmarking a post*

Creating a Stream

Streams allow you to create groupings of specific records that you may want to follow (Figure 6-5). Streams in Chatter are best used when you want to create a custom feed that groups records from various objects into one feed. For example, if you have a new marketing campaign and you want to create a feed that follows records affected by the marketing campaign, you can create a stream that shows you all the Chatter posts on these various objects. To create a new stream, click the plus sign found in your Chatter sidebar next to Streams. First, you will need to name the stream. Next, choose what objects and records you want to include in this stream by first choosing the object and then using the search bar to search a specific record. Streams allow you to see records from the following standard objects, plus all custom objects: Accounts, Cases, Contacts, Files, Groups, Leads, Opportunities, People, and Topics. If you are viewing a record and want to include the individual record to a stream, use the + Follow button and select the stream.

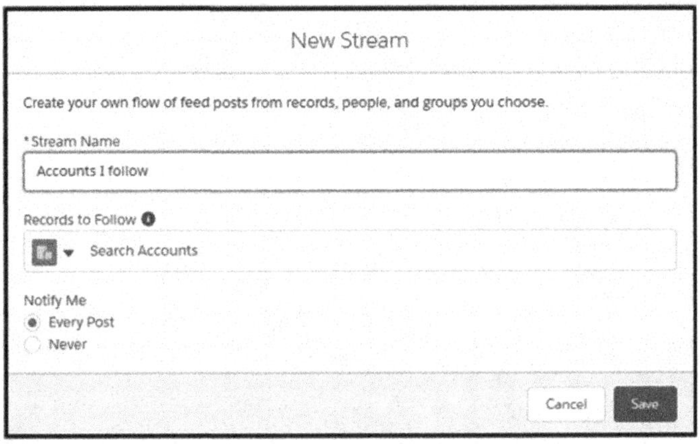

Figure 6-5. *Creating a new stream*

Creating Groups

Chatter user groups in Salesforce provide a central location for users within that group to collaborate (Figure 6-6). Most organizations will create groups for their departments. You can make a group public, private, or unlisted. Public group feeds are seen by customers or Chatter-free users (more on this feature in a bit). Private groups are member-only groups and require a user to request to join and get approved prior to interacting with the group. Unlisted groups provide more privacy than private. Unlisted groups don't allow users to request to join; it is by invitation only. Additionally, unlisted groups don't show up in list views, feeds, profiles, or anywhere unless you are a member of that group or have the permission to modify unlisted groups (even users with Modify All Data can't see these if they aren't members). To create a group, click the plus sign next to Groups on the Chatter sidebar. Next, you'll need to name the group. You can add a description for the group, add information about the group, choose who manages the group in the owner field, determine the access type (public, private, or unlisted), select if customers should be considered for joining the group, select Broadcast Only if you want the posts to only come from managers or owners of the group, and click the Save & Next button. On the next page, upload a group photo for your group.

Figure 6-6. *Creating a Chatter group*

Chatter Feed

Access your Chatter feed by navigating to the Chatter tab or by going to your profile found in the upper-right corner of the screen and clicking your name (Figure 6-7).

Figure 6-7. *Navigating to Chatter*

Your Chatter feed contains all the items you follow, posts directed at you using the @ symbol, or posts that you have created. In your Chatter feed, you can control what you see by using the sidebar.

Creating Posts on Your Feed

To create a post, make sure you are on the Post tab of Chatter (Figure 6-8). You can start typing in the box provided and use any of the stylings it provides, such as the bolding, italicizing, underlying, strikethrough to your text, and bullet points or numbering. You can also add images, tag other groups or users, and attach files. Once your post is complete, click Share. Make a mistake on your post? Not a problem, use the downward-facing arrow (the same as the one used to bookmark) and click Edit or Delete.

Figure 6-8. *Creating a post on your feed*

After you have shared your post, watch other users like, comment, and share your post (Figure 6-9).

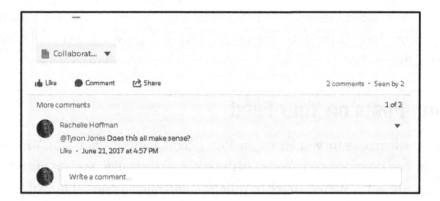

Figure 6-9. *Other users commenting and liking your post*

Creating a Post on a Record's Feed

First, you'll have to search for or find the record you want to write your post on. Next, you'll click the word Chatter that appears on the right when you are on the Related tab of that record. Once you have clicked Chatter, you can start typing in the box provided and use any of the stylings it provides, such as the bolding, italicizing, underlying, strikethrough to your text, or bullet point or numbering. You can also add images, tag other groups or users, and attach files, as shown in Figure 6-10. Once your post is complete, click Share. You can also use the Poll and Questions options (covered later in the chapter).

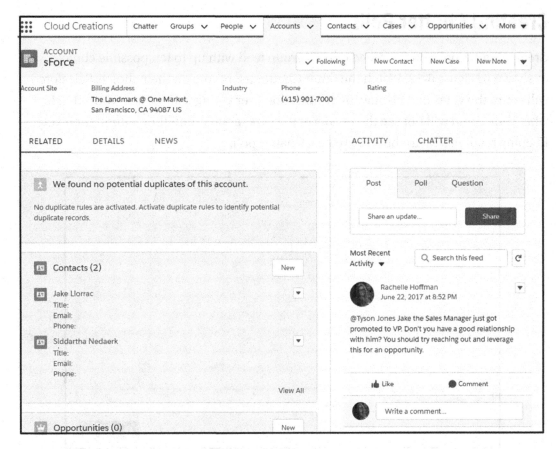

Figure 6-10. *Creating a Chatter post on record*

Creating Topics in Your Post

You can use hashtags just like on Twitter and Instagram to create trending topics in Salesforce. Just add the # symbol in front of any word (with no space) in comments or in posts. For example, use #learning (Figure 6-11).

Figure 6-11. *Using hashtags to create topics*

Creating Chatter Polls

Create Chatter polls on your feed or on a group feed with up to ten possible choices, as shown in Figure 6-12. Watch the other Chatter users vote on their choice. Salesforce will count the votes and display the results. The user voting will not see who voted for what choice and will not see the results of the Chatter poll until they submit their vote. Keeping reading to learn how to create a Chatter poll.

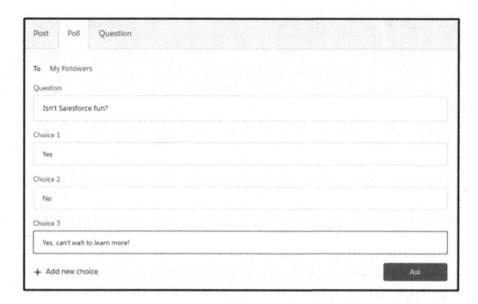

Figure 6-12. *Chatter poll*

To create a Chatter poll, follow these steps:

1. Navigate to the Chatter object or create a poll from within a record by navigating to the Chatter tab.

2. Click the Poll tab found within the Chatter section of the record. Figure 6-13 shows how to access this from a record, and Figure 6-14 shows how to access this from the Chatter object.

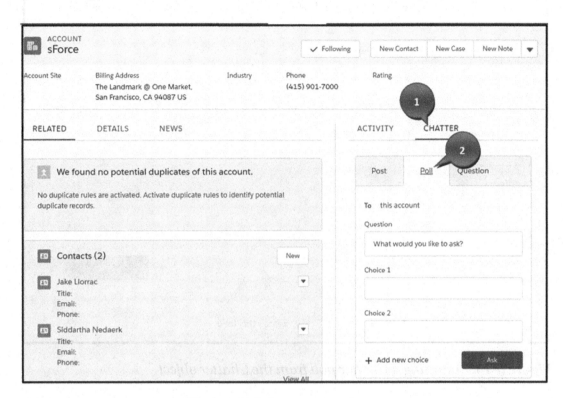

Figure 6-13. *Accessing a Chatter poll from a record*

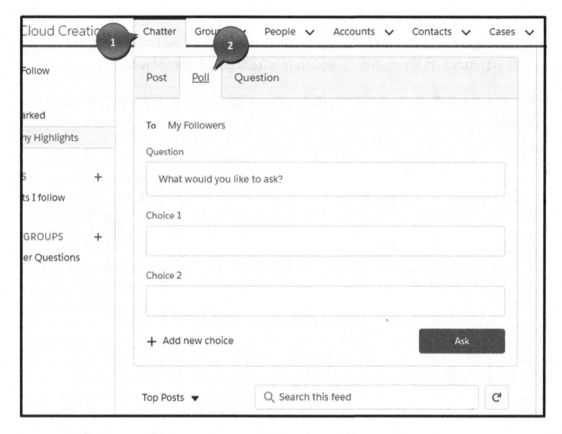

Figure 6-14. *Accessing a Chatter poll from the Chatter object*

3. Enter the poll question you have in mind for your Chatter users.

4. Enter the choices your Chatter users have for the poll.

5. If you need more choices, click the "Add new choice" link.

6. Once finished with your choices, click Ask, as shown in Figure 6-15.

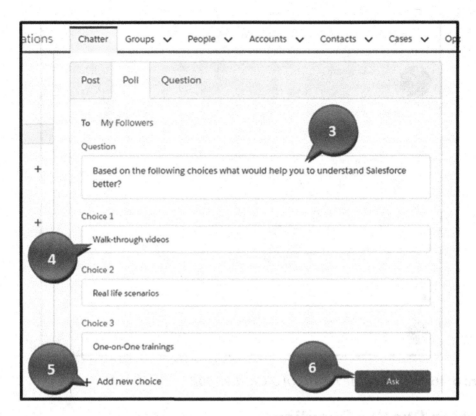

Figure 6-15. *Creating a Chatter poll*

7. Once you have posted your poll, you can click the "View results" link to see your results, as shown in Figure 6-16.

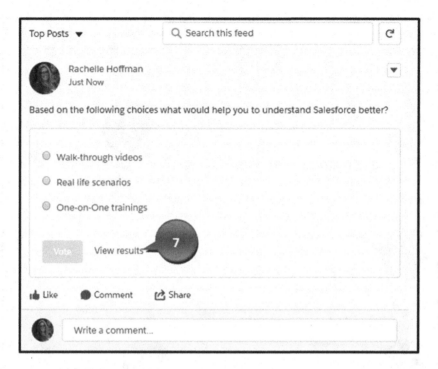

Figure 6-16. *Viewing the results of a Chatter poll*

Creating Chatter Questions

You can use Chatter questions to ask questions that may be beneficial to other users or that other users may have the answer to, as shown in Figure 6-17. Make sure you are on the Question tab of your Chatter feed and post your question. Sit and wait for other users to answer your post. Once you have found the best answer, click the Select as Best link next to the Like link in the comment posted and watch it move to the top of your post under your question for other users to see.

Figure 6-17. *Creating a Chatter question*

Chatter Notifications

Chatter notifications can come in many forms. You can see immediately when someone directs a post at you by the bell icon in the upper-right corner of your browser, as shown in Figure 6-18. You can click the bell icon and see what the latest post to you is or what the comment left is. From here, you can click the "Mark all as read" link to clear your Notifications window, or you can click the comment itself to be taken to the post in Chatter.

Figure 6-18. *Receiving Chatter notifications*

You can also choose to receive daily, weekly, and instantaneous email notifications. If you are a Salesforce mobile (iPhone or Android) user, you can enable notifications to be delivered to your mobile phone, as shown in Figure 6-19.

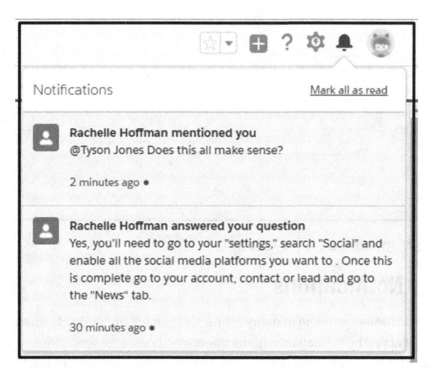

Figure 6-19. *Chatter notifications*

Enabling Chatter Email Notifications

You can enable Chatter email notifications for all your users by following these steps:

1. Go to settings cog icon in the upper-right corner and choose Setup from the drop-down, as shown in Figure 6-20.

Figure 6-20. *Navigating to the Setup menu*

2. In the Quick Find box, type **Email Setting** and click Email Settings found under Chatter, as shown in Figure 6-21.

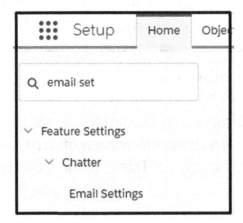

Figure 6-21. *Clicking Email Settings*

3. Select the email setting of your choice, as shown in Figure 6-22.

   - Allow Emails turns on Chatter email notifications for users.

   - Allow Email Replies turns on the ability for your users to reply from within their email to Chatter notifications.

   - Allow Posts via Email allows your users to post to groups using their email.

   - Allow Attachments via Email gives the ability for your users to use attachments in their replies and post from email.

- "Show Salesforce mobile app download badges" adds badges
  for downloading the Salesforce mobile app to all Chatter email
  notifications in your organization.

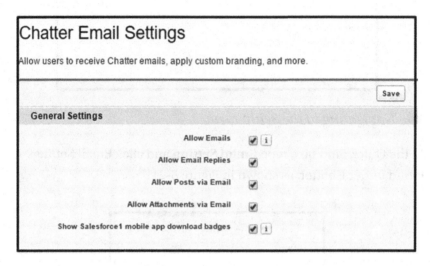

Figure 6-22. *General email settings*

Note   Badges in Salesforce are an internal Chatter recognition technique that users can earn and give. This helps with user adoption by allowing users to give recognition with a Thanks badge. The Thanks badge shows up on the user's profile for everyone to see.

---

4. Click Save.

User's Configuration for Chatter Notifications

The previous settings will allow your users to use Chatter. Now we'll cover how your users can choose to receive the Chatter notifications.

1. Click your profile picture at the top-right corner of the web browser and click Settings, as shown in Figure 6-23.

Figure 6-23. *Accessing your profile*

2. In the Quick Find area, type in **Email Notifications** and select Email Notifications under Chatter.

3. Select the options that best fit your needs.

   - In the General section, you must select "Receive emails" to receive Chatter emails, as shown in Figure 6-24.

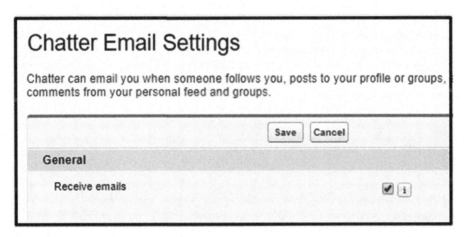

Figure 6-24. *Turning "Receive emails" on*

- In the Personal section, for "Email me when Someone," we recommend the following be selected because your users can become overwhelmed by too many email notices if all of them are selected:

  - *Posts on my profile*: This option will keep you up-to-date on any post that is made on your profile.

  - *Comments on a post on my profile*: This option will notify you on any comment that was left on your post.

  - *Comments on an item I bookmarked*: This will keep you current with any bookmark post so you know the latest.

  - *Mentions me in a post*: This will let you know any time a user uses the @ symbol and directs a post to you or mentions you in a post.

  - *Mentions me in a comment*: This will let you know any time a user uses the @ symbol and directs a comment or mentions you in a comment.

Figure 6-25. *Configuring what Chatter email you receive*

4. Select the frequency of your personal digest. Your personal digest is a summary of the recent activity in Chatter that appears on your own feed. You can choose to receive this daily, weekly, or never, as shown in Figure 6-26.

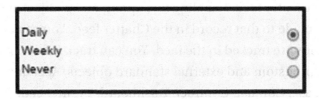

Figure 6-26. *Selecting to receive emails daily, weekly, or never*

5. You can also set how often you receive group Chatter notifications.
    We suggest that you select Limited for new groups; you can
    change your setting for each individual group should you want
    more frequency, as shown in Figure 6-27.

Figure 6-27. *Selecting what to receive from Chatter*

6. You can select how often you receive group customer questions
    as well, as shown in Figure 6-28. We suggest Limited as well here.
    If you choose another option, you may get more emails than you
    want, which can cause more of a distraction than being helpful.

Group	Email on Each Post	Daily Digests	Weekly Digests	Limited
Customer Questions	○	○	○	◉

Figure 6-28. *Selecting what customer questions to be notified from*

Feed Tracking

Salesforce feed tracking with Chatter allows you to see changes made to records that
are recorded in the Chatter feed. Enabling this option on an object allows a user to
follow the changes made to that record in the Chatter feed. You can choose which
object and what fields are tracked in the feed. You can track fields on the following
objects: User, Group, custom and external standard objects, Account, Article Type,
Asset, Campaign, Case, Contact, Contract, Dashboard, Event, Lead, Opportunity,
Product, Report, Solution, and Task.

Note   Field-level security and sharing settings are used in the Chatter feed to
determine what users can see in the feed as well.

Enabling and Customizing Feed Tracking

Follow these steps:

1. Click the settings cog icon in the upper-right corner of the browser and select Setup, as shown in Figure 6-29.

Figure 6-29. *Navigating to the Setup menu*

2. In the Quick Find area, type **Feed Tracking** and select Feed Tracking under Chatter, as shown in Figure 6-30.

Figure 6-30. *Navigating to Feed Tracking*

3. On the left side, click an object you want to configure for feed tracking, as shown in Figure 6-31.

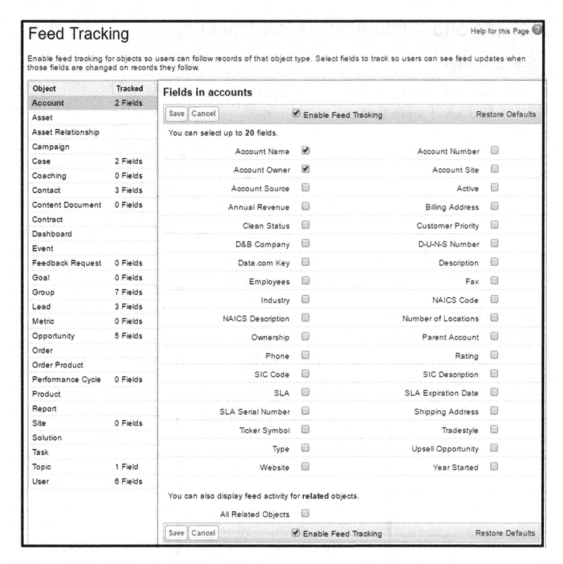

Figure 6-31. *Setting up feed tracking*

4. At the top, make sure to select Enable Feed Tracking.

5. Select up to 20 fields to track per object. You don't need to select any fields here if you don't want to track changes to specific fields in Chatter. By selecting individual fields to track, this will capture the change that was made in Chatter. See Figure 6-32 for an example of feed tracking.

Figure 6-32. *How feed tracking shows up in Chatter*

Note   The more you select, the more cluttered your Chatter record feeds will become. Any field change on the field selection will add a new post to that record feed, pushing older posts lower.

---

6.   Once you have set up all the objects as desired, click the Save button.

Chatter Profiles

Salesforce Chatter profiles allow your users to customize their Salesforce profile that is seen by other Salesforce users and the Chatter-free users (usually customers). They can add a profile picture, write an About Me section, add contact information, and add a header photo. The profile is another way your users can see their Chatter feeds, what groups they are part of, what files they've uploaded in posts, who they are following, and who is following them. They can even add a new post and comment on existing ones from their profiles.

To access your profile, click your profile picture in the upper-right corner and click your name, as shown in Figure 6-33.

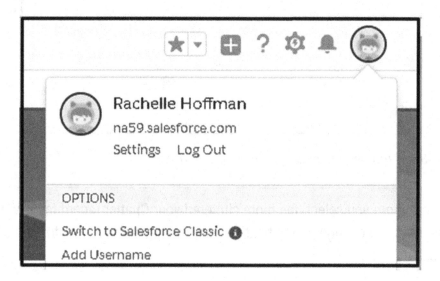

Figure 6-33. *Navigating to your profile*

Other users can access your profile by clicking your hyperlinked name found on records, in Chatter posts, or anywhere else they see your name hyperlinked, as shown in Figure 6-34.

Figure 6-34. *Accessing other users' profiles*

Uploading Your Profile Picture

To upload your profile picture, follow these steps:

1. Once you have reached your profile, you can click the camera symbol and click Update Photo, as shown in Figure 6-35.

Figure 6-35. *Uploading your profile picture*

Note   Your photo must be stored on your computer. It has to be in JPEG, GIF, or PNG format, and the file size must be smaller than 16MB.

---

2. Click the Upload Image button and choose the image from your computer location, as shown in Figure 6-36.

Figure 6-36. *Uploading your profile picture from your computer*

3. Use the slide bar to resize your photo. Select the check box "Show my photo on publicly accessible pages" if you want your photo disabled outside of Salesforce, as shown in Figure 6-37.

4. Once complete, click Save.

Figure 6-37. *Modifying the size of your image*

Editing Your Profile

To edit your profile, follow these steps:

1. Go to your profile by clicking your profile picture found in the upper-right corner of your browser, as shown in Figure 6-38.

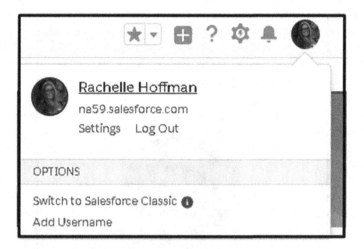

Figure 6-38. *Editing your profile*

2. Click the word Edit found under your tabs on the right side of your browser, as shown in Figure 6-39.

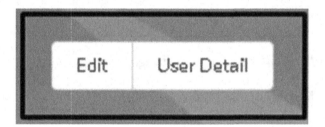

Figure 6-39. *Edit button*

3. You can edit any field here on the profile just like any field in Salesforce. Let others know who your manager is, add the title that you hold with your company, add a phone number and cell phone number, add your office location, and, of course, don't forget to tell your other users a little bit about yourself in the About Me section, as shown in Figure 6-40.

4. Once complete, click Save.

Edit Rachelle Hoffman

* Name   Manager

First Name   Search People

Rachelle

* Last Name

Hoffman

Title   Company Name

Chief Technology Officer   Cloud Creations

Email   Phone

rhoffman@cloudcreations.com   (800) 951-7651

Address   Cell

Street   213-479-4550

130 Cook Ave

City   State/Province

Pasadena   CA

Zip/Postal Code   Country

91107   US

About Me

Cloud Creations Inc. provides Salesforce implementation services, which include data import, integration, documentation, reports, and training. Our clients range from small-and-medium sized businesses to large enterprises.

Cancel   Save

Figure 6-40. *Editing your profile*

Updating Your Header Photo

To update your header photo, follow these steps:

1. Click the camera image in the right corner above the Edit button, click the "Select an image" button, find your image on your computer, and click Open, as shown in Figure 6-41.

Figure 6-41. *Uploading your banner*

Note   Your photo must be stored on your computer. It has to be in JPEG, GIF, or PNG format. For the best results, use a panoramic image that is at least 1280×300 pixels.

---

2.   Adjust your photo to fit the area provided. If you find that the photo won't work, click "Choose a different photo" to upload a new one, as shown in Figure 6-42.

Figure 6-42. *Modifying the size of your banner*

3. Click Save when complete.

After your user completes their profile, it should like Figure 6-43.

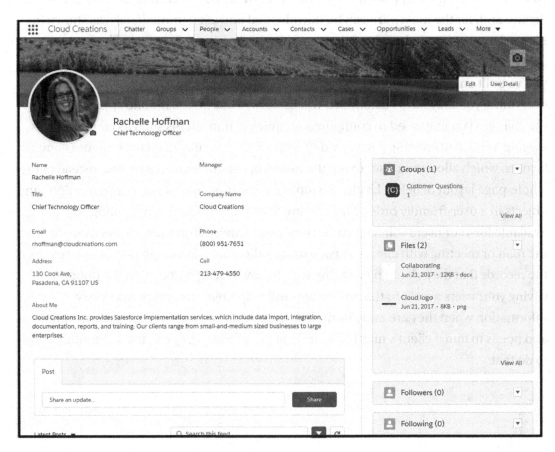

Figure 6-43. *Complete user profile*

Salesforce Mobile App for iPhone and Android Users

Salesforce, the mobile app for iPhone and Android users, is included in every Salesforce license and, for the most part, can be downloaded and used immediately, as shown in Figure 6-44. Users can download the app from the App Store or Google Play and start using it today! Salesforce can work out of the box because it uses metadata to see what you've built and configured in the desktop environment. However, with that said, not everything you may have customized will be easy to use on the mobile app. Some of the changes you may need to configure are "quick action" items such as creating a task, logging a call, and creating a new lead or contact. Or you may need to configure compact layouts, which allow your user to see the most important detail of a record instead of the whole-page layout of fields. Lastly, the mobile navigation allows you to place actions and objects in a user-friendly order. Making sure that the Salesforce app is configured and available for your users will help your users' productivity. If you have users who are on the road or meeting with clients outside of the office, Salesforce app provides access to the records that they would be working with if they were in office or on the phone. Giving your users access to the mobile app will help them to capture necessary information when they are away from their desks. Also, if your user is out of the office and needs to find a client's number quickly or an address, they can use the mobile app to do that.

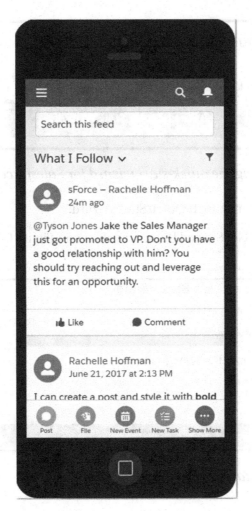

Figure 6-44. Salesforce mobile app

Quick-Start Guide to Setting Up the Mobile App

Salesforce offers a quick-start guide to setting up the mobile app.

1. Click the settings cog icon in the upper-right corner of the browser and click Setup.

2. In the Quick Find box, type in **Salesforce Mobile** and select the option Salesforce mobile Quick Start, as shown in Figure 6-45.

Figure 6-45. *Launching the quick-start wizard for Salesforce mobile configuration*

3. Click the button Launch Quick Start Wizard.

4. Click the Let's Get Started button, as shown in Figure 6-46.

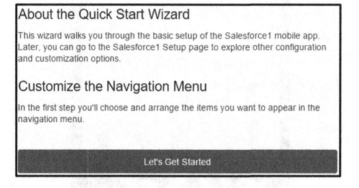

Figure 6-46. *Getting started with the quick start*

5. You can remove or reorder items found on this navigation menu
    by clicking it and using the arrows in the middle or by dragging
    and dropping them into a new place, as shown in Figure 6-47.

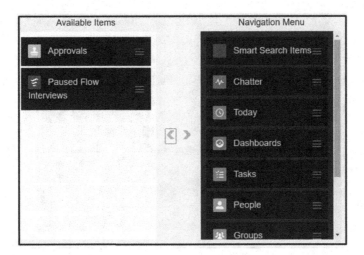

Figure 6-47. Modifying the navigation menu

6. Once you are done with your navigation menu, click Save & Next at the lower-right corner of your screen.

7. Click the Arrange Global Actions button, as shown in Figure 6-48.

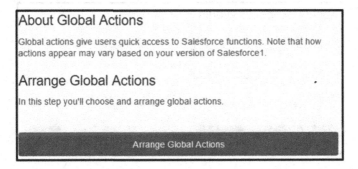

Figure 6-48. Arranging the global actions

8. Move actions that are necessary into the Selected Global Actions area and move ones that aren't needed into the Available Items using the arrows provided between these two areas. Reorder what actions appear first by dragging and dropping them into place, as shown in Figure 6-49.

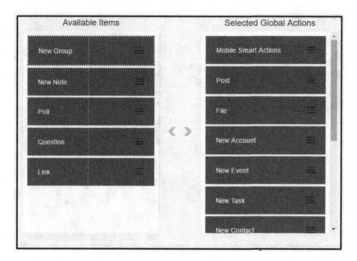

Figure 6-49. *Modifying the order of your actions*

9. Click Save & Next when you are complete.

10. Click the Create Compact Layout button, as shown in Figure 6-50.

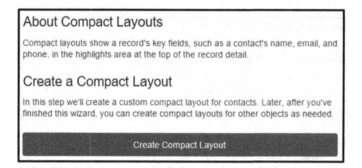

Figure 6-50. *Configuring the contact compact layout*

Note   Through the quick start, you can only create a compact layout for contact records. We'll go over how to make compact layouts for other objects on the next page.

---

11. Move fields into the Compact Layout for Contacts area that you want displayed in your mobile app and move fields to the Available Fields section that you don't want to include. Reorder the arrangement of the fields by dragging and dropping them into place, as shown in Figure 6-51.

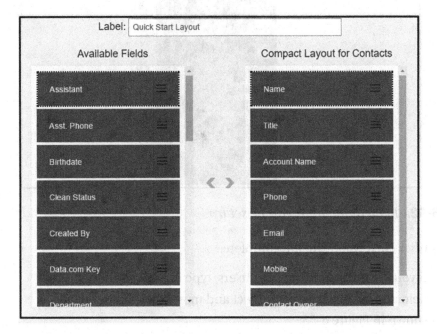

Figure 6-51. *Modifying the order of the fields for your contact compact layout*

12. Click Save & Next when you are complete.

13. In step 4 you can review what you have arranged in this quick start by clicking Navigation Menu, Global Actions, and Contact Compact Layout to see what you created. Do you see that a change needs to be made? Click the Edit button to be taken to that edit screen and make the change, as shown in Figure 6-52.

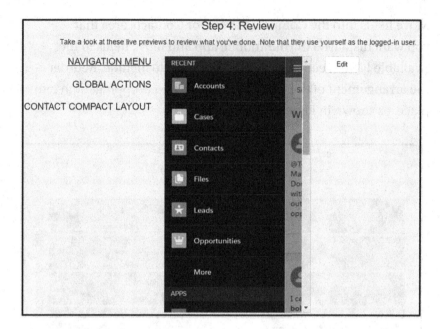

Figure 6-52. *Reviewing what you've set up*

14.   Click Next when you are complete.

15.   If you are ready to invite your users, type in the names in the To field and customize your subject and message. Click Send, as shown in Figure 6-53.

16.   Click Next when complete and Finish.

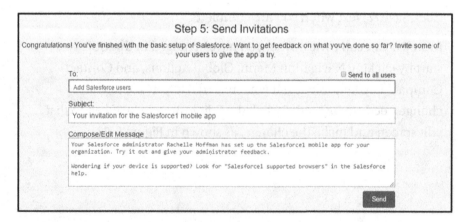

Figure 6-53. *Inviting users to download the Salesforce mobile app*

Creating Compact Layouts

In step 10 previously, we mentioned that you can create compact layouts for other objects as well. Here's how:

1. Click the settings cog icon in the upper-right corner of the browser and click Setup.

2. Select the Object Manager tab found at the top next to the home tab.

3. Select the object that you want to configure a compact layout for and click the hyperlink name of that object, as shown in Figure 6-54.

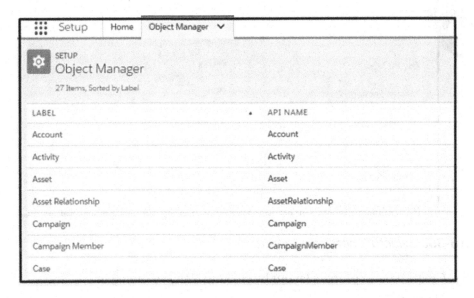

Figure 6-54. *Navigating to the compact layout for an object*

4. On the left side, you'll see various options and actions that can be made within this object. Select Compact Layouts, as shown in Figure 6-55.

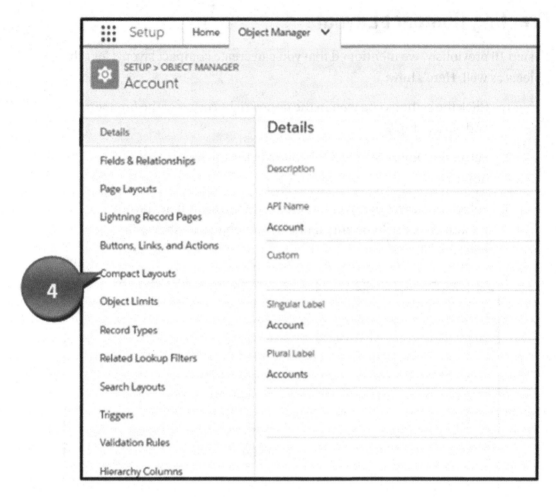

Figure 6-55. *Selecting compact layouts*

5.   Create a new compact layout by clicking New, as shown in
     Figure 6-56.

Compact Layouts 1 Items, Sorted by Label		Find in page		New	Compact Layout Assignment
LABEL	▲ API NAME	PRIMARY	MODIFIED BY	LAST MODIFIED	
System Default	SYSTEM	✓			

Figure 6-56. *Clicking the New button*

6. Create a label for your compact layout and hit your Tab key to automatically create the name. Move the field from the Available Fields area to the Selected Fields area using the arrows in between. Move the order in which a user sees the details up and down by using the arrows next to Selected Fields, as shown in Figure 6-57.

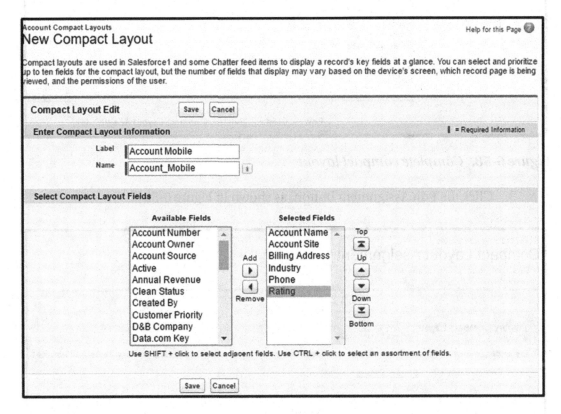

Figure 6-57. *Creating a compact layout*

7. Once complete, click Save.

8. Click the Compact Layout Assignment button, as shown in Figure 6-58.

Figure 6-58. *Complete compact layout*

9. Click the Edit Assignment button, as shown in Figure 6-59.

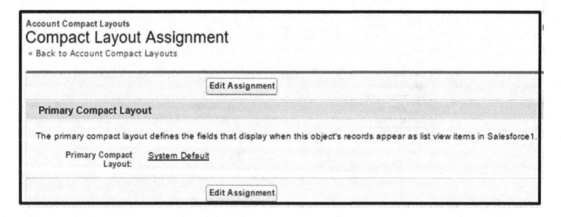

Figure 6-59. *Edit Assignment button*

10. Select from the drop-down the compact layout you created, as shown in Figure 6-60.

11. Click Save.

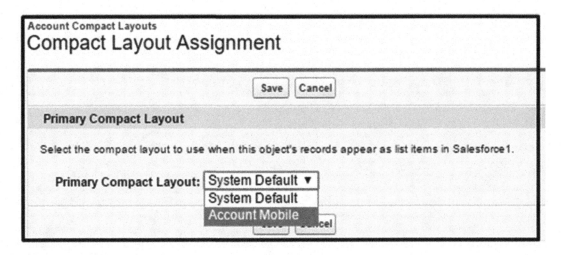

Figure 6-60. *Selecting the compact layout*

Summary

As you can see, there are many ways for your users to interact with each other and with external customers in Salesforce. Collaboration in a business is key to getting sales closed and or projects/tasks moving forward. With the use of Chatter and Salesforce mobile app, your users have all the tools available to work throughout their day.

CHAPTER 7

Lightning Process Builder

Lightning Process Builder is an extremely powerful business process automation tool that can solve a myriad of real-world business issues. Process Builder makes it easy to build logic in one place, with its enhanced point-and-click interface. With Process Builder, you can reduce or eliminate the need to build Apex code for simple processes. You can create automated logic to update related records, update fields, create a task, send an email, and much more. Click New to get started, as shown in Figure 7-1.

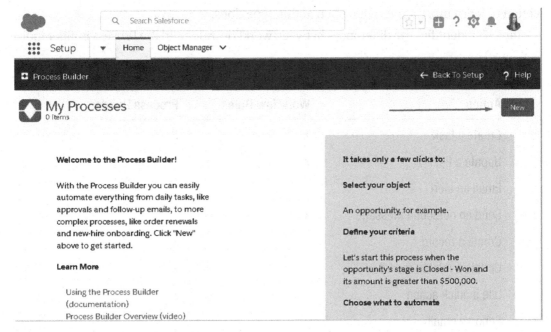

Figure 7-1. Process Builder home page. Click New to get started.

© Felicia Duarte, Rachelle Hoffman 2018

F. Duarte, R. Hoffman, *Learn Salesforce Lightning*, https://doi.org/10.1007/978-1-4842-2994-1_7

Salesforce Workflow Rules vs. Process Builder

Salesforce has multiple solutions to automate your business process, including workflow rules and Process Builder.

Workflow rules are automated actions that take place when a record meets specified criteria and is saved. You can minimize the amount of manual data entry and processes by having a systematic process in place.

Process Builder is supported in Salesforce Lightning and does everything a workflow rule can do and more (with the exception of outbound messages). A Process Builder action can start when a record is changed or when invoked by another process. Both automation types support time-based actions.

If you have a simple single if/then statement, it is suggested that you use a workflow rule to automate your process. In other words, if you have criteria for automation that include simple logic, use a workflow rule. If there is a level of complexity to your automated requirement, Process Builder is best suited for this. Read the "Actions" section to learn more about what each action type does.

Table 7-1 identifies the differences between workflow rules and the Process Builder tool.

Table 7-1. *Actions Available in Workflow Rules and Process Builder*

Action	Workflow Rules	Process Builder
Create a task	X	X
Update a field	X	X
Email an alert	X	X
Send an outbound message	X	
Create a record		X
Update a related record		X
Use a quick action		X
Send an email		X
Launch a flow		X
Post to the Chatter area		
Submit for approval		
Call an Apex method		

Process Builder: Action Types

Process Builder makes it easier to create automated actions because it is a visual designer, as shown in Figure 7-2.

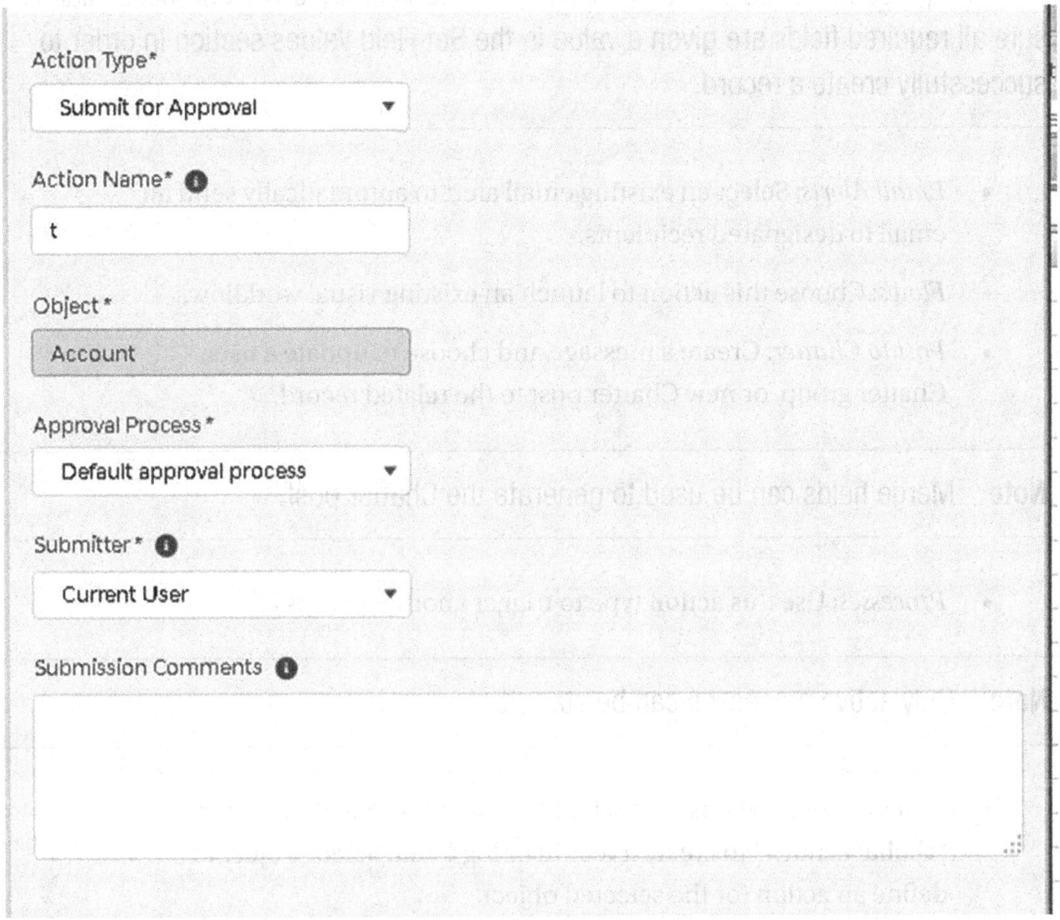

Figure 7-2. *Submit for Approval action type*

The following are the actions that can be completed by a workflow rule or Process Builder:

- *Call on an Apex class*: Apex is a programming language used in Salesforce to develop complex processes. You can use Process Builder to call on an existing Apex class.

- *Create a Record*: Use this action to create a new record from any standard or custom object. Field values can be set to build the record appropriately.

Tip   Required fields are still active when a record is created via a process. Make sure all required fields are given a value in the Set Field Values section in order to successfully create a record.

- *Email Alerts*: Select an existing email alert to automatically send an email to designated recipients.

- *Flows*: Choose this action to launch an existing visual workflow.

- *Post to Chatter*: Create a message and choose to update a user, Chatter group, or new Chatter post to the related record.

Note   Merge fields can be used to generate the Chatter post.

- *Processes*: Use this action type to trigger another process.

Note   Only active processes can be started.

- *Quick action*: Use this action type to start a quick action. Select "Global actions" to create a record or log a call. Select Object to define an action for the selected object.

- *Submit for Approval*: Choose to activate the default approval process or specific approval process for the given record, as shown in Figure 7-2. Control who the submitter is by selecting the appropriate value: Current User, User Field from a Record, or Specific User. Submission comments can be entered.

- *Update records*: Choose to update the existing record or a record related to the corresponding object (shown in Figure 7-3).

Select a Record to Update

○ Select the Account record that started your process

⦿ Select a record related to the Account

| Type to filter list... | ▼ |

Figure 7-3. *Selecting a record to update in Process Builder*

Time-Dependent Actions

When a record meets the criteria, the action can be executed immediately or on a specified schedule.

To control when the action is executed, add a time lapse to the process, as shown in Figure 7-4. Actions can be triggered to run before or after a specified date.

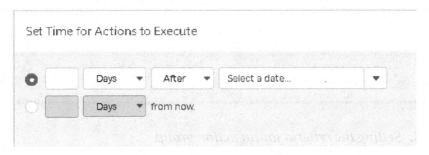

Figure 7-4. *Setting the time for a time-dependent action*

Example

As an example, let's create an automated action to send a "Happy Birthday" card to all active clients one day before birthdate. The Scheduled Actions option is available only when the first node of the process starts the process with "only when a record is created" *or* "when a record is created or edited" is selected *and* the Yes check box is selected in the criteria node in the Advanced section, as shown in Figure 7-5.

Define Criteria for this Action Group

Criteria Name* ⓘ

> Criteria Test

Criteria for Executing Actions *
- ● Conditions are met
- ○ Formula evaluates to true
- ○ No criteria–just execute the actions!

Set Conditions

Field*	Operator*	Type*	Value*	
1 [Account].Na... 🔍	Equals ▼	String ▼	Test	✕

+ Add Row

Conditions *
- ● All of the conditions are met (AND)
- ○ Any of the conditions are met (OR)
- ○ Customize the logic

⌄ Advanced

Do you want to execute the actions only when specified changes are made to the record? ⓘ

☑ Yes

Figure 7-5. Setting the criteria for an action group

Creating a Process Using Process Builder

Follow the steps in this section to create an automated business process.

In this scenario, you will encounter a real-world business problem. Say sales users have to manually create a project record with the same details stored at the opportunity level. Rather than creating a new record and copying and pasting the details, it is beneficial for them to have the tool automatically create a new project record. At the same time, it's beneficial to automatically pull the details stored in the opportunity record into the new project record.

Note   In this use case, project records are records stored in a custom object titled Projects.

For all opportunities that are set to Closed Won, you want to create a new project record and update the Project field Next Step to say Schedule Project Kickoff.

Note   This is a use case you can use while managing projects in Salesforce. These steps can also be tweaked to create the new policy records most commonly used with insurance companies. Those in the financial services industry also use this concept to create new financial accounts records when an opportunity closes. These are just a few examples. The opportunities to use automation in Salesforce are endless!

Follow these steps to create this process:

1. From Setup, select Process Automation in the Platform Tools section, as shown in Figure 7-6.

Figure 7-6. *Process Automation in Setup*

2. Next, select Process Builder to access the Process Builder
    home page.

    All active and inactive processes are listed on this page, as shown
    in Figure 7-7, along with the description of the process, the related
    object, the process type, the last modified date, the status, and the
    actions.

Figure 7-7. *Process Builder home page and list of processes*

3. Click the New button to start a new process.

4. Type the process name and press Tab to generate the API name, as
    shown in Figure 7-8.

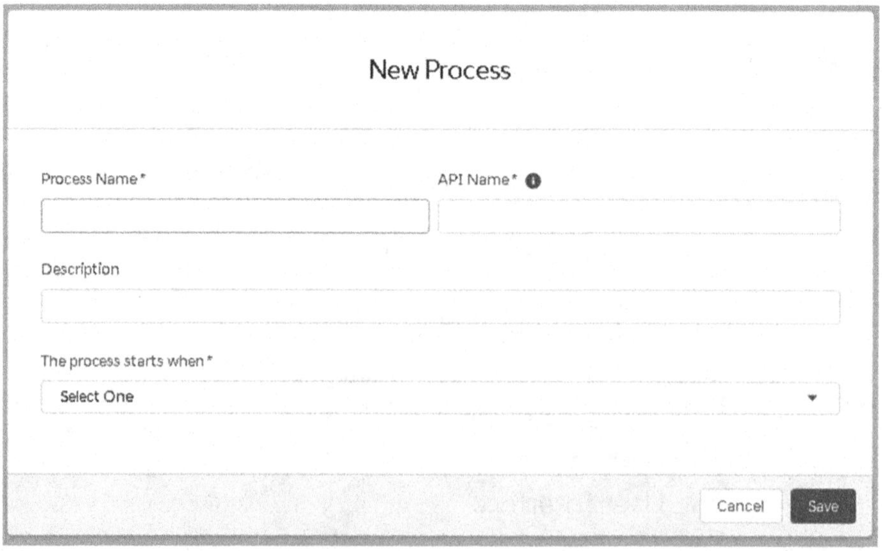

Figure 7-8. *Naming your process*

Note   It is not required but recommended to enter a description for each process. For organizations with numerous automation processes, it can be challenging to find the right process when there are no descriptions.

5. Determine when the process should start. Your options include when "A record changes" and when "It's invoked by another process."

Note   You can break down more complex processes into simpler processes. These processes can be reused and invoked by another process, as mentioned earlier.

With the current scenario, you will start the process when "A record changes." Click Save, as shown in Figure 7-9.

Figure 7-9.   *Starting a process when a record changes*

6. When you first start your process, you must select the object it starts from. Select Add Object, as highlighted in Figure 7-10.

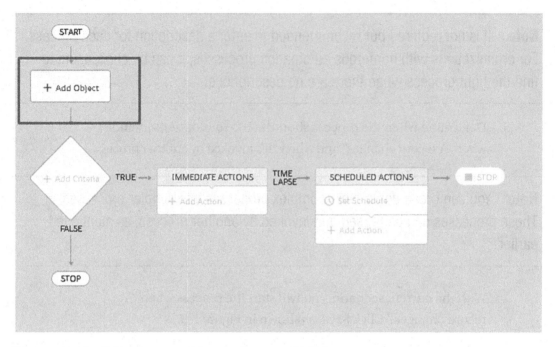

Figure 7-10. *Selecting an object in Process Builder*

7. Choose the object that the process should be evaluated from, as shown in Figure 7-11. In this example, you will select Opportunity.

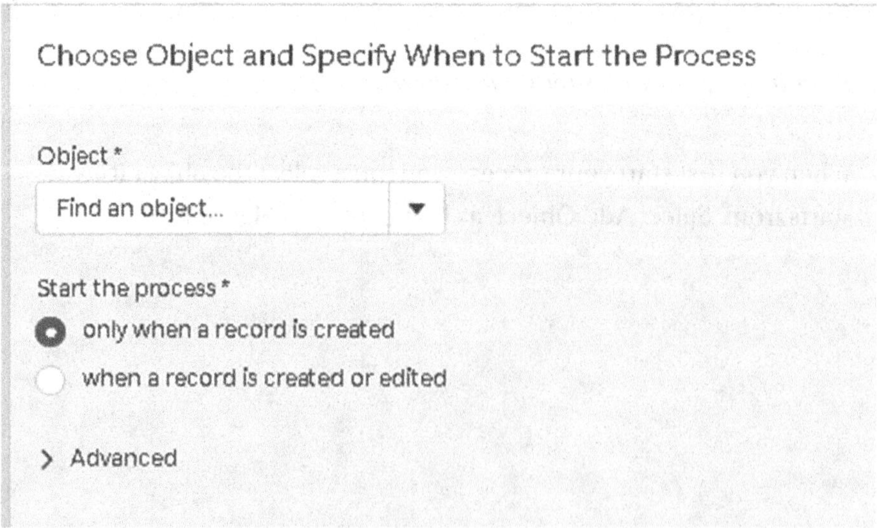

Choose Object and Specify When to Start the Process

Object *

Find an object...   ▼

Start the process *
⦿ only when a record is created
◯ when a record is created or edited

> Advanced

Figure 7-11. *Choosing when to start a process*

8. Select when the process should start, as shown in Figure 7-11.

   a. Select "only when a record is created" to only start the process for new records.

   b. Select "when a record is created or edited" to start the process for new records *and* existing record that are edited upon saving.

9. You can click Yes, as shown in Figure 7-12, to evaluate the record multiple times (up to five times) in one execution.

Figure 7-12. *Click Yes to allow the process to evaluate a record multiple times in a single transaction*

10. Confirm your specification and click ⬛ Save .

11. Select the Add Criteria node shown in Figure 7-13 to set the criteria for this process.

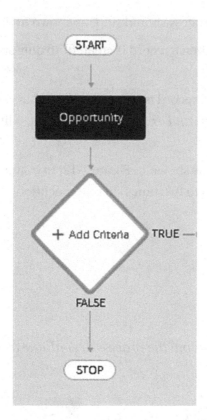

Figure 7-13. *Adding a criteria node to a process*

12. Set the criteria that the record should meet in order for the actions to be executed.

In this example, you want to set the criteria for the process to start only when opportunity records have a stage marked as Closed Won.

Setting the Criteria

Follow these steps to set the criteria for a process:

1. Name your criteria, as shown in Figure 7-14.

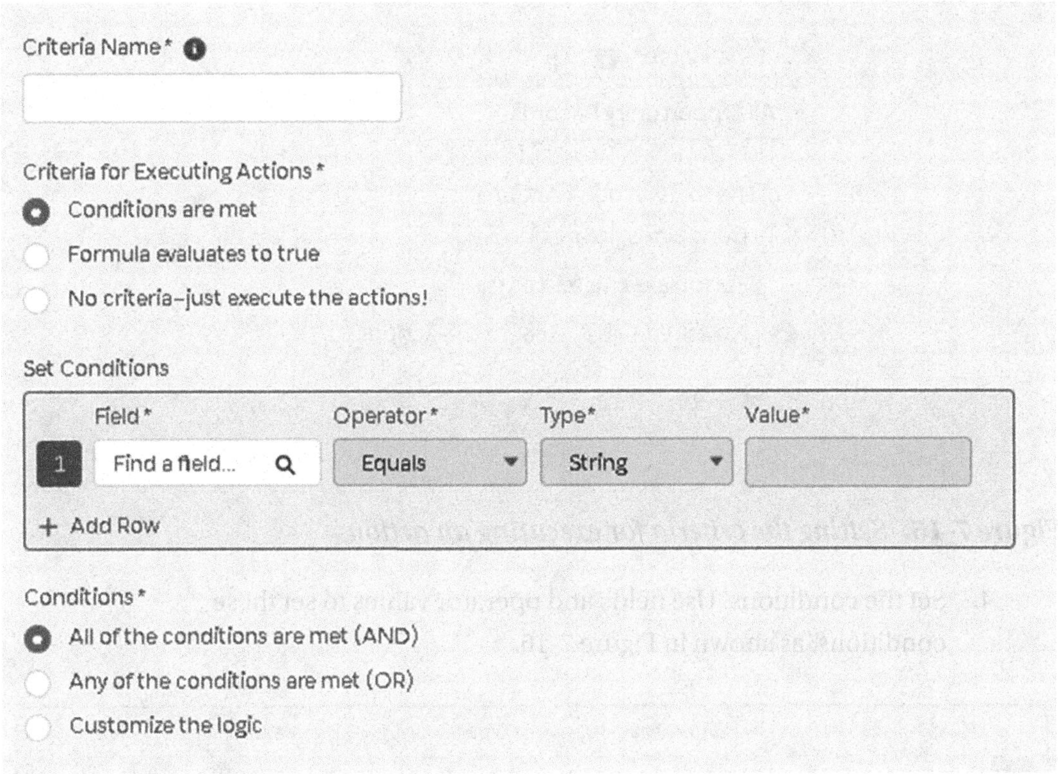

Criteria Name* ⓘ

Criteria for Executing Actions *

⦿ Conditions are met

◯ Formula evaluates to true

◯ No criteria–just execute the actions!

Set Conditions

	Field *	Operator *	Type *	Value *
1	Find a field... 🔍	Equals ▾	String ▾	

➕ Add Row

Conditions *

⦿ All of the conditions are met (AND)

◯ Any of the conditions are met (OR)

◯ Customize the logic

Figure 7-14. *Steps to setting the criteria*

2. Find a field and choose the appropriate operator to set the criteria.

3. Select the criteria for executing the action (shown in Figure 7-15). You can choose to execute the actions only when the criteria are met, when a formula evaluates to be true, or with no criteria; just evaluate the action for that object. In this example, select "No Criteria–just execute the actions!" to execute the action for all opportunity records.

Figure 7-15. *Setting the criteria for executing an action*

4. Set the conditions. Use fields and operator values to set these conditions, as shown in Figure 7-16.

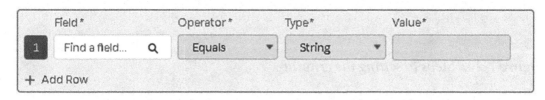

Figure 7-16. *Setting the conditions to invoke a process*

5. Once the criteria are all set, click Save.

6. Choose what the action should be once this criterion is met. Click Add Action, as shown in Figure 7-17.

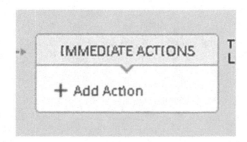

Figure 7-17. *Adding an immediate action to a process*

7. Define the action type.

8. In this scenario, you want to create a new project record. Click Create a Record.

9. Name the action and choose what type of record should be created, as shown in Figure 7-18.

Figure 7-18. *Naming the action and choosing the record type*

10. Set the field values for the new record, as shown in Figure 7-19, In our example, we set all the field values that we want to carry over into the new project record.

Figure 7-19. *Setting the field values when creating a new record*

Note   All required fields must be entered when choosing this action. If a required field value is not entered, the record will not be created.

---

11. Once you confirm that the criteria and actions are correct, click Save [Save].

12. To make this process active. Click Activate, as shown in
Figure 7-20.

Figure 7-20. *Activating a process*

Note   Only one version of the process can be active at a time.

---

13. It is best practice to test the process. Create a test record to test this
new automated process.

Summary

In this chapter, we reviewed the high-level details of what Process Builder can do. You
can automate a lot more than you can with just workflow rules. It's important to know
that there are countless ways you can build automation into your existing setup. Use this
chapter as a guide as to what the practical capabilities are with Process Builder.

CHAPTER 8

Data Management

Salesforce offers an array of data management tools. Lightning Salesforce offers a Data Import Wizard that allows you to update existing records or create new records (Figure 8-1). The Data Import Wizard allows imports, updates, and inserts to be performed using comma-separated value (CSV) files, Outlook CSV, ACT! CSV, and Gmail CSV. Salesforce not only supplies an importing tool but also provides tools to help you export your data into CSV files, mass transfer records from one owner to another based on the criteria of the record, and mass delete records based on the criteria of the record. Salesforce also provides data control tools that help you control the type of data your users are adding to the system. You can create duplication rules to prevent users from adding duplicate records. Data management is hugely important for organizations; in fact, your Salesforce organization is only as good as the data you collect with it. If the data is "dirty," your reports will be too. Having accurate and useful data will allow you to properly analyze your information. This in turn will allow you to better the user and client experience.

Figure 8-1. *Importing can be easy!*

© Felicia Duarte, Rachelle Hoffman 2018
F. Duarte, R. Hoffman, *Learn Salesforce Lightning*, https://doi.org/10.1007/978-1-4842-2994-1_8

Using the Data Import Wizard

The Data Import Wizard that Salesforce has provided allows you to import new records and update existing records. All you need is a CSV file with column headers that match your existing Salesforce fields and your data in the rows of the spreadsheet (Figure 8-2).

	A	B	C	D	E	F	G
1	Account Name	Salutatii ▼	First Nan ▼	Last Nan ▼	Title ▼	Mailing Street ▼	Mailing Cit ▼
2	Burlington Textiles Corp of America	Mr.	Jack	Rogers	VP, Facilities	525 S. Lexington Ave	Burlington
3	Dickenson plc	Mr	Andy	Young	SVP, Operations	1301 Hoch Drive	Lawrence
4	Edge Communications	Ms.	Rose	Gonzalez	SVP, Procurement	313 Constitution Place Austin, TX 78767 USA	
5	Edge Communications	Mr.	Sean	Forbes	CFO	312 Constitution Place Austin, TX 78767 USA	
6	Express Logistics and Transport	Ms.	Babara	Levy	SVP, Operations	620 SW 5th Avenue Suite 400 Portland, Oregon 97204 United States	
7	Express Logistics and Transport	Mr.	Josh	Davis	Director, Warehouse Mgmt	621 SW 5th Avenue Suite 400 Portland, Oregon 97204 United States	
8	GenePoint	Ms.	Edna	Frank	VP, Technology	345 Shoreline Park Mountain View, CA 94043 USA	
9	Grand Hotels & Resorts Ltd	Mr.	Tim	Barr	SVP, Administration and Finance	2335 N. Michigan Avenue, Suite 1500 Chicago, IL 60601, USA	
10	Grand Hotels & Resorts Ltd	Mr.	John	Bond	VP, Facilities	2334 N. Michigan Avenue, Suite 1500 Chicago, IL 60601, USA	
11	Pyramid Construction Inc.	Ms.	Pat	Stumuller	SVP, Administration and Finance	2 Place Jussieu	Paris
12	sForce	Ms.	Siddartha	Nedaerk		The Landmark @ One Market	San Francisco
13	sForce	Mr.	Jake	Llorrac		The Landmark @ One Market	San Francisco
14	United Oil & Gas Corp.	Ms.	Stella	Pavlova	SVP, Production	1303 Avenue of the Americas New York, NY 10019 USA	
15	United Oil & Gas Corp.	Ms.	Lauren	Boyle	SVP, Technology	1304 Avenue of the Americas New York, NY 10019 USA	

Figure 8-2. *CSV file ready for an import into the Salesforce organization*

You can easily create a CSV file with an Excel spreadsheet. Once you save the file, you'll see under the file name that you create a "save as" type. Select the drop-down and change it to "CSV (Comma delimited)." According to your Excel version, the verbiage may change. See Figure 8-3 for an example.

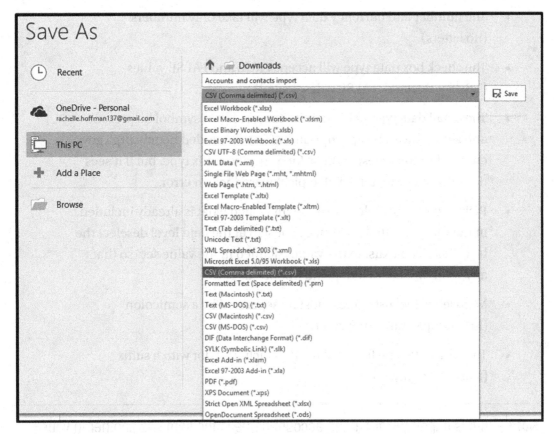

Figure 8-3. *How to save an Excel file into a CSV file format*

Preparing Your Data for an Import

To prepare your data for a contact and account import, you must make sure that in your CSV file there is a column for all the required fields you may have set up or the ones that come standard with Salesforce. You can determine what fields are required by editing a record and looking for the fields with a red line next to them. You can include any field as a column in this CSV file that is found on the object you are importing to. Another important preparation step is to ensure that the data being imported matches the data type of the field. It is important to prepare your data because if it is incorrect, it will give you an error and not import that record. To prevent spending hours on import, follow these tips:

- The date data type can be accepted only with this format: MM/DD/YYYY.

- The date and time data type can be accepted in the following format: MM/DD/YYYY hh:mm:ss. There are other formats accepted as well.

- The number and currency data type will take only numbers (no letters).

- The check box data type will accept TRUE and FALSE values (TRUE = selected, FALSE = deselected).

- The email data type fields require that an at (@) symbol be present and a dot (.) with an appropriate suffix be included (.com, .org, .gov, etc.). Salesforce doesn't check for a specific suffix type, but if it sees no suffix after the dot, it will typically produce an error.

- Picklist data type fields must exactly match what is already included in the values for that picklist, or you can at the field level deselect the box "Restrict picklist to the values defined in the value set" so that any value will be included and imported.

- Multiselect picklist values must be separated by a semicolon (for example, blue; red; green).

- The URL data type field will need to include a dot with a suffix (.com, .org, .gov, etc.).

Note   In this import wizard, if the account name is the same as another in your CSV file, Salesforce will not create a duplicate. If the account name has one extra letter, Salesforce will see this as a new account and create a duplicate.

Additionally, if you label your column headers with the Salesforce field label, the Salesforce import wizard will automatically map your columns to the Salesforce fields (we'll speak about this in step 9).

- Try to match all your column headers to the field names for your import. Most importing tools will "automap" your column headers to the appropriate fields.

Importing Accounts and Contacts with the Data Import Wizard

The Salesforce Data Import Wizard is a great, easy-to-use tool. It provides videos to help walk you through importing and has great a FAQ section. It even gives you a step-by-step process for setting up the import. It is important to keep your Salesforce data accurate and current. Whether you are importing accounts and contacts for the first time or adding new ones to the system, you'll need to know how to do this for data integrity.

1. Prepare your data for import. Accounts in a standard Salesforce setup require the account name. Along with accounts, you can import contacts. Contacts in a standard Salesforce setup will require an account name and the last name. Because an account name is required for a contact, you can in your CSV file set the account and account details in one row and just use the account name for all the contacts related to that account for additional contacts. If you populate different account field details in the account fields to each contact, the last row of the import for that account will reflect in Salesforce. In Figure 8-4, Cloud Creations on row 5 would be the information seen in Salesforce after the import is performed.

	A	B	C	D	E	F	G
1	Account Name	Account Website	Account Industry	Salutati ▾	First Nar ▾	Last Nar ▾	Title ▾
2	Burlington Textiles Corp of America	Burlingtontextilescorpofamerica.com	Clothing	Mr.	Jack	Rogers	VP, Facilities
3	Dickenson plc	Dickenson.com	Clothing	Mr	Andy	Young	SVP, Operations
4	Cloud Creations	Cloudcreations.org	Telecommunications	Ms.	Rachelle	Hoffman	CTO
5	Cloud Creations	Cloudcreations.com	Salesforce Consultants	Mr.	Felicia	Duarte	COO

Figure 8-4. *Data ready for an import*

2.   Navigate to the Setup menu, as shown in Figure 8-5.

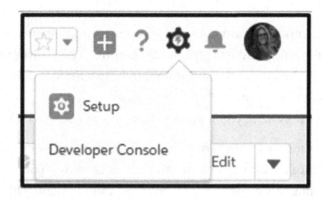

Figure 8-5.   *Navigating to the Setup menu*

3.   In the Quick Find box, type **Data import** (don't hit the Enter key;
the option will populate as you type). Click Data Import Wizard, as
shown in Figure 8-6.

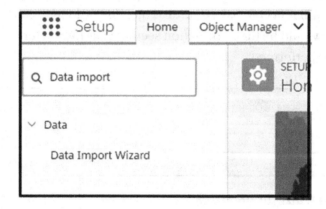

Figure 8-6.   *Searching for Data Import Wizard*

4.   Click the green Launch Wizard! button, as shown in Figure 8-7.

Figure 8-7. *Accessing the Data Import Wizard*

5. Under the "What kind of data are you importing? question, click Accounts and Contacts on the "Standard objects" tab, as shown in Figure 8-8.

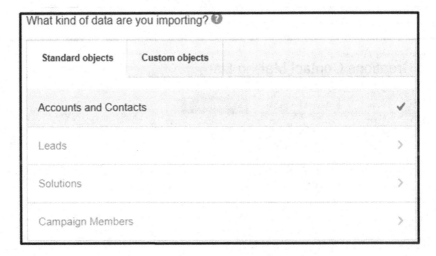

Figure 8-8. *What kind of data are you importing?*

6. Under the "What do you want to do?" question, click "add new records" and the following information will appear:

   • *Match contact by*: This allows you to match your CSV data to an existing contact, if it already exists in Salesforce, by the full name of the contact, email, or any field you have created and made a unique ID or external ID. This helps to prevent duplication when importing. You would want to choose which you think is the best match. Most commonly an email is used.

Note   The unique ID or external ID is an ID or a unique identifier that relates only to that record. When transitioning data from another CRM to Salesforce, your other CRM will contain its own unique ID. You should create a field and mark it as an external ID and import this field to your Salesforce instance. This will allow you to make updates to it in the future should you forget to include something in your original import. Or, for business use integrations to other systems, an external ID is essential to relate the two organizations together and make sure that you have only one record being updated. Salesforce creates its own unique ID for every record created as well; it is a 15- to 18-character alphanumeric ID. You can find this ID for your records in reports; just search for the field ID, as shown in Figure 8-9, or find it in the URL of your browser, as shown in Figure 8-10.

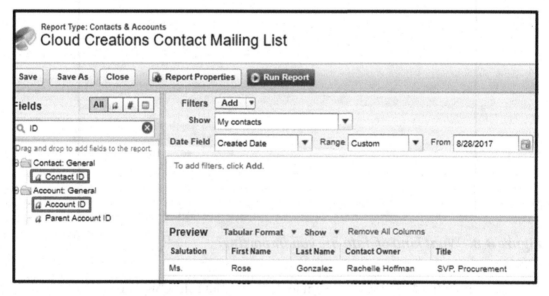

Figure 8-9. *How you can search for the ID for your record in reports*

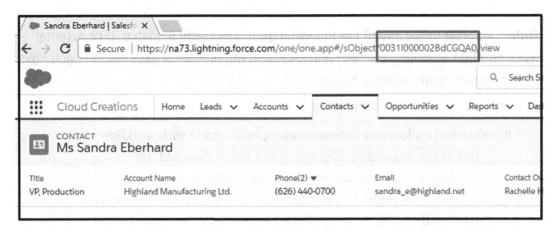

Figure 8-10. *Where you can find your record ID in your browser URL*

7. *Match Account by*: This allows you to match your CSV data to an existing account, if it already exists in Salesforce, by the account name and site (a standard web site field on accounts) or any field you have created and made a unique ID or external ID, as shown in Figure 8-11.

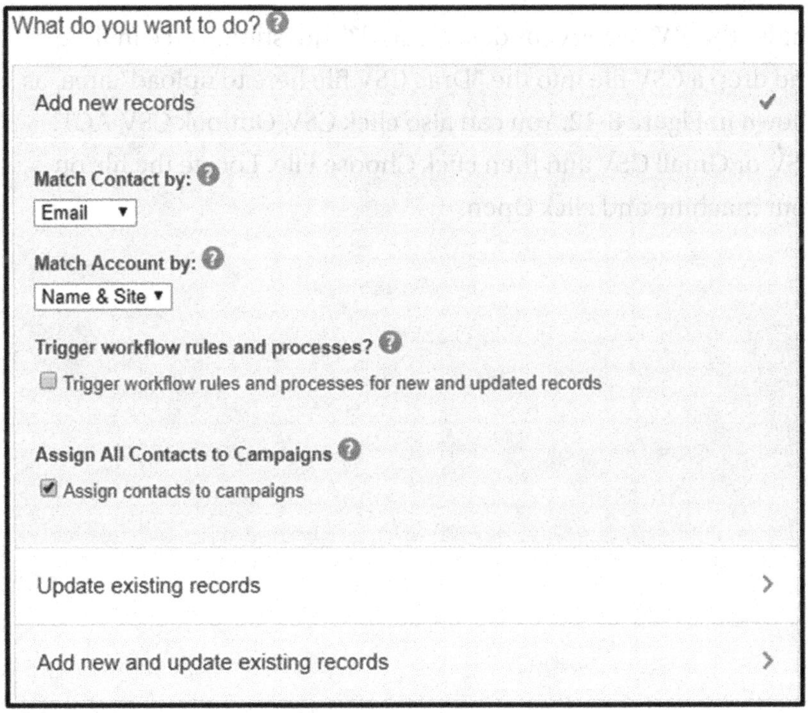

What do you want to do? ❓

    Add new records   ✓

    Match Contact by: ❓
    [Email ▾]

    Match Account by: ❓
    [Name & Site ▾]

    Trigger workflow rules and processes? ❓
    ☐ Trigger workflow rules and processes for new and updated records

    Assign All Contacts to Campaigns ❓
    ☑ Assign contacts to campaigns

    Update existing records   ›

    Add new and update existing records   ›

Figure 8-11. *What do you want to do?*

Note   You can make any of the following data type fields a unique ID or external ID by creating or editing the field and selecting the unique or external ID check box: auto-number, email, number, or text.

8. Salesforce allows for automated processes made with workflow rules or the Process Builder to be enabled or disabled. By checking the box, you are enabling them to be active during this import. This is important to consider if you have created actions that include email and tasks because this could bombard your clients or users. For example, you could have a workflow rule that can email a contact a welcome email every time a contact is created. If you keep this selected, all contacts imported will receive this email.

9. You can also assign all contacts imported to an existing campaign. If you select this option, you need to include a column in your import containing the campaign Salesforce ID.

10. Under the "Where is your data located?" question, you can drag and drop a CSV file into the "Drag CSV file here to upload" area, as shown in Figure 8-12. You can also click CSV, Outlook CSV, ACT! CSV, or Gmail CSV and then click Choose File. Locate the file on your machine and click Open.

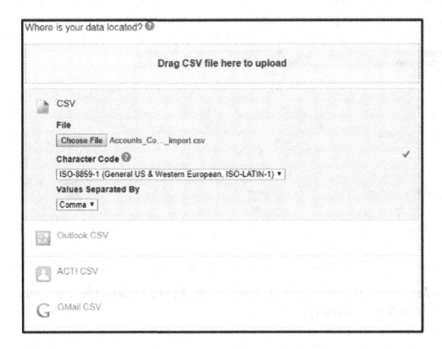

Figure 8-12. *Where is your data located?*

11. Once these steps are complete, click the Next button at the
     bottom-right corner of your screen, as shown in Figure 8-13.

Figure 8-13. *Click the Next button on the screen*

12. In the Edit Mapping field, this is where you choose what column
     header is mapped to what Salesforce field on the accounts or
     contacts. If you set your column headers up correctly, you'll
     see that Salesforce will match all your columns to the fields in
     Salesforce, as shown in Figure 8-14. In Figure 8-15, you'll see that
     the headers didn't match the names of the fields. Steps 13 and 14
     are additional steps to follow should you not match the headers of
     your columns to the field names they are mapping too.

Edit Field Mapping: Accounts and Contacts
Your file has been auto-mapped to existing Salesforce fields, but you can edit the mappings if you wish. Unmapped fields will not be imported.

Edit	Mapped Salesforce Object	CSV Header	Example	Example	Example
Change	Contact: Salutation	Salutation	Ms	Mr.	Mr.
Change	Contact: First Name	First Name	Rose	Sean	Jack
Change	Contact: Last Name	Last Name	Gonzalez	Forbes	Rogers
Change	Contact: Title	Title	SVP, Procurement	CFO	VP, Facilities
Change	Contact: Mailing Street	Mailing Street	313 Constitution Place	312 Constitution Place	525 S. Lexington Ave
Change	Contact: Mailing City	Mailing City			Burlington
Change	Contact: Mailing State/Province	Mailing State/Province			NC
Change	Contact: Mailing Zip/Postal Code	Mailing Zip/Postal Code			27215
Change	Contact: Mailing Country	Mailing Country			USA
Change	Contact: Phone	Phone	(512) 757-6000	(512) 757-6000	(336) 222-7000
Change	Contact: Mobile	Mobile	(512) 757-9340	(512) 757-4561	
Change	Account: Fax	Fax	(512) 757-9000	(512) 757-9000	(336) 222-8000

Figure 8-14. *Field mapping when you matched your column headers to the field names in Salesforce correctly*

Edit Field Mapping: Accounts and Contacts
Your file has been auto-mapped to existing Salesforce fields, but you can edit the mappings if you wish. Unmapped fields will not be imported.

Edit	Mapped Salesforce Object	CSV Header	Example	Example	Example
Map	Unmapped ⊘	Mr/Mrsetc	Ms.	Mr.	Mr.
Map	Unmapped ⊘	F name	Rose	Sean	Jack
Map	Unmapped ⊘	L name	Gonzalez	Forbes	Rogers
Change	Contact: Title	Title	SVP, Procurem	CFO	VP, Facilities
Map	Unmapped ⊘	Street Address	313 Constitution	312 Constitution	525 S. Lexington Ave
Map	Unmapped ⊘	City			Burlington
Map	Unmapped ⊘	State			NC
Map	Unmapped ⊘	Zip			27215
Map	Unmapped ⊘	Country			USA
Map	Unmapped ⊘	#	(512) 757-6000	(512) 757-6000	(336) 222-7000
Map	Unmapped ⊘	cell	(512) 757-9340	(512) 757-4561	
Change	Contact: Email	E-mail	rose@edge.com	sean@edge.com	jrogers@burlington.com
Map	Unmapped ⊘	Company	Edge Communi	Edge Communi	Burlington Textiles Corp of America

Figure 8-15. *Field mapping when you didn't match your column headers to the field names in Salesforce*

13. If you see a triangle with an exclamation mark inside, this means that there is an error with your mapping, as shown in Figure 8-16. Hover over the icon to display the error message. In most cases, it is because you have mapped one column to multiple fields.

| Change | Contact: Mailing Street, Account: Billin... ⚠ | Street Address | | 313 Constitutior | 312 Constitutior | 525 S. Lexington Ave |
| Change | Contact: Mailing City, Account: Billing ... ⚠ | City | | | | Burlington |

Figure 8-16. *Shows the little triangle symbol*

Note   If your import requires that two fields be updated with the same information, you'll need to create two columns with the same data in each and map the columns to the respective fields. Importing tools can link to only one data point at a time.

---

14. If you see a field in bold red like Figure 8-15, this means the field still needs to be mapped. To map a field or change a field already mapped, click the Map or Change hyperlink. You can either type in the field name or use the scroll bar to find the field. Select the appropriate field and click Map, as shown in Figure 8-17.

Figure 8-17. *Mapping fields using the Data Import Wizard*

Note   If you don't create a record owner field in your import, the records created will automatically be assigned to the user performing the import. This could impact your organization if you have security set up that eliminates users from seeing data. For example, if you have a role hierarchy set up that puts you at the top of the hierarchy and you are the importing user, users below you may not be able to see the records you've imported. This ultimately means they can't do their jobs.

15.   Once you have reviewed that all the columns are mapped to the appropriate fields, click the Next button at the bottom-right corner, as shown in Figure 8-18.

Cancel	Previous	Next

Figure 8-18. *Click the Next button to continue*

16.   The Review & Start Import screen summarizes what objects you're importing to, what type of import it is (insert, update, upset), what CSV you are using for your import, how many fields are mapped, and how many are unmapped, as shown in Figure 8-19.

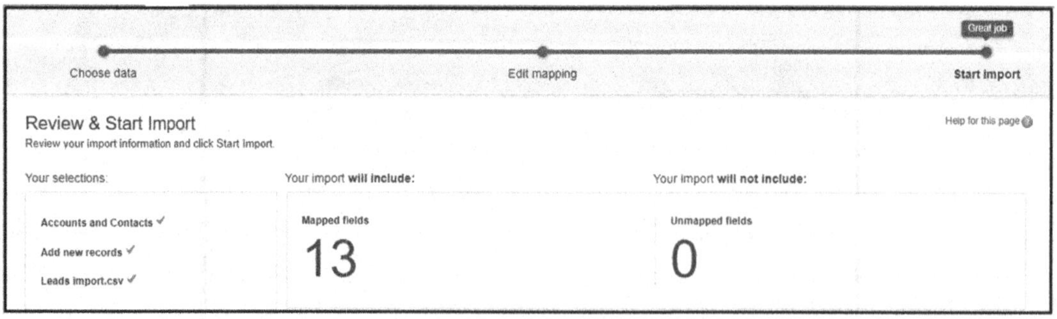

Figure 8-19. *A review of your import before you click Start Import*

17. Once you have reviewed this information and feel that it is correct, click the Start Import button, as shown in Figure 8-20.

Figure 8-20. *Start Import button*

18. Click the OK button on the congratulations page to be taken to the bulk data load job request and status page, as shown in Figure 8-21.

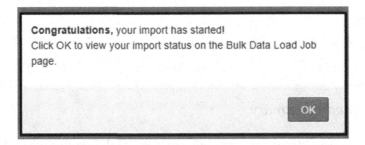

Figure 8-21. *OK button*

19. If the import is a large import (tens of thousands of rows), the job being processed can take up to several hours. If it is a small import, you may find that your job will be finished as soon as you click OK, as shown in Figure 8-22.

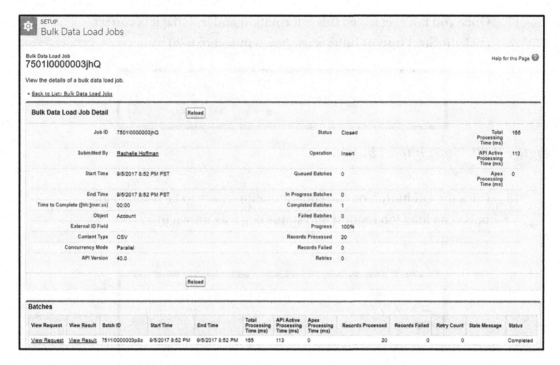

Figure 8-22. *Import summary*

20. Salesforce will send you an email when your job is complete and will attach an error file to review any errors on your import. Some errors could include a data type not matching. Another could be that Salesforce is seeing a blank row, as shown in Figure 8-23.

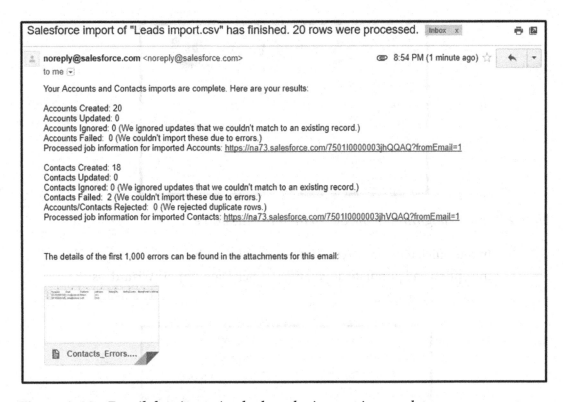

Figure 8-23. *Email that is received when the import is complete*

Importing Leads

Ideally, you'll find that you get to import new leads all the time! Whether you get new leads from a conference you attend or a purchased list, you'll want to import them immediately to get your sales team working on them! The following steps will show you how to quickly make this happen:

1. Prepare your data for the import. Make sure that all the required fields are populated columns in your import. The standard Salesforce setup requires a last name, a company name, and a lead status.

2. Navigate to the Setup menu, as shown in Figure 8-24.

Figure 8-24. *Navigating to the Setup area in Salesforce*

3. In the Quick Find area, type **Data import** (don't hit the Enter key; the option will populate as you type). Click Data Import Wizard, as shown in Figure 8-25.

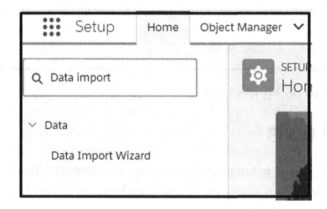

Figure 8-25. *Searching for Data Import Wizard*

4. Click the green Launch Wizard! button, as shown in Figure 8-26.

Figure 8-26. *Launching the Salesforce wizard*

5. Under the "What kind of data are you importing?" question, click Leads on the "Standard objects" tab, as shown in Figure 8-27.

What kind of data are you importing? ❼

Standard objects	Custom objects	
Accounts and Contacts		❯
Leads		✔
Solutions		❯
Campaign Members		❯

Figure 8-27. *What kind of data are you importing?*

6. Under the "What do you want to do?" question, click "Add new records," and the following information will appear:

- *Match Lead by*: This allows you to match your CSV data to an existing lead contact if it already exists in Salesforce by the full name of the lead, email, or any field you have created and made a unique ID or external ID. This helps to prevent duplication from being imported. You would want to choose which you think is the best match. Most commonly email is used.

- *Assign New Leads to this Source*: This allows you to select what lead source all the leads should be assigned to. If you have an import that is not a mixture of lead sources, you can use this function. For example, if you just attended a conference and you want to show that all these leads came from that conference, you would globally assign all the imported leads from this list to that lead source. If you have a mixture of sources where your leads came from, you'll want to ignore this.

- *Assign all leads using Assignment rules*: This allows you to utilize a lead assignment rule you've created to auto-assign the owner. The drop-down should include all your options that you created in lead assignments. If all the leads you are importing need to be assigned to specific users, you can ignore this feature. However, if you purchased a list and these leads are up for anyone, you may want to let your auto-assignment rules handle who gets what.

- *Assign leads to campaigns*: This allows you to add all the imported leads to a campaign. You'll just need to make sure to include a column in your spreadsheet with that campaign ID. If you want to have all the imported leads related to a campaign for an event or a campaign for an email blast, you can do this with this function.

7. Salesforce allows for automated process made with workflow rules or the Process Builder to be enabled to disabled. By checking the box, you are enabling them to be active during this import. This is important to consider if you have created actions that include email and tasks as this could bombard your clients or users.

8. Under the "Where is your data located?" question, you can drag
and drop a CSV file into the "Drag CSV file here to upload" area,
as shown in Figures 8-28 and 8-29. You can also click CSV, Outlook
CSV, ACT! CSV, or Gmail CSV. Then click Choose File, locate the
file on your machine, and click Open.

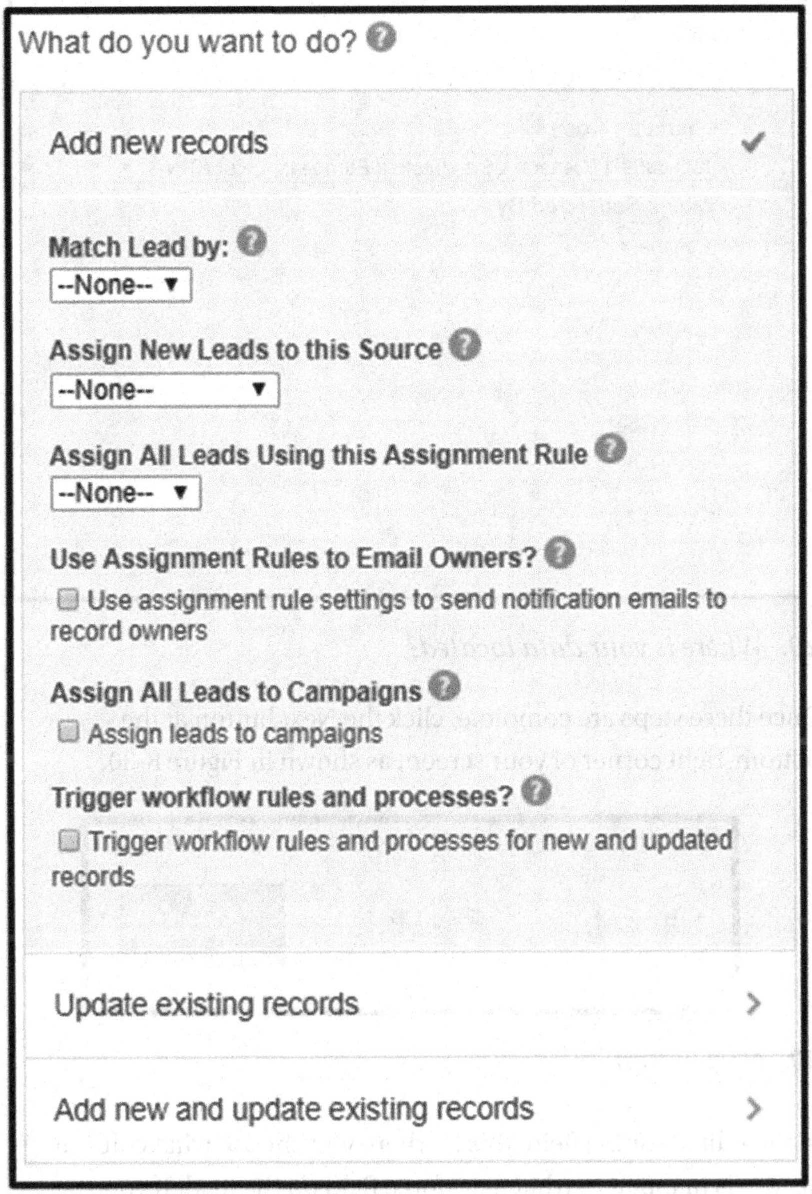

Figure 8-28. *What do you want to do?*

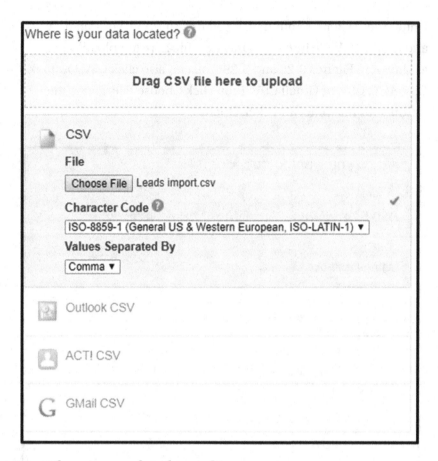

Figure 8-29. *Where is your data located?*

9.   Once these steps are complete, click the Next button at the bottom-right corner of your screen, as shown in Figure 8-30.

Figure 8-30. *Next button*

10. In the Edit Mapping field, this is where you choose what column header is mapped to what Salesforce field on the lead. If you set your column headers up correctly, you'll see that Salesforce will match all your columns to the fields in Salesforce, as shown

in Figure 8-31. In Figure 8-32, you'll see that the headers didn't match the names of the fields. Steps 11 and 12 are additional steps to follow if you did not match the headers of your columns to the field names they are mapping to.

Edit Field Mapping: Accounts and Contacts
Your file has been auto-mapped to existing Salesforce fields, but you can edit the mappings if you wish. Unmapped fields will not be imported.

Edit	Mapped Salesforce Object	CSV Header	Example	Example	Example
Change	Contact: Salutation	Salutation	Ms.	Mr	Mr.
Change	Contact: First Name	First Name	Rose	Sean	Jack
Change	Contact: Last Name	Last Name	Gonzalez	Forbes	Rogers
Change	Contact: Title	Title	SVP, Procurement	CFO	VP, Facilities
Change	Contact: Mailing Street	Mailing Street	313 Constitution Place	312 Constitution Place	525 S. Lexington Ave
Change	Contact: Mailing City	Mailing City			Burlington
Change	Contact: Mailing State/Province	Mailing State/Province			NC
Change	Contact: Mailing Zip/Postal Code	Mailing Zip/Postal Code			27215
Change	Contact: Mailing Country	Mailing Country			USA
Change	Contact: Phone	Phone	(512) 757-6000	(512) 757-6000	(336) 222-7000
Change	Contact: Mobile	Mobile	(512) 757-9340	(512) 757-4561	
Change	Account: Fax	Fax	(512) 757-9000	(512) 757-9000	(336) 222-8000

Figure 8-31. *Field mapping when you matched your column headers to the field names in Salesforce correctly*

Edit Field Mapping: Accounts and Contacts
Your file has been auto-mapped to existing Salesforce fields, but you can edit the mappings if you wish. Unmapped fields will not be imported.

Edit	Mapped Salesforce Object	CSV Header	Example	Example	Example
Map	Unmapped	Mr/Mrsetc	Ms.	Mr.	Mr.
Map	Unmapped	F name	Rose	Sean	Jack
Map	Unmapped	L name	Gonzalez	Forbes	Rogers
Change	Contact: Title	Title	SVP, Procurem	CFO	VP, Facilities
Map	Unmapped	Street Address	313 Constitution	312 Constitution	525 S. Lexington Ave
Map	Unmapped	City			Burlington
Map	Unmapped	State			NC
Map	Unmapped	Zip			27215
Map	Unmapped	Country			USA
Map	Unmapped	#	(512) 757-6000	(512) 757-6000	(336) 222-7000
Map	Unmapped	cell	(512) 757-9340	(512) 757-4561	
Change	Contact: Email	E-mail	rose@edge.con	sean@edge.con	jrogers@burlington.com
Map	Unmapped	Company	Edge Communi	Edge Communi	Burlington Textiles Corp of America

Figure 8-32. *Field mapping when you didn't match your column headers to the field names in Salesforce*

11.   If you see a field in bold red, this means that the field still needs to be mapped, as shown in Figure 8-33. To map a field or change a field already mapped, click the Map or Change hyperlink. You can either type in the field name or use the scroll bar to find the field. Select the appropriate field and click Map, as shown in Figure 8-34.

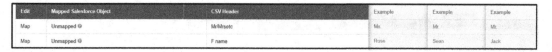

Edit	Mapped Salesforce Object	CSV Header	Example	Example	Example
Map	Unmapped ⊘	Mr/Mrsetc	Ms.	Mr.	Mr.
Map	Unmapped ⊘	F name	Rose	Sean	Jack

Figure 8-33. *Fields shown as unmapped*

Figure 8-34. *Selecting a field*

Note   If you don't create a record owner field and you don't choose to use your lead assignment rules in the import, the records created will automatically be assigned to the user performing the import. This could impact your organization if you have security set up that eliminates users from seeing data. For example, if you have a role hierarchy set up that puts you at the top of the hierarchy and you are the importing user, users below you may not be able to see the records you've imported. This ultimately means they can't do their jobs.

12. Once you have reviewed that all the columns are mapped to the appropriate fields, click the Next button at the bottom-right corner, as shown in Figure 8-35.

Cancel   Previous   Next

Figure 8-35. *Next button*

13. The Review & Start Import screen summarizes what objects you're importing to, what type of import it is (insert, update, upsert), what CSV you are using for your import, how many fields are mapped, and how many are unmapped, as shown in Figure 8-36.

Great job

Choose data   Edit mapping   **Start import**

Review & Start Import   Help for this page

Review your import information and click Start Import.

Your selections: Your import **will include:**   Your import **will not include:**

Accounts and Contacts ✓   **Mapped fields**   **Unmapped fields**

Add new records ✓   13   0

Leads import.csv ✓

Figure 8-36. *Import review*

14. Once you have reviewed this information and feel that it is correct, click the Start Import button, as shown in Figure 8-37.

Figure 8-37. *Start Import button*

15. Click the OK button on the congratulations page to be taken to the bulk data load job request and status page, as shown in Figure 8-38.

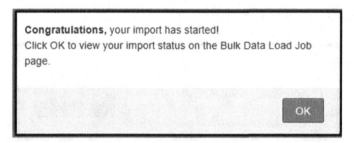

Figure 8-38. *OK button*

16. If the import is a large import (tens of thousands of rows), the job being processed can take up to several hours. If it is a small import, you may find that your job will be finished as soon as you clicked OK, as shown in Figure 8-39.

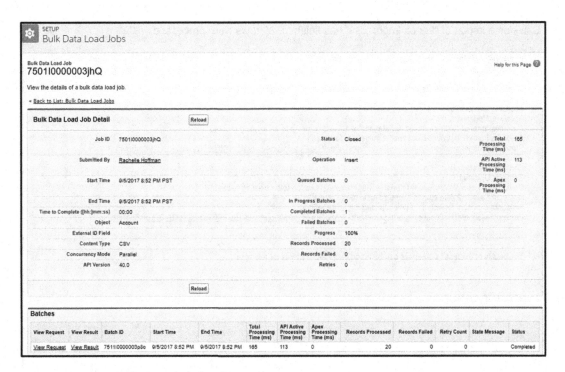

Figure 8-39. *Bulk data load job review*

17. Salesforce will also send you an email when your job is complete
     and will attach an error file to review any errors on your import.
     Some errors could include data type not matching. Another could
     be that Salesforce is seeing a blank row, as shown in Figure 8-40.

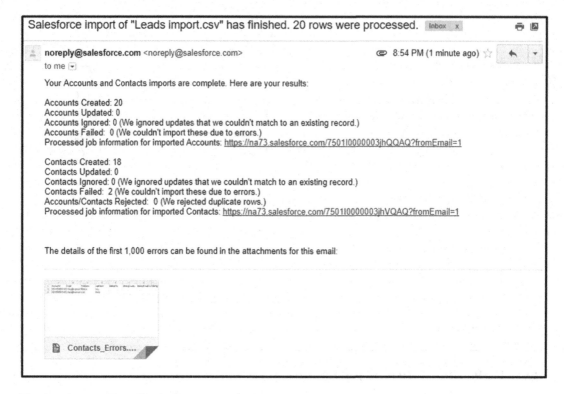

Figure 8-40. *Email confirmation*

Scheduling a Data Export

Salesforce is a cloud-based CRM and development platform that can be accessed
anywhere you have an Internet connection. If there is a drop in your Internet service or
you need to work offline for the time being, Salesforce allows you to export your data into
a CSV file. Or, if you're like us and you like to keep a backup of your data, you can do so.
You can schedule an export to run monthly (free of charge for all Salesforce editions),
weekly, or daily (which may have a charge depending on the Salesforce edition), and you
can have it emailed you. Or you can perform one-time exports.

1.   Navigate to the Setup menu, as shown in Figure 8-41.

Figure 8-41. *Navigating to the Setup area*

2. In the Quick Find area, type **Data Export** (don't hit the Enter key; the option will populate as you type). Click Data Export, as shown in Figure 8-42.

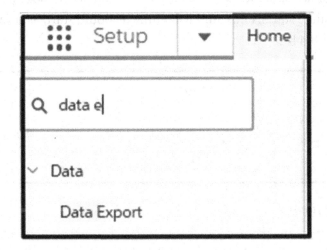

Figure 8-42. *Searching for Data Export*

3. To schedule an export, click the Schedule Export button, or to create a one-time export, click Export Now, as shown in Figure 8-43.

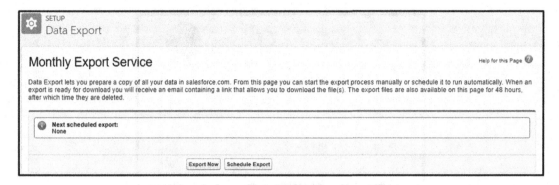

Figure 8-43. *Monthly export service options*

4. To schedule the export, choose what frequency the export should be delivered at. For a monthly export, you can choose what day of the month it should be delivered on, or the first, second, third, fourth, or last specific day of the week. You can also choose when the schedule starts, ends, and what time it should start, as shown in Figure 8-44.

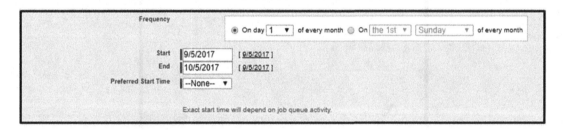

Figure 8-44. *Frequency*

Note   The start time doesn't ensure that it will be delivered at that time. Depending on the amount of data you have, it can take up to several hours to complete.

---

5. You can choose to include images, documents, attachments, Salesforce files, and CRM content document versions with your export by selecting the boxes at the top of the page, as shown in Figure 8-45.

Schedule Data Export

Schedule Data Export	Save Cancel
Export File Encoding	ISO-8859-1 (General US & Western European, ISO-LATIN-1) ▼
Include images, documents, and attachments	☐ ⓘ
Include Salesforce Files and Salesforce CRM Content document versions	☐ ⓘ
Replace carriage returns with spaces	☑

Figure 8-45. *Choosing what to include*

6. You can also select specific objects to be exported only, or you can choose the option at the top-right corner to have all data included, as shown in Figure 8-46.

Action	File Name	File Size
download	WE_00D1I0000002ulLUAY_1.ZIP	55.3K

Figure 8-46. *Objects to export*

7. Once the export is all set, click the Save button.

8. If you have scheduled your export, you should see a yellow box with the time your next scheduled export should run, as shown in Figure 8-47. If the export is scheduled for now, there will be a note for who scheduled, what time, and in what format the information will be received in, as shown in Figure 8-48.

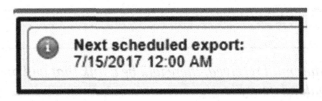

ⓘ **Next scheduled export:**
7/15/2017 12:00 AM

Figure 8-47. *Export now response*

	Your export has been queued. You will receive an email notification when it is completed.
Scheduled By	Rachelle Hoffman
Schedule Date	9/5/2017
Export File Encoding	ISO-8859-1 (General US & Western European, ISO-LATIN-1)

Figure 8-48. *Export scheduled response*

9. Once the export is ready, Salesforce will email you with a link to
    the data export in the Setup menu, as shown in Figure 8-49.

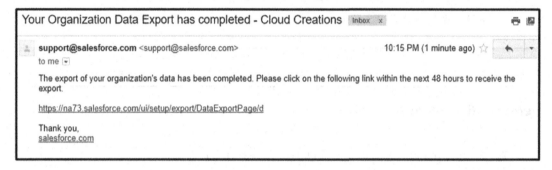

Figure 8-49. *Email sent from Salesforce that your email has been received*

10. Here the download hyperlink will need to be clicked to download
    the file that will then need to be stored on a machine, as shown in
    Figure 8-50.

Action	File Name	File Size
download	WE_00D1I0000002uILUAY_1.ZIP	55.3K

Figure 8-50. *In the email received, there will be a link that will direct you back in*
Salesforce to download your file

11. It will be downloaded to a zip file that will need to be unzipped for your use. All objects will be broken out into individual CSV files, as shown in Figure 8-51.

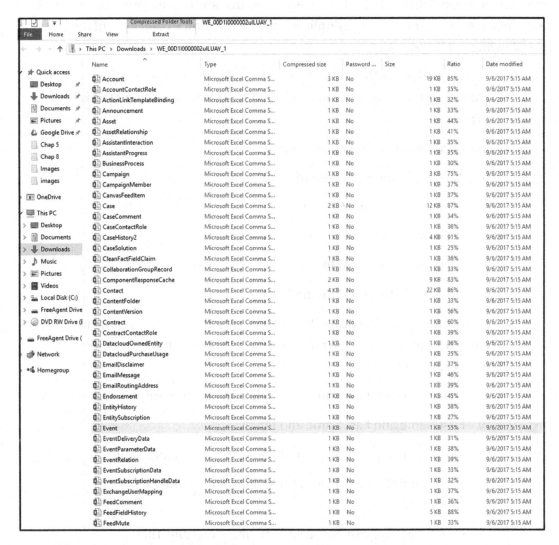

Figure 8-51. *Shows all objects broken out into individual CSV files*

Duplicating Data Management

Another great feature in Salesforce is the ability to set up duplicate rules. Duplicate rules allow you to create criteria that will be checked against any new account, contact, or lead and prevent a user from creating a duplicate record. Salesforce comes out of the box with the following duplicate rules:

- *Standard Account Duplicate Rule*: Will verify if the new account being created matches any of the following combinations of account fields to an existing account:

  a. Account Name and Billing Street

  b. Account Name and City and State

  c. Account name and Zip code

  d. Account name and Phone

  e. Account Website and Phone

  f. Account Website and Billing Street

- *Standard Contact Duplicate Rule*: Will verify if the new contact being created matches any of the following combinations of contact fields to an existing contact:

  a. First Name and Last Name and Title and Account Name

  b. First Name and Last Name and Email

  c. First Name and Last Name and Phone and Company Name

  d. First Name and Last Name and Mailing Street and (City or Zip code or Phone)

  e. First Name and Last Name and Mailing Street and Title

  f. First Name and Last Name and Title and Email

  g. First Name and Last Name and Phone

- *Standard Lead Duplicate Rule*: Will verify if the new lead being created matches any of the following combinations of lead fields to an existing lead:

328

a.   First Name and Last Name and Title and Account Name

b.   First Name and Last Name and Email

c.   First Name and Last Name and Phone and Company Name

d.   First Name and Last Name and Mailing Street and (City or Zip code or Phone)

e.   First Name and Last Name and Mailing Street and Title

f.   First Name and Last Name and Title and Email

g.   First Name and Last Name and Phone

If the standard rules don't work for your company, you can also create your own. For example, perhaps you have another combination of fields that would work better for account duplication rules. Maybe your business can match an account based on the account name and a custom field you are collecting. To create a new rule, follow these steps:

1.   Go to your Setup menu and search for *Duplicate Rules*. Click Duplicate Rules, as shown in Figure 8-52.

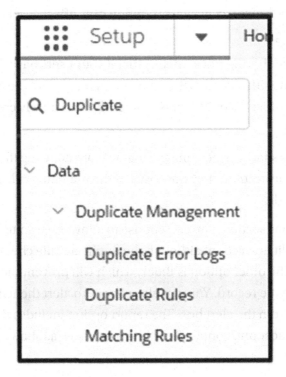

Figure 8-52. *Selecting Duplicate Rules*

2. From the New Rule drop-down, choose the object, in this example Account, as shown in Figure 8-53.

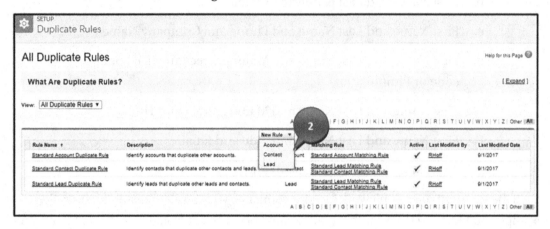

Figure 8-53. *New account rule*

3. Name your duplicate rule.

4. Add a description.

5. Set the record-level security. This option only affects users who have sharing rules.

    a. "Enforce sharing rules" means that if your users have limited visibility with accounts they don't own, they won't be able to see the other account that is matching to this newly created account.

    b. "Bypass sharing rules" means that you are allowing the user to see the account they don't own if the matching rule is activated.

6. In the Actions section, you can choose to allow the user to create or edit an account although the duplicate rule check was activated. The other option is Block, which will prevent the user from saving the record. You can also choose to alert them with a message from the alert box. The report option includes the duplicated account/contact/lead into a list view, as shown in Figure 8-54.

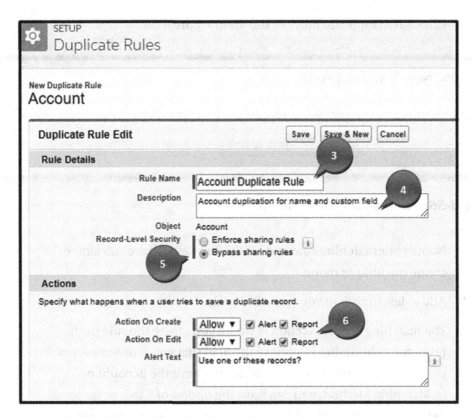

Figure 8-54. *Duplicate rule, steps 3 to 6*

7. You can choose a preexisting matching rule you've created or you can pick from the drop-down Create New Matching Rule, as shown in Figure 8-55.

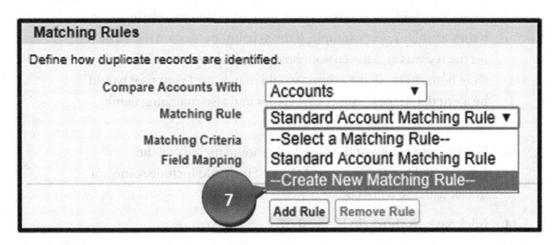

Figure 8-55. *Creating a new matching rule*

8.   Click Save Duplicate Rule, as shown in Figure 8-56.

Create New Matching Rule

Save your duplicate rule and we'll redirect you to create your new matching rule.

Save Duplicate Rule   Cancel

Figure 8-56. *Saving your duplicate rule*

9.   Name your matching rule and hit the Tab key to have Salesforce create the unique name.

10.   Add a description to your matching rule.

11.   The matching criteria section is where you create the rule itself. From the column fields, choose the field that you'll use as part of your matching rule. In this example, you have the account name. In Matching Method, you can have the option of Exact or for some fields Fuzzy. The method Fuzzy will strip the account name of *Inc* or *Corporation* and see if it can match two accounts without these in the name. The Fuzzy method changes per field; to see a full list of these methods, go to `https://help.salesforce.com/` and search *matching methods used with matching rules*.

12.   Select Match Blank Fields to allow your criteria to match the fields if they are blank. For example, if the account names are the same for the records and the custom field on both is blank and these were both checked, the criteria would match, and your user would be alerted. I suggest using exact values and also matching blank fields.

13.   You can also choose if the filter logic should include all the previous fields with the word AND or if it should include some but not all with the word OR.

14.   Click Save, as shown in Figure 8-57.

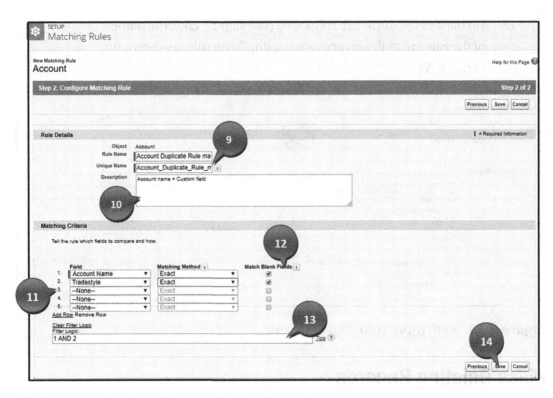

Figure 8-57. *Creating the matching rule*

15.   Make sure to activate your matching rule by clicking the Activate
       button, as shown in Figure 8-58.

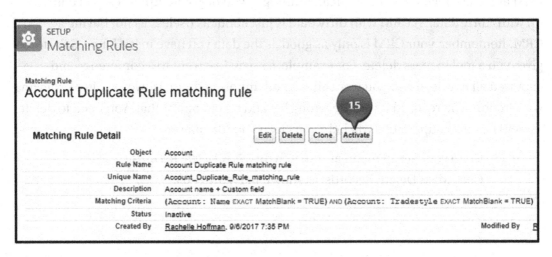

Figure 8-58. *Activating your matching rule*

16. Go back to the duplicate rules area (see step 1), click the name of the rule created, and activate the duplicate rule, as shown in Figure 8-59.

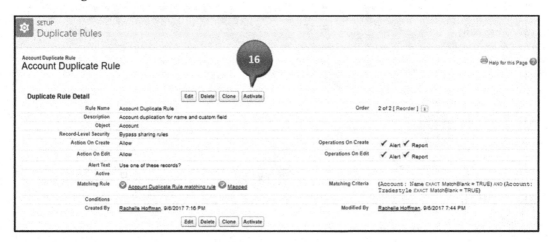

Figure 8-59. *Activating your duplicate rule*

Mass Deleting Records

Salesforce offers a Mass Delete Records option for accounts, leads, activities, contacts, cases, solutions, products, and reports. This option is especially important because it allows you to clean up your database. If you allow or do not maintain your Salesforce CRM and leave records in it that mean nothing to you or your employees, you end up with "dirty data." A CRM with dirty data is just about as useless as not having a CRM. Remember, your CRM is only as good as the data you have in it. Hence, Salesforce gives you a tool to mass delete. For example, say you just went to a conference and captured all new leads, so you went ahead and imported them. However, after reviewing your import, you realized it was the wrong list and an old one at that. You need to delete these! The next couple steps will help you clean your database:

1. Go to your Setup menu and search for *Mass Delete Records*. Click Mass Delete Records, as shown in Figure 8-60.

Figure 8-60. *Finding Mass Delete Records*

2. Click the option for the objects you want to delete the records
    from. In the previous example, it was Leads, as shown in
    Figure 8-61.

Figure 8-61. *Mass delete record choices*

3. Determine the criteria of the data that needs to be deleted. In this
    example, we know the created date was yesterday. Or perhaps the
    lead source was the specific conference. Almost any field on the
    object can be used as the criteria to find the records that need to
    be deleted.

4. In the first column, select the field.

5. In the second column, choose the method.

6. In the third column, enter your value.

7. Click Search, as shown in Figure 8-62.

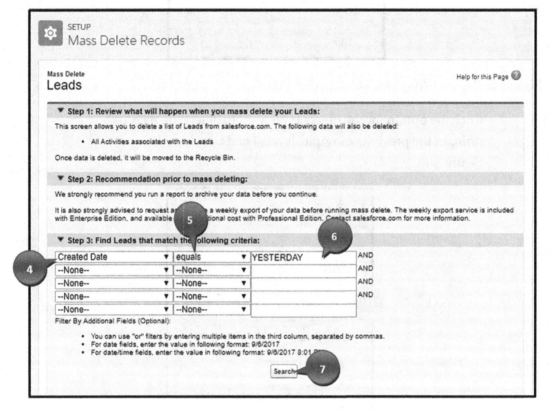

Figure 8-62. *Set up the criteria to find the records needing to be deleted*

8. Select the records you want to delete or select the box at the top to select all the records.

9. Select the box Permanently Delete if you are sure you never want to retrieve these again.

Note   Deleted records go to your recycle bin and will autodelete after 15 days, or if your recycle bin is full, the oldest record will be deleted.

---

10.   Click the Delete button when you are ready to delete the records, as shown in Figure 8-63.

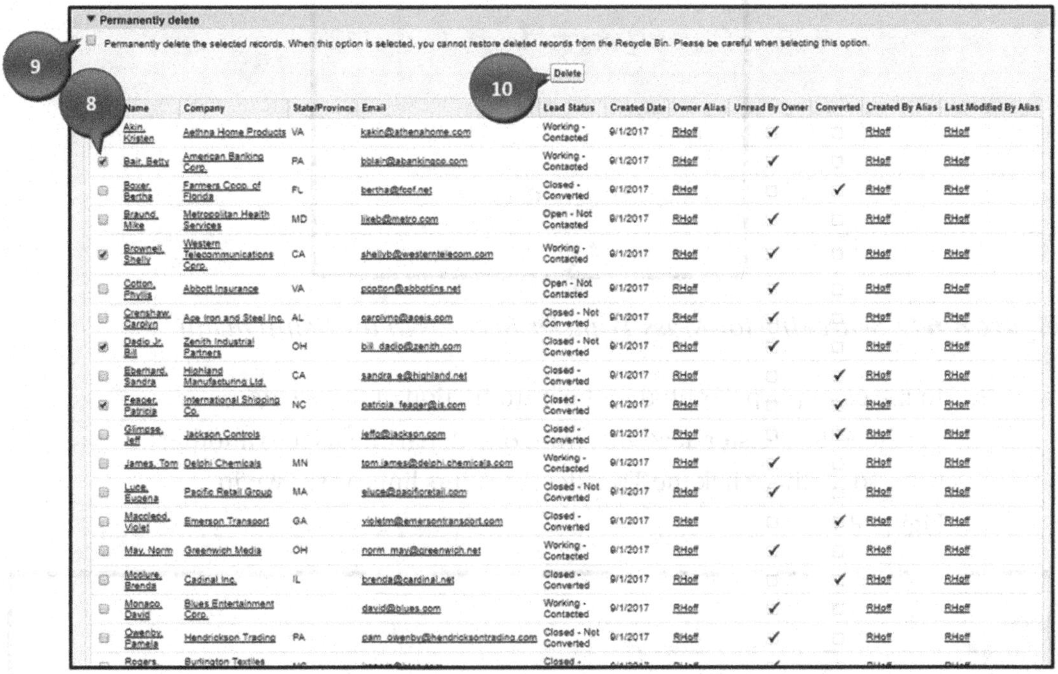

Figure 8-63. *Mass deleting your records*

Note   You can only mass delete 250 records at a time.

Mass Transferring Records

Salesforce offers a tool to help you transfer the ownership of accounts, leads, macros, or streaming channel records to another user. This allows you to transfer every record a user owns to another and can be based on the criteria of the record. This is an important tool if you have an employee who leaves your company or if one gets promoted! For example, if an employee is leaving your company and owns many accounts that now need to be managed by another employee, you can use this tool to transfer those accounts to new users.

1.   Go to your Setup menu, search for *Mass Transfer Records*, and click the phrase, we shown in Figure 8-64.

Figure 8-64. *Searching for Mass Transfer Records in the Setup menu*

2. In the example presented in the introduction of this section, you need to transfer accounts from one departing user to another user. To do this, click the Transfer Accounts link, as shown in Figure 8-65.

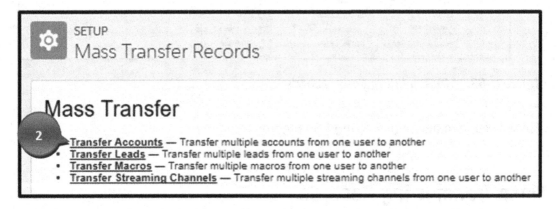

Figure 8-65. *Transfer Account Records screen*

3. Using the magnifying glass icon, search for the user you want to transfer the ownership of the records from.

4. Using the magnifying glass icon, search for the user you want to transfer the ownership of the records to.

5. It is a general rule that you shouldn't transfer records that are closed or completed from one user to another. We recommend that you keep the history of your business this way. Therefore, in Figure 8-66, you'll see we only select "Transfer open opportunities" and "Transfer open cases."

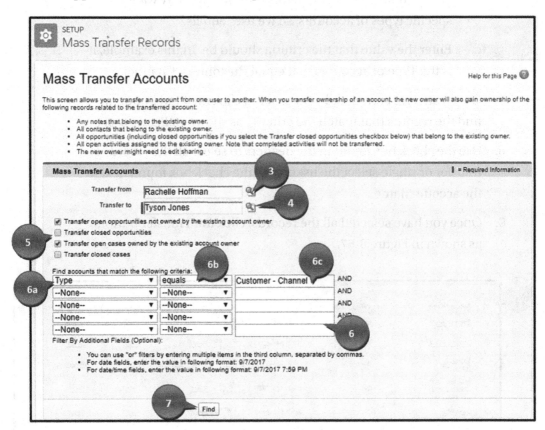

Figure 8-66. *Setting up the mass transfer of records*

6. If you want all records that one user owns transferred to the other, you can leave this section blank. Otherwise, if you want to transfer only specific records based on the criteria of the record, you'll need to use this section. Notice that you can only use the logic AND. This means that every set of criteria you build here will have been on the record it is a search for. For example, if you set the Type field to Customer – Channel and Billing State to California, this will require that the record has both of these values for it to be available to transfer.

a.   Find the field that you want to filter from. For example, if you use a Type field on the account and you only want to transfer specific types of accounts to the new user.

b.   Use the appropriate method: equals, contains, less than, greater than, and so on. In this example, we only want specific types of accounts, so we use "equals."

c.   Enter the value that the criteria should be. In this example, it is the Type of accounts that equal Customer – Channel.

7.   Once you have completed your criteria, click the Find button to find the records that match the criteria, as shown in Figure 8-66.

8.   Use the check box found in the headers to select all the records to transfer or single select the users with the check box found next to the account name.

9.   Once you have selected all the records, click the Transfer button, as shown in Figure 8-67.

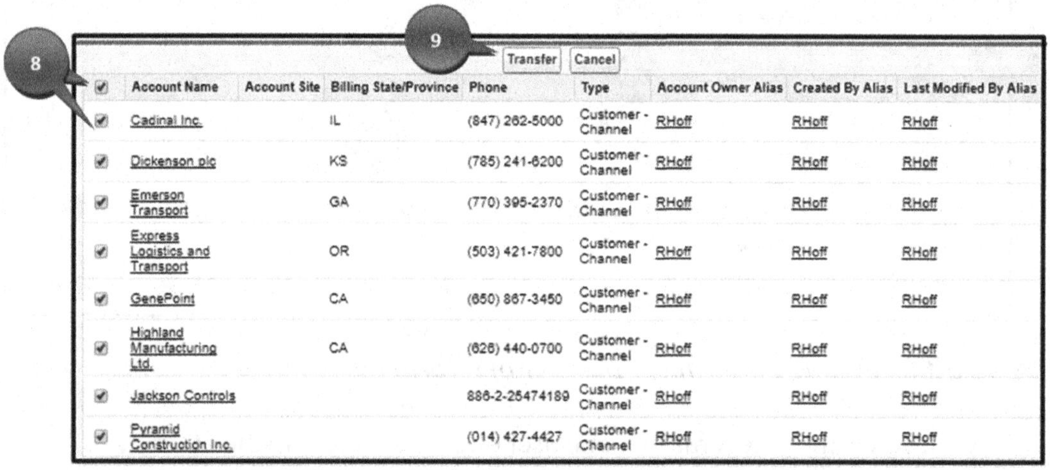

Figure 8-67. Selecting the records to transfer

Once complete, you should get the record count of the transferred records, as shown in Figure 8-68.

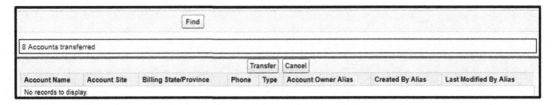

Figure 8-68. *Record count of transferred records*

Summary

Salesforce offers so many tools right at your fingertips. With all the data tools presented, you shouldn't have any issues with dirty data. If you let dirty data get out of control, it can become a burden to you and your users. With the proper tools at hand, you'll never have a reason to let it get this way.

CHAPTER 9

Security Overview

Salesforce is committed to running the most secure cloud platform. Protecting data integrity and privacy is at the forefront of Salesforce's business model. Salesforce approaches security with a multitiered architecture, which supports greater flexibility and protection. System administrators have complete control over the level of access delivered to end users. You can protect sensitive information and manage end user accessibility with profiles, permission sets, field-level security, sharing rules, and more. Visit the Salesforce Trust web site at `http://trust.salesforce.com` (Figure 9-1) for transparent access to security threats and advisories.

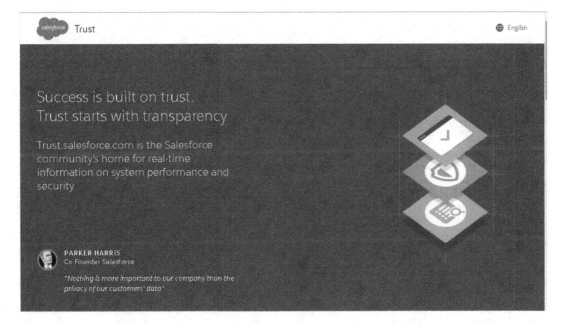

Figure 9-1. *Salesforce Trust web site*

© Felicia Duarte, Rachelle Hoffman 2018
F. Duarte, R. Hoffman, *Learn Salesforce Lightning*, https://doi.org/10.1007/978-1-4842-2994-1_9

Salesforce Security Model

Controlling the level of access to your Salesforce organization is vital to ensuring client and data protection. While Salesforce is committed to the highest levels of data protection, your system administrator should configure the security settings to make the system as secure as possible. Design a security plan by considering what the primary risks to your data are and then learn about the Salesforce sharing architecture and its components to properly configure your security settings.

Fundamentals Data can be secured and layered at different levels in Salesforce. Access is secured in three ways: at the object level, at the field level, and at the record level. In database terms, an object is a table. *Objects* hold groupings of information that may be related. This includes the records that live in them. *Records* are the rows of information that are found within a table.

Accounts, contacts, and opportunities are just a few examples of standard Salesforce objects. Figure 9-2 shows a list view of account records in the account object. Cloud Creations HQ is an example of an account record in the Account object, as shown in Figure 9-2.

Figure 9-2. *Identifying objects, records, and fields*

Each record stores key pieces of information. These are called *fields*. In database terms, fields are the columns found within a table. In Figure 9-2, Account Name, Account Site, and Phone are all examples of fields in an account record. Refer to Figure 9-2 to identify the difference between objects, records, and fields.

Profiles and Permission Sets

Profiles contain a collection of settings for determining what a user or group of users can see and do in Salesforce. A permission set contains the same collection of administrative settings but can be assigned to an individual user or groups of users as an extra layer of permission.

Note   Rather than create countless profiles to assign the appropriate settings and permissions for an individual user, it is best practice to assign a permission set.

Profiles

All users must be assigned a profile, and profiles can be assigned to multiple users. However, users can be assigned only one profile. Typically, profiles are assigned to users by their job function. This is usually because those with the same job description often require similar levels of access.

For example, you may have different security requirements for your marketing users, service agents, sales reps, and developers. It's recommended that you create or modify profiles to meet their specific requirements.

Profile Home Page

We suggest familiarizing yourself with the different profile settings on the profile home page. This page is broken down into the following permissions and settings.

Console Settings

Click Edit to control the console settings for each profile (shown in Figure 9-3).

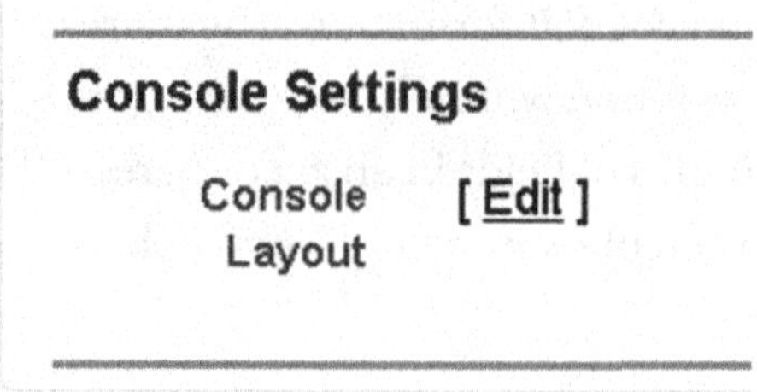

Console Settings

Console   [Edit]
Layout

Figure 9-3. *Console Settings*

Page Layouts

Page layouts can be configured for each profile. Click View Assignment next to each desired object to configure a different page layout for a profile (shown in Figure 9-4).

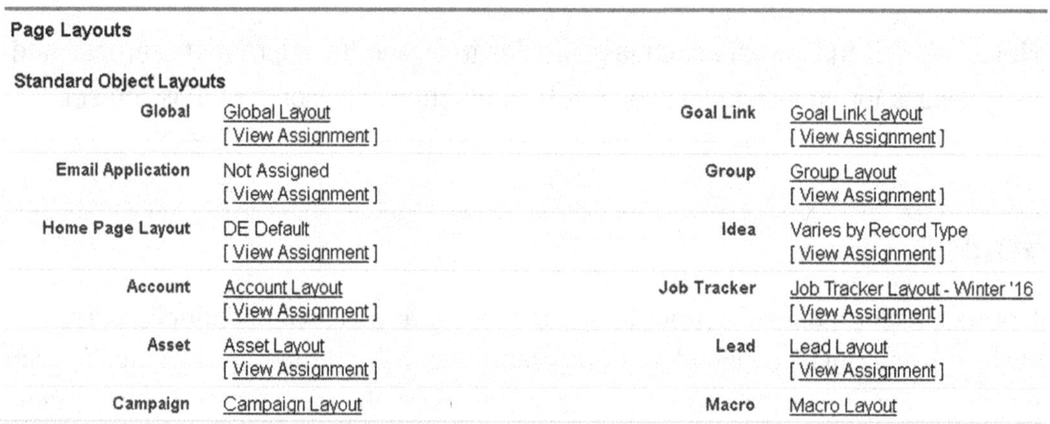

Page Layouts

Standard Object Layouts

Global	Global Layout [View Assignment]	Goal Link	Goal Link Layout [View Assignment]
Email Application	Not Assigned [View Assignment]	Group	Group Layout [View Assignment]
Home Page Layout	DE Default [View Assignment]	Idea	Varies by Record Type [View Assignment]
Account	Account Layout [View Assignment]	Job Tracker	Job Tracker Layout - Winter '16 [View Assignment]
Asset	Asset Layout [View Assignment]	Lead	Lead Layout [View Assignment]
Campaign	Campaign Layout	Macro	Macro Layout

Figure 9-4. *You can control page layouts for each object at the profile level.*

Field-Level Security

Once object-level access and record-level access are granted, you can control what fields are visible at the profile level. Navigate to the field level and click View next to the desired object to control the level of access that a profile should have to a field. Once you click View, you will see a list of all fields related to that object and the current field-level permissions. Click Edit to make changes to the appropriate field (shown in Figure 9-5).

Account Field-Level Security for profile			Help for this Page ⑦
Standard User			

Edit	Back to Profile

Field Name	Field Type	Read Access	Edit Access
Account Name	Name	✓	✓
Account Number	Text	✓	✓
Account Owner	Lookup	✓	✓
Account Site	Text	✓	✓
Account Source	Picklist	✓	✓
Active	Picklist	✓	✓
Annual Revenue	Currency	✓	✓
Billing Address	Address	✓	✓

Figure 9-5. *Field-level security at the account level*

Click Read Access to make a field visible. Select Edit Access to allow users to view and edit a field. Deselect Read Access and Edit Access to make a field hidden.

Let's look at an example. Say Michael Scott Paper Co. uses Salesforce to track sales and accounting information. However, the CEO, Michael Scott, does not want sales representatives to see sensitive financial information such as credit card and Social Security numbers.

To solve this, create a profile for sales representatives and another profile for accounting. For each profile, click View Assignment next to the account and edit the field security. For the sales representatives profile, deselect Read Access and Edit Access in the Credit Card and Social Security fields. This will hide both fields from users assigned to the sales representative profile. Log in as a user assigned to the sales representative profile to test your work.

App and Tab Settings

Specify what apps are visible and set the default in the Custom App Settings section of the profile (shown in Figure 9-6).

Standard Object Permissions

	Basic Access				Data Administration	
	Read	Create	Edit	Delete	View All	Modify All
Accounts	✓	✓	✓	✓	☐	☐
Assets	✓	✓	✓	✓	☐	☐
Campaigns	✓	☐	☐	☐	☐	☐
Cases	✓	✓	✓	☐	☐	☐
Coaching	✓	✓	✓	☐	☐	☐
Contacts	✓	✓	✓	✓	☐	☐
Contracts	✓	✓	✓	✓	☐	☐
D&B Companies	✓	☐	☐	☐	☐	☐
Documents	✓	✓	✓	✓	☐	☐
Duplicate Record Sets	☐	☐	☐	☐	☐	☐
Feedback	✓	✓	✓	☐	☐	☐
Feedback Questions	✓	✓	✓	☐	☐	☐
Feedback Question Sets	✓	✓	✓	☐	☐	☐
Feedback Requests	✓	✓	✓	☐	☐	☐
Feedback Templates	✓	✓	✓	☐	☐	☐

Figure 9-6. *Custom App Settings area in a profile*

Record Type Settings

Record types can be assigned at the profile level. For objects with record types, add the record type next to the appropriate object.

Administrative and General User Permissions

Profiles have two types of permissions: Administrative and General, as shown in Figures 9-7 and 9-8. Familiarize yourself with the granular types of permissions so you can better administer a secure organization.

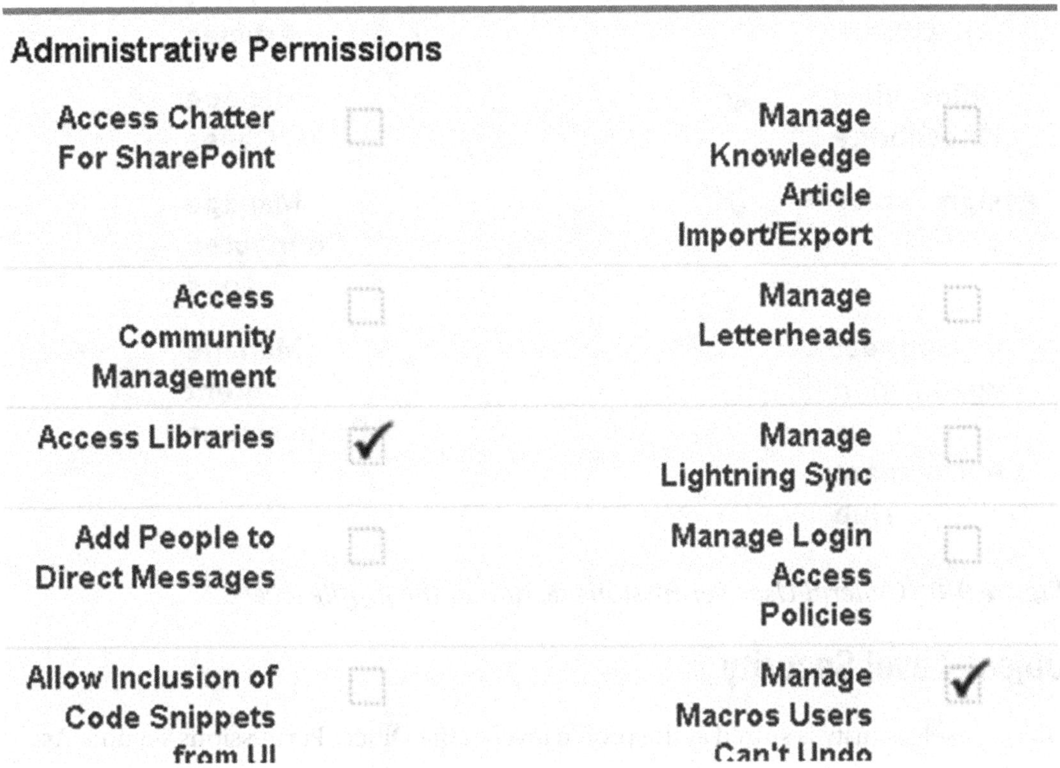

Administrative Permissions

Access Chatter For SharePoint	☐	Manage Knowledge Article Import/Export	☐
Access Community Management	☐	Manage Letterheads	☐
Access Libraries	✓	Manage Lightning Sync	☐
Add People to Direct Messages	☐	Manage Login Access Policies	☐
Allow Inclusion of Code Snippets from UI	☐	Manage Macros Users Can't Undo	✓

Figure 9-7. Administrative Permissions section located in a profile

349

General User Permissions

Activate Contracts	☐	Lightning Login User	☐
Activate Orders	☐	Manage Articles	☐
Allow View Knowledge	✓	Manage Cases	☐
Assign Topics	✓	Manage Connected Apps	☐
Connect Organization to Environment Hub	☐	Manage Content Permissions	☐

Figure 9-8. *General User Permissions section at the profile level*

Object-Level Security

Object-level security is stored at the profile level in the Object Permissions section. As a starting point, a user must have the appropriate level of access to an object to see the object and the records inside of it. You can control object-level security in profiles, as shown in Figure 9-3.

The following are different permission types used to set the level of access users have with each object:

- *Read*: Users can view records.

- *Create*: Users can create records.

- *Edit*: Users can read and edit records stored in this object.

- *Delete*: Users have permission to read, edit, and delete records.

- *View All*: Users can view all records stored within this object.

- *Modify All*: Users can modify all records stored within this object.

Set the object-level security for standard and custom objects. Define whether a profile should have Read, Create, Edit, Delete, View All, or Modify All, as shown in Figure 9-9.

Standard Object Permissions

	Basic Access				Data Administration	
	Read	Create	Edit	Delete	View All	Modify All
Accounts	✓	✓	✓	✓	☐	☐
Assets	✓	✓	✓	✓	☐	☐
Campaigns	✓	☐	☐	☐	☐	☐
Cases	✓	✓	✓	☐	☐	☐
Coaching	✓	✓	✓	☐	☐	☐
Contacts	✓	✓	✓	✓	☐	☐
Contracts	✓	✓	✓	✓	☐	☐
D&B Companies	✓	☐	☐	☐	☐	☐
Documents	✓	✓	✓	✓	☐	☐
Duplicate Record Sets	☐	☐	☐	☐	☐	☐
Feedback	✓	✓	✓	☐	☐	☐
Feedback Questions	✓	✓	✓	☐	☐	☐
Feedback Question Sets	✓	✓	✓	☐	☐	☐
Feedback Requests	✓	✓	✓	☐	☐	☐
Feedback Templates	✓	✓	✓	☐	☐	☐

Figure 9-9. *Setting object-level security*

Password Policies, Login Hours, and IP Ranges

You can specify when passwords should expire, password requirements, session timeouts, and much more. You can also control the login hours and acceptable IP ranges for each profile.

Assigning a Profile

There are six different types of standard profiles:

- *System Administrator*: Assign this profile to a user who needs access to all functionality within license. This profile has access to view and modify all data.

- *Standard User*: This profile has core platform functionality. They can view, edit, and delete records they have access to.

- *Solution Manager*: This is the same functionality as a Standard User plus additional permissions to manage published solutions.

- *Marketing User*: This is the same functionality as a Standard User plus permission to import leads, manage campaigns, and manage communication templates.

- *Contract Manager*: This is the same functionality as a Standard User plus permission to manage and approve contracts.

- *Read Only*: This profile can only view records they have access to and run reports and export.

Create a Custom Profile

Create custom profiles to build a unique set of permissions for different groups of users. Follow these steps to create a custom profile:

1. Search for and select Profiles from the Setup menu (shown in Figure 9-10).

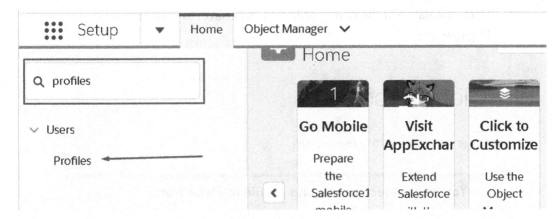

Figure 9-10. *Navigating to Profiles in Salesforce*

2.   To create a new profile, click New Profile, as shown in Figure 9-11.

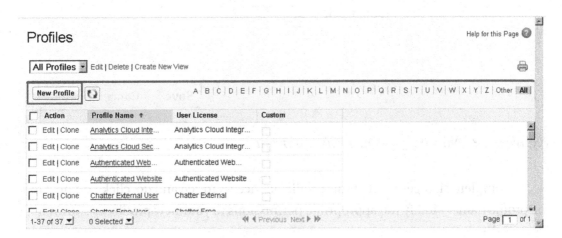

Figure 9-11. *New Profile button on the Profiles home page*

3.   To create a custom profile, you must clone one from an existing standard profile. Choose a standard profile to clone from and click Clone.

4. Enter the name of the new profile and click Save, as shown in Figure 9-12.

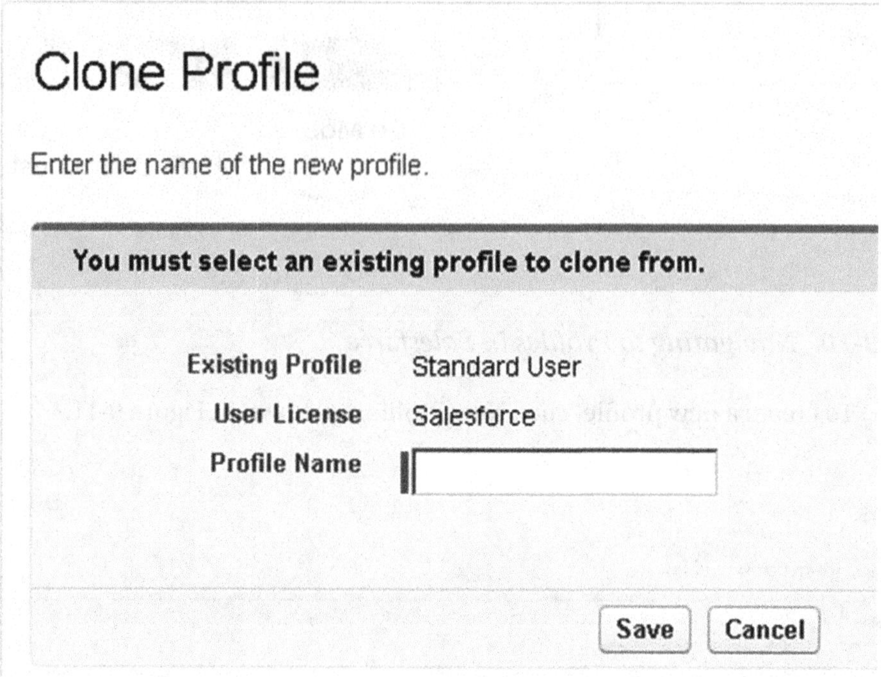

Clone Profile

Enter the name of the new profile.

You must select an existing profile to clone from.

Existing Profile	Standard User
User License	Salesforce
Profile Name	

| Save | Cancel |

Figure 9-12. *Naming your new custom profile*

To complete changes to what this profile has access to see and do, click Edit next to the profile name. Modify the appropriate permissions to your new profile, as shown in Figure 9-13.

Figure 9-13. *Home page of a profile*

Note   All users must have an assigned profile, and profiles can be assigned to multiple users. However, users can be assigned only one profile.

So, what do you do when you need to give additional permissions to an individual user?

For example, let's say you want to extend the permission Create Reports to an individual user. Rather than creating a new profile or editing permissions on an existing profile, we suggest creating a permission set.

Permission Sets

Permission sets are a collection of permissions and settings that can be assigned to the users who need it.

Follow these steps to create a permission set:

1. Search Permission in Setup and click Permission Set.

2. Click the New button to create a new permission set, as shown in Figure 9-14.

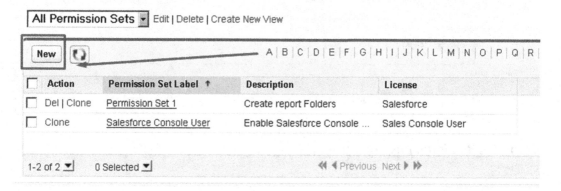

Figure 9-14. *Permission Sets home page*

3. Enter the name of your permission set in the Label field and provide a detailed description, as shown in Figure 9-15.

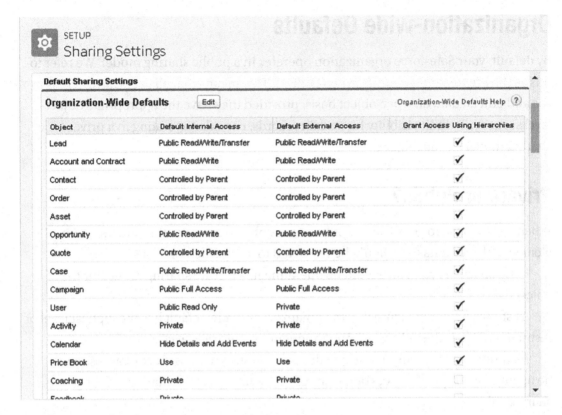

Figure 9-15. *Steps to create a permission step*

4.   Choose the type of user who will use this permission set.

Tip   It is best practice to give your permission set a description. This makes it easier to find when many permission sets exist.

Record-Level Security

Record-level security specifies what records a user has access to view and edit in each object.

Record Ownership

Each record in Salesforce must have an owner. This can be either a user or a queue. By default, the owner of a record has full access capabilities. This means they can view, edit, delete, transfer, and share the record.

Organization-wide Defaults

By default, your Salesforce organization operates in a public sharing model. We refer to this as the *organization-wide defaults* (OWDs). This means that all users have access to see and edit all data on a per-object basis, provided they have the appropriate object-level security. To limit visibility for certain records, consider operating in a private sharing model for that object.

Private or Public?

When considering to go private or public on an object, consider this: are there any elements of your data that should be restricted to any particular user?

If the answer is yes, you should be operating in a private sharing model for that object.

As shown earlier in Figure 9-2, the organization-wide default has the highest level of restriction. This is the only security component that restricts access.

All other security components are designed to share access. Record access can be opened up to specific users or groups of users through roles, manual sharing, and sharing rules.

Change Sharing Settings

To modify your organization-wide defaults, navigate to Sharing Settings in Setup.

To control the sharing settings for external users, you must first enable external sharing. Select Sharing Settings in the Setup area's Quick Find, and click Enable External Sharing.

From here, you can view the level of access both internally and externally by object, as shown in Figure 9-16.

SETUP
Sharing Settings

Default Sharing Settings

Organization-Wide Defaults   [Edit]   Organization-Wide Defaults Help ⑦

Object	Default Internal Access	Default External Access	Grant Access Using Hierarchies
Lead	Public Read/Write/Transfer	Public Read/Write/Transfer	✓
Account and Contract	Public Read/Write	Public Read/Write	✓
Contact	Controlled by Parent	Controlled by Parent	✓
Order	Controlled by Parent	Controlled by Parent	✓
Asset	Controlled by Parent	Controlled by Parent	✓
Opportunity	Public Read/Write	Public Read/Write	✓
Quote	Controlled by Parent	Controlled by Parent	✓
Case	Public Read/Write/Transfer	Public Read/Write/Transfer	✓
Campaign	Public Full Access	Public Full Access	✓
User	Public Read Only	Private	✓
Activity	Private	Private	✓
Calendar	Hide Details and Add Events	Hide Details and Add Events	✓
Price Book	Use	Use	✓
Coaching	Private	Private	☐
Feedback	Private	Private	☐

Figure 9-16. Default organization-wide settings

External users include community users, guest users, web site users, Chatter external users, and portal users. You can split the sharing settings for each object for internal and external users.

Select Edit to change the settings to any of these options:

- *Private*: All records in this object are private and can be visible only to the record owner, role, or sharing rule.

- *Public Read Only*: All records in this object are visible as read-only records.

- *Public Read/Write Only*: All records in this object are visible and can be modified by all users.

- *Public Read/Write/Transfer*: All records in this object are visible and can be modified and transferred by all users.

- *Controlled by Parent*: Users have the same level of access on the detail of a master-detail relationship.

359

Select Standard Report Visibility to enable visibility to data in reports that may not be accessible because of organization-wide defaults.

Select Manual User Record Sharing to allow users to manually share a record to additional users.

Select Manager Groups to allow users to share records with their manager groups, as shown in Figure 9-17.

Figure 9-17. *Additional security settings*

Role Hierarchies

Once OWDs are in place to restrict data, you can use role hierarchies to open up visibility and share record access. Roles define the level of access a user or groups of users have from the top down. Record access rolls up through the hierarchy.

As an example, create a branch under Sales Managers called Sales Reps to give sales managers access to the sales reps beneath them, as shown in Figure 9-18.

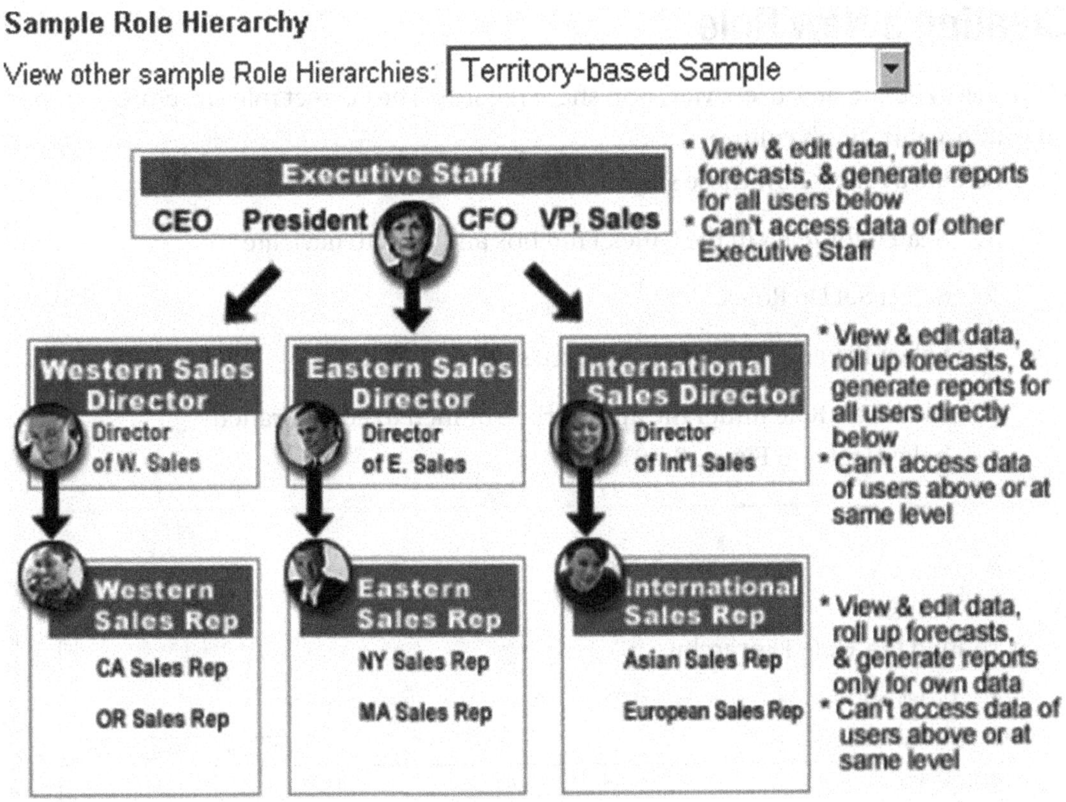

Sample Role Hierarchy

View other sample Role Hierarchies: | Territory-based Sample ▼

Figure 9-18. Understanding the roles home page

Note   When considering your role chart, keep in mind that role hierarchies aren't necessarily the same as your executive organizational chart. Typically you create roles for every level in the hierarchy, not for every position.

If a role sits above someone else in the role hierarchy tree, that role is granted the same level of access to all records that fall beneath that branch. So if the access is read-only, that same level of record access is granted.

Creating a New Role

Use roles to define how users view and share records. The correct role structure depends on your organization's culture.

To create a role, follow these steps:

1. Search for *Roles* in the Quick Find box and click to navigate.

2. Select Set Up Roles.

3. Select Expand All to see Salesforce's default setup.

4. Click Add Role under the appropriate branch to add a branch below (refer to Figure 9-19).

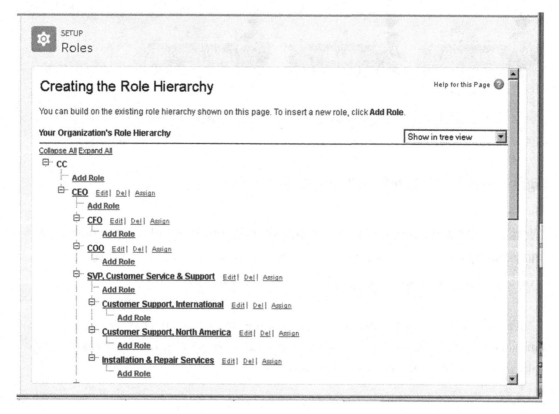

Figure 9-19. *Tree branch view expanded*

5.   Fill in the following details to successfully save a new role, as shown in Figure 9-20:

   a.   *Label*: This is the name used to title the role. Examples can include VP of Sales, Regional Managers, and so on. Press Tab to autopopulate the role name.

   b.   *Role Name*: This is the unique API name. This role reports to the name of the role above this role.

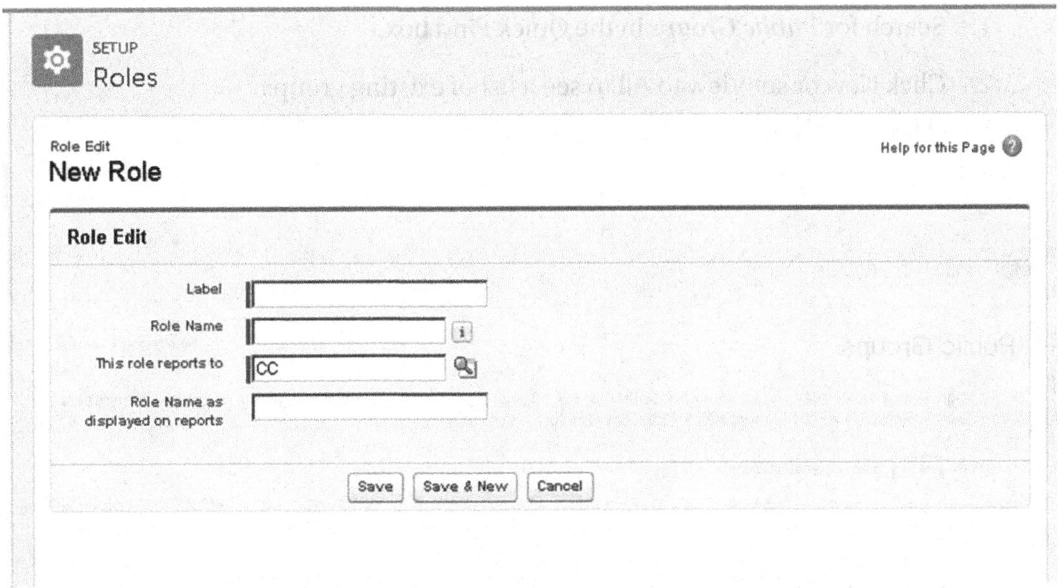

SETUP
Roles

Role Edit
New Role   Help for this Page

Role Edit

Label

Role Name

This role reports to   CC

Role Name as
displayed on reports

[Save] [Save & New] [Cancel]

Figure 9-20. Steps to creating a new role

6.   Assign users to specified roles.

By selecting to assign, you can search for unassigned users to connect them to a proper role. You can also navigate to a user's profile and select Edit to assign a role.

Sharing Rules

You can use sharing rules to give roles, groups, or individual users access to data that they may be excluded from. Sharing rules can be used to override the existing security restrictions.

Public Groups

Groups can be created to simplify sharing and security. This can include a combination of individuals, users with specific roles, or members of other public groups.

Creating a Public Group

Before creating a sharing rule, you must create a public group. Follow these steps to create a public group:

1. Search for *Public Groups* in the Quick Find box.

2. Click New or set View to All to see a list of existing groups (Figure 9-21).

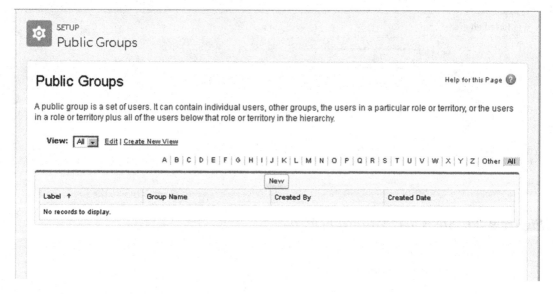

Figure 9-21. *Setting up public groups*

3. Fill in the following details, as shown in Figure 9-22.

    •   Enter the name of the public group in Label.

    •   Enter the unique API name in Group Name.

    •   To add members to a public group, move them from Available Members to Selected Members.

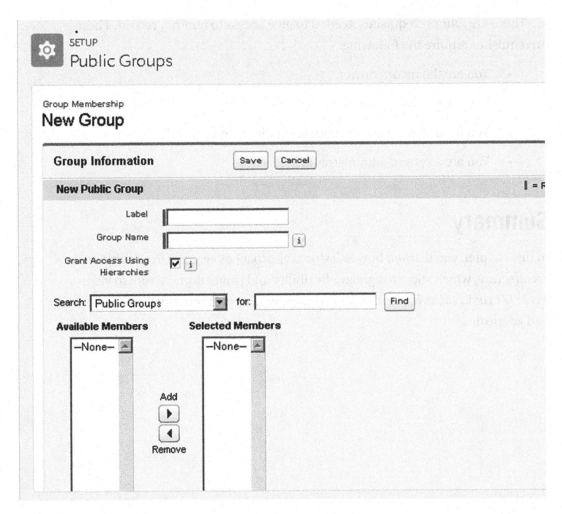

Figure 9-22. *Adding members to a public group*

4.   Click Save. Now you have a new public group with members.

Manual Sharing

Manual sharing can be used to provide individual access to records through a sharing button.

There are four prerequisites needed to give access to another record. These prerequisites require the following:

- You are the record owner.

- You are in a role higher than the record owner.

- You have "full access" permission to the record.

- You are a system administrator.

Summary

In this chapter, you learned how Salesforce approaches security in a multitiered architecture, which supports greater flexibility and protection. Be sure to visit `http://trust.salesforce.com` for transparent access to security threats and advisories.

Index

© Felicia Duarte, Rachelle Hoffman 2018
F. Duarte, R. Hoffman, *Learn Salesforce Lightning*, https://doi.org/10.1007/978-1-4842-2994-1

D, E

N

O

P, Q

Get the eBook for only $5!

Why limit yourself?

With most of our titles available in both PDF and ePUB format, you can access your content wherever and however you wish—on your PC, phone, tablet, or reader.

Since you've purchased this print book, we are happy to offer you the eBook for just $5.

To learn more, go to http://www.apress.com/companion or contact support@apress.com.

Apress®

Printed in the United States
By Bookmasters